Fidel!

Latin American Perspectives Series

Ronald H. Chilcote, Series Editor

†Available in hardcover and paperback

Also by Sheldon B. Liss

Radical Thought in Central America (1991)

Roots of Revolution: Radical Thought in Cuba (1987)

Marxist Thought in Latin America (1984)

Diplomacy and Dependency:
Venezuela, the United States and the Americas (1978)

Man, State and Society in Latin American History
(coeditor, 1972)

The Canal: Aspects of United States–Panamanian Relations (1967)

A Century of Disagreement: The Chamizal Conflict, 1864–1964 (1965)

FIDEL!

Castro's Political and Social Thought

Sheldon B. Liss

Westview Press

Boulder • San Francisco • Oxford

Latin American Perspectives Series, Number 13

Copyright © 1994 by Sheldon B. Liss

Published in 1994 in the United States of America by Westview Press, Inc., 5500 Central Avenue, Boulder, Colorado 80301-2877, and in the United Kingdom by Westview Press, 36 Lonsdale Road, Summertown, Oxford OX2 7EW

Library of Congress Cataloging-in-Publication Data
Liss, Sheldon B.
    Fidel! : Castro's political and social thought / Sheldon B. Liss.
    p.   cm. — (Latin American perspectives series ; no. 13)
    Includes bibliographical references and index.
    ISBN 0-8133-8678-0 — ISBN 0-8133-8679-9 (pbk.)
    1. Castro, Fidel, 1927–   . 2. Cuba—Politics and government—1959–   —Philosophy. 3. Marxism—Cuba.   I. Title.
II. Title: Castro's political and social thought.   III. Series.
F1788.22.C3L57   1994
972.9106'4—dc20
                                                                    93-32735
                                                                         CIP

Printed and bound in the United States of America

∞ The paper used in this publication meets the requirements
    of the American National Standard for Permanence of Paper
    for Printed Library Materials Z39.48-1984.

10   9   8   7   6   5   4   3   2   1

For Susan

Contents

Preface

Over the past three decades Fidel Castro has been the subject of numerous articles and books, most of them polemical in nature. Scholarly objectivity, which is always filtered through an ideological prism, has been rare when writers dealt with the charismatic Cuban leader. Generally, in the United States, journalists, some covertly subsidized by the state, and at times predisposed to sensationalism and character assassination, have done a worse job than academicians in treating Castro fairly. U.S. reporters have tended to conform to the often erroneous and negative attitudes of their government toward Fidel. Their opinions have usually reflected the anticommunism of the advertisers who support their newspapers, magazines, and radio and television stations and who indirectly pay their salaries. One perspicacious student of Cuba pointed out that among academicians once a view about how to properly study a subject is accepted as objective, it rules the field. Those who reject it are pushed to the periphery of the discipline and often considered radical, too ideological, or naïve by those who follow the "official" paradigm.[1]

To understand Fidel Castro one must comprehend the history of Cuba and Latin America as well as the philosophical underpinnings of Marxism and Leninism. Many people in the United States who write about Cuba have some comprehension of the country's history and can place it in a Latin American context, but few understand Marxism and Leninism, nor are they sufficiently flexible to even accept its democratic and egalitarian aspects. Thus the majority, including liberal academics, tend to analyze Fidel from a cold war, anti-Marxist perspective.

What follows is not a biography, nor an account of how Castro came to power, a tale told often and well by others. It is not a history of Cuba's Communist party, a book on revolutionary strategy, or a text on guerrilla warfare. This volume examines Fidel's endeavors to build socialism in Cuba, but it is not a theoretical tract. Cuban Marxism, as we shall see, is more a product of the political and social thought and praxis of Fidel Castro than a defined doctrine. This book enhances understanding of the Cuban Revolution by viewing it through the political and social thought of its primary motivator.

The creative spirit for the Revolution has, to a great degree, emanated from Fidel's intuitively radical beliefs, many of them predicated upon Cuba's historical reality. I approach the Revolution as a historical process and explore the role of its central figure in Cuba's revolutionary theory and practice.

This volume lets Castro explain his vision of Cuban Marxism and does not evaluate the Revolution by employing a scholarly model. Occasionally, I refer to established typologies that Fidel's ideas happen to fit. I also realize that political, social, and economic exigencies have often forced Cuba's leader to change his views.

I started collecting material for this study in 1977 when preparing a section on Castro for my *Marxist Thought in Latin America,* and I acquired additional data on a 1981–1982 research trip to Cuba while working on *Roots of Revolution: Radical Thought in Cuba.* Numerous documents collected and interviews conducted in Cuba in 1992 helped to clarify my thinking. Over the years, I have waded through thousands of speeches, transcripts, articles, and essays by and about Fidel and have reviewed dozens of interviews with him by individuals representing diverse ideologies. No act of Castro's goes unrecorded. Whenever he breathes, someone measures the oxygen count. Some remarks attributed to Fidel might have been written by others, although he approves just about everything that goes out over his name.

Fidel Castro, like Karl Marx, has never tried to formulate a comprehensive philosophical or historical system explaining everything. This book is not designed to show that his ideas constitute a coherent whole but to illustrate how they have been affected by, adapted from, and organized according to diverse Marxist beliefs and how they have been applied practically in Cuba. The book explores three decades of Castro's thought and touches the most salient aspects of Cuban life under the Revolution. The emphasis is on political and social thought, with the understanding that political economy is central to Cuban thinking.

Rather than a critique of Fidel Castro's political and social actions and accomplishments, this book is an explication of his thoughts in those areas. For instance, I am more interested in what Fidel has to say about the role of women in the Revolution than in appraising the gains they have made in Cuba over the past three decades. Critical comments appear throughout the text. They are designed to enhance the reader's appreciation of Fidel's thoughts, that is, to place his comments in clearer perspective. This is not a volume written to diminish Castro or to make him into an icon. It examines and reflects Fidel's thinking and in so doing naturally shows Cuba and its Revolution in a more positive than negative light. Fundamentally, my worldviews and Castro's coincide. That is not to say that we agree on every subject or that I condone all of Fidel's actions or policies.

Neither I nor any other honest student of the Cuban Revolution knows to what extent Fidel directs the entire show in Cuba. It is my intention to enable the reader to gain insight into the extent of Castro's control by explaining his views on a myriad of topics. Through Fidel's eyes the reader can decide what the *jefe máximo* (principal leader) has sought to achieve, why he has pursued various policies, and to a lesser extent whether he has failed or succeeded.

Castro has ignored many significant topics in his voluminous writings and speeches, and others he has examined only cursorily. This book conforms to his interests and tastes. It emphasizes what he has stressed in his writings, speeches, and interviews. I have always considered it bad form for book reviewers to write about what authors choose to omit from their works. I believe that writers generally have good reasons for disregarding certain topics and do not do so out of ignorance. Thus I cannot in good conscience write about what Fidel has elected to ignore or keep to himself.

Where there does not exist strong and honest evidence to contest or counterbalance Castro's views, I let them stand on their own so that the reader can assess them for her or himself. Where necessary, I note why I believe that he is wrong. The majority of this book consists of comments by Fidel, generally paraphrased by me and annotated, so the reader can see when and under what conditions he spoke or wrote. I also use numerous direct quotations from him. For example, all of the epigraphs in this book are his sayings. In some places, for the sake of clarity, I bridge gaps in his thought with my own ideas. I refrain from commenting on every point he makes. To do so would destroy the flow of his ideas, which this book is basically designed to present.

It is difficult to make the depth and clarity of this work exceed that of Fidel's thought. I use his words and expressions wherever possible and try not to read into his thoughts ideas that he did not intend. Moreover, this volume is arranged topically, not chronologically, and chapters and subsections do not have to be read in sequence to understand them. To avoid cumbersome repetition, what is mentioned in one section will usually not be repeated in another even it if is germane to the topic.

This is not a formal psychological profile or a character analysis. I stay away from psychological postulates such as the "hubris-nemesis complex," designed to prove that Fidel is driven by personal ambition and that his actions derive primarily from the fact that he detests the United States.

The following paragraphs occasionally move from one subject to another without precisely defined transitions. This reflects Fidel's loose style of speech and writing mannerisms and the fact that his agile mind often makes quantum leaps from one related topic to another. Bear in mind that he is not a formal *pensador* (thinker). In fact, this book contains a great deal of rhetoric, which is characteristic of the organized Left, and at which Fidel Castro is a master.

Finally, unlike many books written by academics, this one is not directed to a handful of experts in the field or only to intellectuals but to a broad spectrum of readers who want to know more about the thinking of Cuba's long-time leader.

Sheldon B. Liss

Acknowledgments

Insights derived from discussions with dozens of individuals in the scholarly and government communities in Cuba and the United States enabled me to clarify my thinking and to write with greater precision. The names of those who have written about the Cuban Revolution and have contributed to my understanding of it appear throughout the text, notes, and bibliography. Special thanks go to journalist Lionel Martin, who has lived and worked in Cuba for over three decades, has written an excellent book on Fidel Castro's early years, and read and commented on my manuscript. His extraordinary knowledge of the Cuban leader prevented me from making at least one egregious error of interpretation. The majority of my ideas concerning Fidel's political and social thought come from analyzing his printed writings, speeches, and interviews, most of which have been made public by the government of Cuba.

Many people from the Faculty of Philosophy, History, and Sociology at the University of Havana and the Center for Cuban Studies in New York City helped me to obtain materials for my research. Ronald H. Chilcote, editor of *Latin American Perspectives* and the Westview Press series of the same name, suggested worthwhile revisions and expedited the publication of this book. Westview Press editors Barbara Ellington, Jane Raese, and Marian Safran provided valuable assistance in their respective areas of expertise. Sarah Lorenz Akers supervised the efficient processing of my numerous interlibrary loan requests. Edie Richeson typed the original manuscript from my often illegible longhand. Patricia Davis and Maryann Hamilton rapidly and accurately corrected subsequent drafts on the word processor and enabled me to complete the book on schedule.

S.B.L.

1

The Revolutionary Leader

Aristotle said that a man is a social being, and it seems I belong to that species.
—Fidel Castro

"Fidel! Fidel! Fidel!" chant a million people gathered in Havana's José Martí Revolution Square to hear Castro speak. Cuba's citizens engage in a one-sided dialogue with the man who has guided their nation for over three decades and has attracted more attention than any other Latin American leader of the twentieth century. As loved and respected in Cuba as he is loathed and suspected in the United States, Fidel Alejandro Castro Ruz engenders debate and controversy in many quarters. To the million approving voices he epitomizes revolutionary legitimacy. Although he denies that he is synonymous with the Revolution, his political and social philosophy pervade contemporary Cuba.

Cuba has a long tradition of radicalism expressed through trade unions, mass participation in cooperative actions, and worker uprisings.[1] The rhetoric of dissent, at which Fidel excels, has been an integral part of Latin American politics. His strong personality and political dominance make it difficult to deal with him dispassionately. Even his critics are often beguiled by this man who can be simultaneously enchanting and manipulative. Using sociologist Max Weber's categories, we find that his charisma evolves from personal qualities, as opposed to the charisma of office, which arises from some sacred nature ascribed to the position.

Castro is constantly in demand. At times he has on his desk as many as three hundred requests for interviews. He likes to talk and repeatedly tells his revolutionary story to interviewers. One of his friends, novelist Gabriel García Márquez, insists that he rests from talking by talking.[2] Despite a fragile voice that sometimes sounds uncertain, he has great oratorical powers. He fre-

1

quently uses the words "let us analyze it," indicating that to him socioanalysis is the highest form of communication. He speaks Spanish with impeccable syntax and avoids using English, which he reads but speaks haltingly. Those who converse with him receive undivided attention. Interviewers find that what he says has been thought out in advance and is presented logically. He is forthcoming, controls interviews, and prefers to deal with reality, not theory. One can irritate him by constantly couching questions in terms of Marxist doctrine. In writing his speeches he has a knack for shifting the burden of proof to his adversaries. Foreign interviewers who cast questions in the ethnocentric vein of their own nation frustrate Fidel, who, for example, does not like to see European suppositions injected into interviews about Cuba.[3] He refuses to get pinned down unless he so desires, evading answers by delivering long-winded diatribes.

Castro, a master of mass psychology, designs his speeches to be heard. They tend to be repetitious, often lack literary quality, and are tedious when read. Unlike V. I. Lenin and Leon Trotsky, who wrote speeches for party cadres, Fidel writes both speeches and articles for the masses. Seventy to 75 percent of his hundreds of writings and speeches are pep talks with little theoretical content. He refers to his speeches as conversations or exchanges with the public and adapts them to specific audiences. His comrade Ernesto "Che" Guevara said that one had to witness Fidel in action in big public meetings to appreciate how he integrated with the masses. Che drew an analogy to "two tuning forks whose vibrations summon forth new vibrations each in the other. Fidel and the masses begin to vibrate in a dialogue of growing intensity which reaches its culminating point in an abrupt ending crowned by our victorious battle cry."[4] His charisma seems to be absorbed by the people, who in return grant him authority. From another vantage point, one might call his public dialogues monologues wherein he asks and answers questions.

Fidel has delivered hundreds of orations sprinkled with historical allusions to previous Cuban struggles like the 1868 uprising against Spain. His speeches reveal broad literary and classical interests and always reflect a Cuban point of view. He uses the language of his generation, often more positivist in nature than Marxist, and does not continuously invoke class analysis.[5] Those who listen to him feel that he inspires dignity. His extemporaneous remarks respond to the mood of the audience. Although he improvises some speeches, his major talks are usually written out. He spends hours correcting and rewriting them, putting new meanings in the margins, striving to use language artfully.[6] When not working from a script, he has the basic ideas and the order of presentation in mind. He rarely deals with ideas or situations he does not fully comprehend.

Fidel's speeches have a didactic quality. His orations put greater emphasis on historical description than analysis, whereas his interviews have greater conceptual depth. He feels obligated not to use abstract or highly technical terms when addressing the masses, but he does use polysyllabic words. In demagogic fashion, he encourages his followers, raises civic and revolutionary consciousness, and criticizes his enemies. He also contradicts himself occasionally.

The *Jefe Máximo*

Fidel Castro, the unifying force of the Cuban Revolution and its political and ideological leader, stands as a constant reminder of the military victory over bourgeois dictatorship and imperialism. Holding the rank of *comandante en jefe* (commander in chief), he almost always wears battle dress as a reminder of the ongoing revolution. He mixes Latin America's revolutionary tradition with Marxist ideology to produce "*Fidelismo*," or "Castroism." *Fidelismo* reflects his personal mysticism, not the impersonal aura of the Communist party. His followers, or *fidelistas*, deviate from traditional Communist adherence to a narrow and inflexible party. Instead, they represent broad national interests.

With the overthrow of Paraguay's Alfredo Stroessner in February 1989, Castro became the longest-ruling head of state in the Americas. Following the Latin tradition of strong chief executives, Fidel has presided over Cuba with a dynamic style of personal governance and has built close ties to the masses. His relationship to the people in some ways approximates that of China's Mao Zedong, whom Fidel saw as a sincere and brilliant revolutionary and thinker, but one who lacked humility and created a cult of personality.[7]

Everyone in Cuba calls him Fidel. Some others, including opponents in the United States, refer to him as Castro. Throughout this book I use Fidel and Castro interchangeably. To a few he is "Fifo," or *el caballo* (the horse), a name connoting indestructibility. Those who recall his missives from the guerrilla days in the Sierra Maestra remember him by the pseudonym Alex. Whether acting as Cuba's *jefe supremo* (supreme chief), *líder máximo* (maximum leader), president of Cuba's Council of Ministers, head of the National Assembly and Council of State, first secretary of the Communist party, or commander in chief of the Revolutionary Armed Forces, he responds toward his compatriots as a concerned father or family head. Most Cubans react positively to that relationship and look upon him as a benevolent, sometimes puritanical, patriarch. Hero worship and wishful thinking have led many Cubans to regard Castro as infallible, an attribute that even during the early years of the Revolution he denied vehemently.

Those who know Fidel see him as a tireless worker, a man of iron discipline, someone with wonderful political instincts, but also as someone at times unable to delegate authority and with a propensity to interfere in well-designed plans made by others. García Márquez has said that what Castro hates most is to lose; thus in most situations he struggles vehemently to get the upper hand.[8] In order to do so, he feels a great need to be well informed, and García Márquez noted that Fidel breakfasts with two hundred pages of world news.[9] He probably has detailed knowledge of more facets of life in his country than has any other modern national leader. He recites correct harvest yields, describes school curricula, or tells you how much toilet paper Cuba produces annually. He believes that no two people are alike; thus he allows for individual differences. In order to attain flexibility, he believes it necessary to stress the practical aspects of revolutionary thought, eschewing dogma. He talks about individual worth and dignity more than collective duties.

He characterizes himself as a "revolutionary politician,"[10] or a "professional revolutionary," meaning that he cannot stand injustice.[11] He primarily thinks politically, not militarily. He sees himself as an internationalist whose blood is that of all others. According to one biographer, Tad Szulc, he displays Latin mysticism, believing it his destiny to play a major role in public affairs.[12] Considering himself a teacher of the Cuban people, he rarely misses an opportunity to explain and expound upon his views.[13] Ever since his days fighting in the Sierra Maestra, he has never issued orders in a military way, preferring to be pedagogical and to give reasons for his directives.[14] To him, it is unimportant who leads; what counts is how well one governs.[15] Szulc, a kindred spirit of Fidel's Miami opponents, admits that Castro likes José Martí's expression "all the glory in the world fits inside a kernel of corn," meaning that the revolutionary does not fight for personal ambition.[16] Fidel has always resented the phrase "Castro's regime," rejecting the idea that he is a "strong man" in the classical sense of making all decisions.[17] He repeatedly notes, "We have never preached a personality cult. You will not see a statue of me anywhere, nor a school with my name, nor a street, nor a little town, nor any type of personality cult because we have not taught our people to believe, but to think, to reason out."[18]

In Cuba, he says, people think, but in the United States they believe things.[19] Disclaiming omnipotence, he insists that more checks on his power exist than on that of the president of the United States, who can enter thermonuclear war without congressional approval.[20] To charges that he is a dictator, he replies, "A dictator is someone who makes unilateral arbitrary decisions, one who is above all institutions and the law." He says that no one would call the pope a dictator, yet he makes unilateral decisions and governs by decree.[21] He asserts that decisions are made collectively in Cuba but is not so naïve as to think that his authority, granted collectively, and his prestige do not give him extra clout.[22] He opposes the idea that one small faction should have disproportionate power in any sector of society and even stopped publication of the newspaper *Lunes de Revolución* in 1961 because its editors were acquiring too much power.[23] Naturally, his critics can claim that he closed the paper because it vied with him for power and contradicted his wishes. He asserts that the distribution of power in society must favor the working-class majority. To him a genuine revolution requires the support of the masses. When confronted with the fact that the military phase of the Revolution was conducted by a minority, he responds that the latter had majority support or approval. He says that from the early 1950s on, he never intended to seize power with a handful of men but by mobilizing the masses.[24] When Gabriel García Márquez implied that Fidel operated on his own and referred to his "solitude of power," he disagreed: "I don't know what loneliness is when I can be with the people and that's what I always try to do."[25]

Fidel understands the nature of power, and from his extensive reading of history he has learned that it is easier to win power than to retain it and govern. He also feels that as one gets older, one gains experience and can be more useful to society.[26]

Even critical supporters who feel that it is time for Fidel to prepare successors concede that he has been a courageous, morally and physically strong, creative, and audacious hero who accomplished what seemed impossible by overthrowing tyranny, breaking dependence on the United States, and instituting socialism ninety miles from the world's most powerful capitalist state.

Some have claimed that Fidel's road to power was based on tactics, not ideas.[27] Subsequent pages should enable the reader to determine if that is so and to what extent independent leadership and thinking can develop in a nation dominated by one man for over three decades. Readers will eventually have better answers to the following questions raised by Cubanologist Max Azicri: How democratic are political institutions in Cuba? Is the populace well served? And who wields power, Fidel alone, the Political Bureau, or the National Assembly of People's Power?[28] The readers should be able to discern whether these questions represent universal concerns or merely bourgeois-democratic ones. We might also determine whether Fidel fears institutionalization, which would strip him of some power and limit his capacity for action, a question posed by his severe critic Carlos Montaner, who claimed that Castro rules by conducting public dialogues with the people and accepting their acquiescence as a note of confidence.[29] Montaner and other opponents concluded that Fidel suffers from a messiah complex. Supporters see nothing wrong with his desire to save Latin America from capitalist exploitation and foreign domination. Some scholars have accused Fidel of Bonapartism, Karl Marx's idea that Louis Napoleon Bonaparte exercised power on behalf of the masses, who were too factionalized and disengaged to do it themselves, and strove to protect them from the ravages of other classes. Political scientist Samuel Farber labeled Fidel a Bonapartist because he took and maintained control, stripped power from the elites, turned against his former supporters from the upper and middle classes, encouraged working-class hostility toward them, and forced the transition to socialism.[30]

The Man

Undoubtedly, the daring warrior of Cuba's revolutionary epic possesses extraordinary qualities. A natural leader who perpetually urges his team onward, Fidel has managed to make his charisma a routine part of daily life in Cuba. Castro is always vibrant, not just a politician who turns the electricity off and on when needed. An extrovert in public, in private he is surprisingly soft-spoken. Possessed of enormous self-esteem, at times he employs what appears to be false modesty. For example, endeavoring to serve Marxist theory, he quotes from the German master: "An individual cannot make history. The masses make it."[31] His critics might surmise that Castro, by using this technique, is attempting to ingratiate himself with people of lesser talents. But his supporters feel that he genuinely believes in this dictum.

Fidel does not generally reveal his innermost self to the public or to most interviewers. But no one can doubt that he has always been a radical, one with enormous optimism and faith, based on reality, in what he does.[32] He is by nature a decisive person, and his experiences in the guerrilla war enhanced his ability to act and react swiftly. A lifelong risk taker, he delights in challenging and beating the odds but does not plunge into ventures carelessly. He has a compulsive dedication to detail and a general's propensity for planning and thinking one step ahead of his adversaries.

One must separate Castro's personal characteristics from state policies. For instance, at times his language reflects the male chauvinism of his generation, but his policies are never chauvinistic. He dislikes small talk, likes to tell simple but poignant stories, and does so with fluidity, with almost a hypnotic quality. He monopolizes conversations and asks rhetorical questions and answers them.[33] He does not hesitate to render opinions on a multitude of subjects and will admit, in the face of evidence that contradicts something he said, that he erred because he was too glib. For instance, I recall a 1982 meeting on health care where Fidel interjected spontaneously his view on hospital supplies. A knowledgeable health care professional disagreed strongly and not too politely with Castro, citing statistics to prove Fidel wrong. Fidel apologized for his errors, which he said came from his heart but reflected ignorance, and promised henceforth to have better control of his facts before speaking.

Castro is warm and soft-hearted and does not hesitate to speak to strangers about anything that pops into his head. Upon hearing personal appeals, he has released prisoners from jail. His spontaneity often drives to distraction those responsible for his safety. He stops at neighborhood playgrounds to shoot baskets with children, drops into local ice cream parlors and tries out half a dozen scoops of various flavors, and, when exhausted, goes for a two-hour swim to relieve tension.

Fidel's sense of humor is legendary. He likes to joke verbally. Upon entering a huge ceremonial hall in Quito, Ecuador, where he was the center of public attention, he noted that he did not know what to do with his hands, put them in his pockets or cross his arms. He said to the apostolic nuncio to Colombia: "Listen Monsignor, do you know how I feel? I feel as if I were in a Roman circus." The nuncio replied, "Yes, but as a lion." Fidel answered, "No, as a Christian."[34]

Opponents call him "emotional"; supporters prefer "highly passionate." With adversaries he can be an effective bully. He claims that he has never felt personal hatred for opponents. That does not imply some sort of Christian love for humanity. He states that enemies exist as a result of history, which apportions conflicting social statuses to individuals. He believes that which occurs is a combination of predetermined factors. He admits to hating the class system and the fascism it spawns.[35]

He relates well to people on all levels, perhaps because he is not judgmental. He demonstrates great respect for all, regardless of their education or intellectual capacity. He believes that the length of time it takes a person to learn something bears little relationship to his or her ability to use it.[36] His considerable charm enables him to make friends out of enemies and to attract loyalty. He is suspicious and at times appears preoccupied with plots, sabotage, or actions directed against the Revolution. Fidel despises parasites, those who want something for nothing, those who he believes do not live communally.[37] He especially distrusts middle-class liberals and displays a vivid contempt for bourgeois characteristics and behavior.

Fidel's bravado and mastery of invective, coupled with a style devoid of pretense, particularly appeals to peasants. They love the fact that he drives around the countryside in an open jeep, unprotected and seemingly unafraid, and point out that he does so in a country where most people have access to arms. No matter how hard Cubans work, they know that Fidel works harder. They trust him and feel that he is not manipulable and does not play favorites. He even avoids having a close circle of friends for fear that it will be perceived as too influential.[38] His most trusted confidant is his younger brother, Raúl, who exhibits total loyalty and will do anything Fidel asks of him. Castro fits in well with Cubans of all types and feels most comfortable with Third World people who share his anti-imperialist perspective.

All observers agree that Fidel has an enormous capacity for reflection, rapidly assimilates the meaning of new experiences, and can master almost any subject. Immediately after he announced in 1961 that the Revolution was moving to socialism, his opponents tried to portray him as a violence-prone macho character with average intelligence. I recall hearing the respected historian Herminio Portell Vilá, a Cuban exile, claim that his former student always packed a pistol while at the university and managed to graduate only because of assistance from his wife, who was smarter. This proved to be a fallacy, probably concocted by the Central Intelligence Agency (CIA). In recent years, even Fidel's detractors admit that he was always an outstanding student. Carlos Montaner, one of his most vociferous opponents, attests to Fidel's great memory and ability to recall conversations from two decades ago.[39] Castro accumulates information quickly, digests over fifty documents daily,[40] and has considerable dexterity with figures. He claims that he knows so much because he has been running things for more than thirty years. He also takes great pride in examining and learning from the mistakes of the past, which he often calls "idealistic" or "utopian" errors. His methodical mind enables him to apply lessons from his omnivorous reading of history to his own interpretations of life and revolution. He reads extensively in the areas of political theory, philosophy, and political economy and can refer readily to passages from such thinkers as Immanuel Kant, Albert Einstein, and René Descartes. He continuously integrates old knowledge with new and refines his thoughts.

For diversion from serious reading, Fidel enjoys classical and protest music[41] and novels. His favorite authors are Miguel de Cervantes, and Ernest Hemingway, who lived in Cuba off and on. He likes Hemingway's realism, sense of adventure, willingness to break with convention, and the human quality of his characters. Fidel particularly favors *A Farewell to Arms* and *The Old Man and the Sea* and likes Hemingway's saying, "A man can be destroyed but never conquered."[42]

Like many revolutionaries, Fidel has a conservative moral stance. He takes life and work seriously, places a high value on the family, honesty, and integrity, and looks unfavorably upon drugs, excessive alcohol, gambling, and prostitution.[43] While a schoolboy, he developed a concept of good and evil, which he, in non-Marxist fashion, expresses with phrases like "God spare me from …" Fidel believes that altruism is vital to progress and has faith in the human capacity to develop morally. To him, the Revolution, free of the Christian ethic of original sin, stresses the extraordinarily high ability of people to develop.[44] He has an almost mystical conviction that humanity can be changed for the better.[45]

Ideas and opportunities for human progress, not material wealth or prestige, motivate Fidel.[46] To him, seemingly unsurmountable obstacles can be overcome through sacrifice and struggle. He is fond of noting that the spirit of Don Quixote's madness and the madness of revolution are similar. In both, the knight-errant stops the unbeatable foe.

One student of the early Fidel called him a radical voluntarist, implying that his decisions were not entirely the result of external conditions.[47] In other words, he determined what warranted action. This line of thinking corresponds to that of another observer, who felt that the Cuban leader demonstrated an "aristocratic spirit, a faith in the role of the elite" to decide what necessitates action.[48] But, as noted above, Fidel stands by the contention that the people, not the individual, make history. In self-critical fashion he reiterates, "The masses transform men into symbols and attribute to the individual what is not deserved by him alone, but by the many."[49]

Although he has a high opinion of himself and sometimes does not explore all sides of an issue if his mind is made up, he does listen to others and, upon reflection, is willing to change his views. For example, in 1986 a worker told him that production at a textile plant lagged because people had to travel long distances on poor transportation to work there. The workers suggested that housing close to the factory would solve the problem of employee turnover. Fidel in reply asked where the funds for housing would come from, if not production. He insisted that production came first. The worker disagreed. Six months later, after thinking the problem through, Fidel argued for building housing near to workplaces.[50]

Matters of significance to the community interest him. Those pertaining to individuals—or himself—do not. In a 1977 interview, broadcast journalist Barbara Walters, obviously enamored, and a bit in awe, of Fidel, asked him a series of personal questions. He replied: "What is the importance of my being married or not, and who cares? These are my problems. They do not belong to international opinion, they belong to me. I can tell you the following: I'm a man that is totally free, that owns my own life. The rest is detail, intranscendental details that have nothing to do with the Revolution nor politics."[51]

Fidel, the rare Cuban who dislikes private parties and does not sing or dance, lives for the Revolution and what it can accomplish. His greatest joy comes from contributing positively to the lives of others. For over thirty years he concluded each speech with the shout "*venceremos*" (we shall overcome) or "*patria o muerte*" (homeland or death), which attests to his dedication to progress for the Cuban people and unwillingness to accept defeat, despite continuous states of national emergency.

2

Preparing for Socialism

We have had the market economy since the days of Christopher Columbus. We have had the market economy for centuries and what has been the result? What did colonialism, the direct offspring of capitalism leave us? Nothing! ... Four billion hungry people. That's what capitalism, colonialism and the market economy left us.

—Fidel Castro

The Spanish arrived armed with the sword and the cross to subjugate and exploit the heathen, who should have been regarded as God's children, asserts Fidel. To him, Spain conquered with a messianic faith, and then imposed Christianity and civilization through bloodshed. He resents the Spanish, who believed that they possessed the truth, spread it by murder and enslavement, and remained in Cuba for approximately four centuries. He sees Cuba as the first conquered and the last freed of Spain's colonies in America.[1] During the colonial era, Spaniards and wealthy Cubans controlled the plantations, which were worked by slave labor, and dominated the island's commerce. This ruling class subordinated national independence to its own interests in the retention of slavery. Some of the rulers even favored the annexation of Cuba to the United States to maintain slavery and socioeconomic privileges.[2]

According to Fidel, the first phase of the active struggle for freedom in Cuba was started in 1868 by Carlos Manuel de Céspedes and lasted until 1898 and the Cuban-Spanish-American War, which replaced the original colonial master with another, the United States.[3] The battle for freedom reached a critical turning point in the 1933 upheaval, which overthrew dictator Gerardo Machado and installed a short-lived progressive government under Ramón Grau San Martín. Castro's 26th of July Movement continued the progressive struggle in the early 1950s.[4]

When Fidel first read the history of Cuba's protracted struggle for independence, he wished that he had lived in the nineteenth century and had participated as a freedom fighter. He related emotionally to his predecessors' attempts to bring justice to the majority.[5] Filled with romantic notions about the struggle for independence, Castro dreamed about bringing the work of the previous century's heroes, such as José Martí, to fruition. Today, when he reflects upon the past, he draws analogies between twentieth-century Vietnam and nineteenth-century Cuba. The latter, an island with a population of barely a million, fought nearly three hundred thousand Spanish soldiers,[6] and relatively small Vietnam was confronted by a huge force that the United States sent to block independence.[7]

Fidel's radical worldview and his penchant for actively pursuing social justice are not necessarily consistent with his middle-class background. His political attitudes developed as a result of his observations, reading, and adult political involvements. Some of his social beliefs are responses to his boyhood environment. He was born on August 13, 1926, on the family farm "Las Manacas" in Oriente Province. His father, Angel Castro, had come from Galicia to Cuba in the 1890s as a Spanish soldier. Subsequently, Angel raised cattle and sugarcane, sold what he produced to the United Fruit Company, whose plantations surrounded his farm, and continually added to his holdings. By the 1950s, Angel owned about 2,000 acres, rented an additional 25,000, and had an estate valued at approximately U.S. $500,000.[8] Lina Ruz González, a maid in Angel's house, bore him three children out of wedlock, including Fidel. She later married Angel, but their offspring suffered the ridicule reserved for bastards in Cuba's moralistic Catholic society.[9] Fidel's mother prayed daily, but his father, who often ignored society's conventions, had little time for religion.

At age six Fidel went to school in Santiago de Cuba. Two years later he enrolled in a school run by Christian Brothers, where he displayed superior academic and leadership ability and considerable tenacity. He later attended a Jesuit junior high school in Santiago and a fashionable Jesuit high school in Havana. He states that from his teachers he learned the spirit of adventure, discipline, sacrifice, and disdain for the profit motive. He found Jesuit education to be overly oriented to faith and not enough to reason. He maintains that all of his Jesuit teachers were pro–Francisco Franco reactionaries.[10]

Reflecting on his childhood, Fidel recalls that he lived in a remote area surrounded by class divisions and that he learned about capitalism, which never harmed him, by observation. His playmates were children of the poor who worked for his father, whose lives were pervaded by injustice and inequities.[11] He recalls his early classmates as extremely poor, with average intelligence; they dropped out of school into "a bottomless, hopeless sea of ignorance and penury," and he notes that "their children will follow in their footsteps, crushed under the burden of social fatalism."[12]

As a child he developed a special love for history and particularly liked biographies of Latin American heroes such as the "Liberator," Simón Bolívar. His classmates and teachers remember him as a feisty child who loved to be in the midst of action, a youngster who often used athletics as an outlet for his unbridled enthusiasm. In his teens he began to develop an analytical mind. He came to regard the church as a hypocritical institution obsessed with maintaining its power and privileges. Nevertheless, according to biographer Richard Bourne, Christian values remained a lens through which he viewed the world.[13] In high school, he excelled in academic areas and received the 1943–1944 award as Cuba's best all-around athlete. He participated in soccer, track, basketball, and baseball.

The University Years

Fidel entered the University of Havana in 1945 as an unsophisticated political novice.[14] But he quickly delved into the primary student preoccupation—politics. He called the opportunity to attend the university, where one out of a thousand matriculated, a process of "social selection," meaning that he came from a well-off family and did not gain access to the university by a process of natural selection.[15]

At the university, he drew ideological sustenance from Cuban leftist thinkers Julio Antonio Mella, Juan Marinello, Raúl Roa, Blas Roca, and Carlos Rafael Rodríguez.[16] From the outset of his stay at the university, he was attracted to the Ortódoxo party, which took a strong stance against political corruption.[17] The Ortódoxos did not blame capitalism or imperialism for many of Cuba's ills because, as Fidel noted, Cubans were taught respect and gratitude toward the United States.[18] In 1947 he joined the Ortódoxo party; he remained a member until 1955. He organized its Radical Action component[19] and worked for nationalism, economic and political independence, social justice, and better distribution of the wealth. His radicalism far exceeded that of the party's leader, Eduardo Chibás, but he stayed in the organization, which he viewed as a vehicle for progress.[20] Lionel Martin, perspicacious author of the excellent book *The Early Fidel,* saw Chibás as a catalyst, not as an ideological mentor of Castro, especially since the Ortódoxo leader took a cold war anticommunist stance, which Castro never followed.[21] Fidel did draw on Chibás's style of moral denunciation.

At the university, Fidel operated independently of the Communist party. He befriended its members and received books on credit from their bookstore, but he believed that he could not convince the party members, some of whom were political elitists, to use the masses to launch a revolution. He thought of the Communists as potential allies.[22] He also associated with the Puerto Rico Pro-Independence Committee and the Committee to Fight Racial Discrimination. In the university government, where he represented the

Law School, he referred to the institution as "a place where ideas were handled as if they were merchandise, where ideals are manipulated and
mocked."[23]

While a student in 1947, Fidel joined the Caribbean Legion, an abortive ex-
pedition of Latin American democrats who hoped to invade the Dominican
Republic and overthrow its long-standing dictator Rafael Trujillo.[24] The following year he attended an international student congress in Bogota, Colombia. There he witnessed the "Bogotazo," the riots that occurred after the
murder of liberal presidential candidate Jorge Elíecer Gaitán. Castro concluded that the CIA or other imperialists had killed Gaitán because he was a
popular democratic figure who advocated nationalistic reform. Fidel then
thought of Gaitán as a revolutionary, but not a communist revolutionary, and
decided that the United States opposed nationalism and all progressive reforms that could have a negative affect on the profits of its corporations.[25] Today, he might prefer to categorize Gaitán as a reformer.

The "Bogotazo" provided him with deeper insights into popular uprisings.
He felt that the Colombian people had a rebellious spirit but lacked organization and the political education necessary to rebel successfully.[26] Although he
had no contact with Colombia's Communist party in Bogota,[27] upon returning to Havana he sought out Cuban Marxists in order to learn more
about their views on revolution and mass organizing. Years later, when questioned about his role in the "Bogotazo" and whether he was a Communist at
that time, he replied that in 1948 he read Marxist literature and studied political economy and had a socialist and anti-imperialist conscience, good relations
with the few Communists at the University of Havana, but no connection
with the Communist party.[28] He had begun to question the rationality of the
capitalist system and rejected the idea of the crisis of overproduction and unemployment as "inexorable and immutable laws of society." For example, he
found it difficult to understand why in England, with a surplus of coal in the
ground, unemployed workers froze.[29] The Colombian experience stimulated
him to explore radicalism further.

He became a utopian socialist, then a communist, on his own, before reading a book by Marx, Engels, or Lenin. He says that he became a communist,
as did Marx, by studying capitalist political economy: "When I had some understanding of the problem, it actually seemed to me so absurd, so irrational,
so inhuman, that I simply began to elaborate on my own formulas for production and distribution. That was when I was a third-year student at the University of Havana."[30]

During this period of intellectual growth he married Mirta Díaz Balart, a
philosophy student from a wealthy family. In 1949, he regularly attended a
Marxist study group organized by the Communist party. There he read Volume 1 of Marx's *Capital,* which he purchased on his honeymoon in the
United States, and Lenin's *The State and Revolution* and *Imperialism: The*

Highest Stage of Capitalism. He learned the fundamentals of Marxism-Lenin-ism, the theory of surplus value, the concepts of class struggle, and how the state and revolution related to capitalism.[31] He later explained: "Back in my university days, my contact with Marxist ideas led me to acquire a revolution-ary outlook. From then on my entire political strategy was worked out with a Marxist framework."[32] He kept his newfound ideology and revolutionary goals to himself[33] and worked under a reformer's façade. By then, he was con-vinced of the Marxist dictum: "When ideas take possession of the masses, they become a material force."[34]

Castro's only child, Fidelito, was born on September 14, 1949, at a time when Fidel was refining his radical anti-imperialist views. He pondered the questions of the struggle between workers and machines and wondered, "How could there exist a conflict between man's technical possibilities and his needs for happiness, and why did it have to exist?"[35] His anticapitalist, prosocialist character was fully formed by the time he graduated from the uni-versity with a Doctor of Laws degree in the summer of 1950. With two class-mates he established a law firm in Havana to represent poor and politically progressive people. At this point, he was convinced that political change could best be effected by taking direct action.

Direct Action

When dictator Fulgencio Batista took over Cuba in 1952 and violated the na-tion's constitution, Fidel invoked the ideas of Montesquieu, Saint Thomas Aquinas, John Locke, Jean-Jacques Rousseau, and the U.S. Declaration of In-dependence and argued the people's right to rebel against despotism.[36] He denounced the takeover in *El Acusador,* calling Batista a "faithful dog of im-perialism and an ally of great Cuban and foreign interests."[37] He began build-ing a movement to overthrow the tyrant, and within fourteen months he or-ganized 1,200 people. He did not intend to lead the struggle, since numerous well-known political opponents of Batista existed. He sought only to organize the overthrow,[38] to continue the battle that had begun in 1868. While build-ing an insurrectionary movement, he took into consideration Cuba's lack of national identity, its legacies of personalism, Spanish authoritarianism, trade unionism, anarchism, radicalism, class conflict, and political instability. He saw a need for structural change in Cuba's social and economic system and ex-pressed a desire to terminate all forms of subservience to the United States. Realizing that his program would elicit opposition from the United States, he moved quickly to build popular support for it.[39]

Fidel believed that an uprising would unleash a class struggle[40] and thought that eventually a political party would be needed to lead the revolution.[41] He knew that in an insurrection the support of the well-established Cuban Com-munist party would be useful, and he communicated his intentions to it.[42] He made it clear that revolutions are based on morals, not money, and refused to work with politicians who had previously enriched themselves at public expense.[43] He even declined to accept pay from a leading Havana newspaper and wrote for free for journals that opposed the government.[44] These actions negate the theory that Fidel learned the value of moral over material incentives from Argentine physician Ernesto "Che" Guevara, whom he had yet to meet.

Fidel admits that he and his cohorts were unaware of their inexperience when they began the Revolution and were willing to take risks that enabled them to succeed.[45] Observers have speculated that Castro's revolutionary plans began to unfold after the cancellation of the 1953 congressional election in which he appeared certain to win a seat for the Ortódoxo party. He claims that he had intended, if elected, to introduce revolutionary legislation. Paradoxically, he indicated that he also doubted that Cuba's problems could be rectified by parliamentary action.[46]

He filed a legal brief against the Batista takeover in 1952 and stated, "Without a new conception of the state, of society, of the judicial order based on profound historical and philosophical principles, there will be no revolution that generates laws."[47] He believed in the legitimacy of revolution when he led the abortive July 26, 1953, assault on the Moncada army barracks at Santiago, which he hoped would spark a national uprising against the Batista regime. He asserted that the Revolution could not allow "the return of power to men who were morally and historically finished and who were responsible for the country's plight."[48]

A Marxist might construe the attack on Moncada as part of the bourgeois-democratic stage of revolution, but Fidel never intended Cuba to pass through the requisite Marxist phases of revolution. Some have argued that Fidel took a Leninist approach,[49] but the evidence shows that Castro started the struggle against the state apparatus and its U.S. connection without a coherent theoretical program. This was the point of view adopted by Cuba's Communist party at that time.[50] Although he did not adhere to standard Marxist-Leninist practice, Fidel perceived the need for radical social restructuring in Cuba. He spoke about adherence to the 1940 constitution, which would have necessitated changes in the social order. For example, the constitution stipulated that subsoil resources were public property, to be used for the good of the people.[51]

Fidel's rebels, known as the Centennial Generation because the Moncada attack corresponded to the hundredth birthday of José Martí, were led by people with advanced political awareness. They knew something about scientific socialism, had read Lenin, and were aware of the long radical tradition in Cuba, but they refrained from using Marxist terminology because of the prevailing anticommunist atmosphere in Cuba.[52] They chose not to impose ideology on anyone. Fidel noted, "There are things that, in order to be achieved, must be hidden ... proclaiming what they are would only raise difficulties that would make it hard to attain the desired ends."[53] Castro referred to the attempt to capture Moncada as starting up a small engine to help ignite the big engine.[54] To him, the Moncada program was national liberationist but very advanced and near to socialism.[55]

Personally, at the time of Moncada, Fidel had a rather complete Marxist worldview,[56] but he did not convey his innermost revolutionary ideas even to close associates. He thought of the Moncada program as "an antechamber to a socialist revolution. To get to the third floor, one must start from the ground floor."[57] The unifying theme of the 26th of July Movement was not Marxism-Leninism, but armed struggle that would lead to radical political and social transformations.[58] In a manifesto to be issued if the Moncada attack succeeded, Fidel included the democratic, anti-imperialist ideas of José Martí and of the 1934 progressive organization Joven Cuba,[59] examined in Chapter 3. He intended to proclaim five revolutionary laws after taking Moncada. (1) The government would return power to the people and restore the 1940 constitution, until such time as the people decided to change it. (2) Land would be expropriated from larger owners and transferred to sharecroppers, tenants, and squatters. (3) Workers would be given rights to share 30 percent of the profits of all large sugar, industrial, mercantile, and mining enterprises. (4) All sugar planters would have the right to share 55 percent of sugar production, and a portion would be granted to all small tenant farmers. (5) The wealth of those with ill-gotten gains would be confiscated, and half of the property recovered would go to workers, the other half to hospitals, asylums, and orphanages.[60]

Fidel included the aforementioned manifesto in a tract he issued after his capture by government forces. In explaining his actions, rallying support for his embryonic movement, and telling the world about his plan for an anti-imperialist national liberation struggle, he made famous the statement, "Condemn me, it does not matter. History will absolve me." In the *History Will Absolve Me* speech, delivered at his trial and later revised and distributed in pamphlet form, Fidel asserted that "the only remedy against force without authority is to oppose it with force."[61] The speech analyzed the class composition of Cuban society and emphasized the need to mobilize mental and manual workers and the petty bourgeoisie against the Batista government. Castro called the speech the expression of a progressive, not a Marxist, mind. It was, in his words, a living denunciation of what existed in Cuba.[62] He proposed a popular dictatorship to effect revolutionary change, to unite Cuba's 600,000 unemployed, 500,000 small farmers, 20,000 small business people, and 10,000 young professionals. In order to appeal to the widest possible constituency, he did not couch the program in Marxist terminology.

By no stretch of the imagination could one label *History Will Absolve Me* as a socialist tract. It provided for capitalist land reform, profit sharing for employees, and a major role for private funds. Only the proposals for the nation-alization of utilities, the confiscation of misappropriated moneys, and the es-tablishment of public welfare and retirement funds could be construed as so-cialist oriented.[63] To all intents and purposes, Cuba would operate on the principles of state capitalism.

Fidel saw Cuba in 1953 as primarily an agricultural nation in need of indus-trialization. He noted, "We export sugar to import candy, we export hides to import shoes, we export iron to import plows."[64] He believed that the neces-sary economic and social transformations could be made with the help of "the unredeemed masses to whom everything is offered but nothing is given ex-cept deceit and betrayal."[65] He anticipated U.S. opposition but did not ex-pect that the northern neighbor would try to impede the Revolution by force.[66]

In October 1953, as a result of his activities at Moncada, Fidel received a fif-teen-year jail sentence. He remained in prison on the Isle of Pines until re-leased via an amnesty in May 1955, an action that Batista, who misjudged Castro's revolutionary potential, lived to regret. Fidel smuggled the full text of *History Will Absolve Me* out of prison. Careful scrutiny of it revealed that its statistics appeared to be based on *Los fundamentos del socialismo en Cuba* (1943), a book by Blas Roca, Communist party secretary-general.[67] While on the Isle of Pines, Castro immersed himself in Marxist political theory. He read Karl Marx's five-volume *Capital*[68] and proclaimed the author a political ge-nius. He particularly liked Marx's ability to bring the work of the utopian so-cialists to a head and to synthesize German idealism and materialism.[69] He also read Victor Hugo's study of the 1848 revolution in France and its after-math—*Napoléon le petit.* After comparing it to Marx's *The Eighteenth Brumaire of Louis Bonaparte,* he commented, "One could appreciate the enormous difference between a scientific and realistic conception of history and a purely romantic interpretation." For Hugo, "History is chance, for Marx a process governed by laws."[70] "While Hugo sees only a lucky adven-turer, Marx sees the inevitable results of the social contradictions and the con-flict of interests prevailing in those days."[71]

In addition to Marx, Fidel read Brazilian Jorge Amado's biography of Bra-zil's Communist leader Luis Carlos Prestes. For recreation, he also read the novels of Amado as well as some by Fyodor Dostoevsky, Somerset Maugham, Ivan Turgenev, Honoré de Balzac, Anatole France, Maxim Gorky, and A. J. Cronin. Castro reread Lenin and José Martí and examined the work of José Carlos Mariátegui, the Peruvian who adapted Marx's ideas for industrializing nations to predominantly rural Latin America. Fidel went over the works of nineteenth-century *pensador* Félix Varela y Morales, the first Cuban to stress ideology and political thought and to advocate social and political analysis. He read the writings of progressive nineteenth-century Cuban philosopher José de la Luz y Caballero, who implored his countrymen to search for causation in the past behavior of society and to draw historical comparisons. Castro also carefully perused volumes on Cuba's nineteenth-century military struggle against Spain. He familiarized himself with the writings of Immanuel Kant, Sigmund Freud, Albert Einstein, and the social legislation of Franklin Roosevelt.[72] He found interesting Max Weber's *Economy and Society* and Karl Mannheim's *Liberty, Power and Democratic Planning.* He delved into Victor Hugo's *Les Misérables*, André Maurois's *Memoirs*, and Axel Munthe's *The Story of San Michele*, a book about commitment to struggle against social injustice.[73] He tackled the work on exploration by Alexander von Humboldt and Charles Darwin, Plutarch's *Parallel Lives*, Suetonius's *Lives of the Caesars*, and assorted studies on soils, biology, engineering, genetics, finance, history, international relations, and political economy.[74]

Fidel turned his months in prison into an educational experience for himself and his associates. He organized the Abel Santamaría Ideological Academy, where he and fellow inmates explored world history, philosophy, and political economy.[75] They kept abreast of world affairs and were particularly interested in the 1954 CIA-sponsored overthrow of Guatemala's ten-year experiment with democracy. The Guatemala episode convinced Castro that the United States would not permit capitalist nationalist reforms to occur in nations with heavy U.S. investment. It became clear that the United States would endeavor to destroy such movements on the grounds that they were Soviet inspired. He realized that a reform movement similar to that of Guatemala could not succeed in Cuba and that radical restructuring of the Cuban system and the seizure of control from foreign capitalists and their native partners were the only answer to the nation's myriad problems. In years to come, he often noted that Cuba was not Guatemala and should not suffer a similar fate.

The 26th of July Movement coalesced during Castro's imprisonment. By means of exceptional organizing throughout the country, directed by Fidel from jail, the radical organization prepared to fight the dictator Batista. Castro proclaimed:

> We are not professional troublemakers, nor are we blind proponents of violence. We would not resort to violence if the better homeland that we yearn for could be achieved with the weapons of reason and intelligence.
>
> No people would follow a group of adventurers who sought to plunge the country into civil strife unless injustice held sway, unless there were no peaceful legal means provided to all citizens in the civic battle of ideas. We agree with Martí that "he who starts a war that can be avoided is a criminal, and so is he who fails to start a war that is inevitable."[76]

Through the 26th of July Movement, Castro condemned Cuba's establishment politics and appealed in the name of the dispossessed for a better life and the end of exploitation and privilege.[77] In private he exuded socialist optimism and trust in human genius to advance society scientifically,[78] but in public he masked his ideology. Wayne S. Smith, a young U.S. foreign service officer in Cuba at that time, characterized Fidel as one with "gargantuan ambitions, authoritarian tendencies, and not much in the way of an ideology of his own" in 1956.[79] In November of that year the 26th of July Movement issued its *Programme Manifesto*. It stipulated that the organization sought to avoid abstract formulas; "The ideology of the Cuban Revolution must arise from its own roots and the particular circumstances of the people and the country." It stated that the movement's ideology was homegrown, embodied in the ideas of José Martí, which Cubanologist Nelson Valdés calls essentially populist.[80]

After his release from the Isle of Pines, Castro went into exile in Mexico to prepare for his return to Cuba and the revolutionary struggle. While there he read Joseph Stalin's views on capturing power. Castro concerned himself more with revolutionary tactics and strategy than with political theory. In Mexico, he also met Alberto Bayo, a Cuban veteran of the Spanish Republican Army and subsequently author of *Ciento cincuenta preguntas a un guerrillero* (A hundred and fifty questions to a guerrilla). Bayo helped train Castro and his new *compañero* Ernesto "Che" Guevara in the art of guerrilla warfare.

Fidel considered the government of Cuba bereft of ideological foundations. Basically, it was run by corrupt politicians who used the cult of personality to control a society that had little civic awareness and considerable political alienation. Fidel searched for a plan or model for a "new Cuba" but could find nothing better than Cuba's existing corpus of radical thought, which included a somewhat ill-defined socialism stressing anti-imperialism, agrarian reform, and a better way of life for workers. Cuba's radical *pensadores* provided a guide to revolution and an option to the positivism that dominated the country.[81]

In Castro's estimation, there existed three political forces in Cuba: (1) the large landowners, capitalists, reactionary clergy, and multinational companies, which held political power; (2) a national bourgeoisie, which often found itself in conflict with imperialism, but which could not lead the fight against the oligarchy and imperialism because it was paralyzed by the fear of social revolution; and (3) Castro's potential supporters, the masses who aspired to justice, change, fruitful work, and a better future, as well as small, heavily indebted, businessmen and young professionals with university degrees who could not find satisfactory employment.[82]

Fidel won over the third group after he returned to Cuba and established a guerrilla base in the Sierra Maestra in November 1956. While in the hills, Fidel hid his radical philosophy and projected an underdog democratic social reformer image in order to win support in Cuba and in the United States. He also hoped that such a posture would cause the latter to withdraw its backing from Batista. He gambled that his guerrilla victories would elicit mass support for his antidictatorial stance, but at the outset of the military phase of the Revolution he had no specific idea of how to deal with capitalism if he ousted Batista. During the course of the guerrilla struggle, he came to concur inadvertently with Trotsky's idea that the proletariat did not have the task of interpreting the world anew, but of remaking it completely, and he decided to eliminate capitalism.[83]

Fidel and his compañeros added a humanitarian dimension while fighting in the Sierra. As a result, they attracted proportionately more attention than Cuba's size or wealth would normally warrant. They became known as compassionate liberators and guerrilla fighters par excellence, especially in the Third World, where the Revolution merited mention along with that of China. Ironically, Fidel admits that at the time he had not read Mao Zedong's writings on guerrilla warfare.

Castro finally read Mao's *Problems of Strategy in Guerrilla War Against Japan* late in 1958 and found that he was doing what the Chinese leader advocated.[84] He concurred with Mao's axiom that in revolution practice is primary and theory is secondary. He came to admire Mao's leadership ability but found him guilty of abusing his power.[85]

Like Mao, Castro demonstrated that a militant, unorthodox Marxist approach to revolution could succeed in a nonindustrialized society. Fidel freed Cuba from dictatorship and the imperial relationship to the United States that had existed since before the turn of the century. The Cuban Revolution proved that non-communists could overthrow capitalism. It defied the belief that revolution against the army was impossible and that only a rebellion within the military could succeed. In reference to the successful takeover of Cuba on January 1, 1959, Fidel stated that the objective conditions for revolution existed and that the 26th of July Movement created the subjective ones.[86] Unlike earlier Communist takeovers in Eastern Europe, Cuba's had the support of the majority.

Fidel asserted that winning the war was not the Revolution, but provided the right to make the Revolution. He indicated that January 1, 1959, altered the history of Latin America, that the destiny of sister republics no longer remained in Washington's hands.[87] He sought change and development in Latin America within a humanist framework. He wanted to restructure Cuba, which he characterized as a nation with a relatively large petite bourgeoisie and a large culturally backward and illiterate sector and as a U.S. colony economically and ideologically. He deplored the social order that had been maintained by force of arms and the omnipotence of the dominant economic elite, which spread reactionary ideas and political bias among the masses.[88] He moved immediately to disassemble the existing military apparatus in order to eliminate the possibility of its destroying the Revolution.[89]

Castro put power into the hands of the proletariat, directed it from above, and received support from most quarters. He declared the cult of personality and *caudillismo* (bossism) dead, yet he epitomized both. He spoke of an inalienable revolutionary and historical process that could not be thwarted. He initiated social and economic reforms that were favored by most Cubans but that frightened a few.[90] When he supported the suspension of the right of habeas corpus so that criminals could not flee to Miami, he caused some apprehension.[91] When assorted Batista henchmen and criminals went on trial, he explained that revolutionary justice is not based on legal precepts but on moral convictions.[92] The flashy public trials that ensued created consternation in the United States, where some observers feared that justice could not be meted out so swiftly.

The Provisional Government that took over Cuba in early 1959 technically did not include Fidel. His loyal 26th of July members ran the nation. Their *jefe máximo* gave direction from the background. He insisted that the revolutionary program could be conducted without the assistance of the United States, which supported anticommunist reactionaries in Latin America such as Dominican dictator Rafael Trujillo.[93] Fidel assured his people that "this time the Revolution will not be frustrated. It will not be as it was in 1898 when the Americans came and became the masters of the Country. ... It will not be as it was in 1933, when the people began to believe that the Revolution was being made when Mr. Batista came, betrayed the Revolution, installed himself in power and established a ferocious dictatorship."[94]

In April 1959, Fidel warned that counterrevolutionaries would use communism as their pretext to destroy the Revolution. He noted that communism coexisted with capitalism in France and Italy but might not in Cuba. He noted that the anticommunist tactics used in Guatemala in 1954 to thwart nationalist social reforms were being used in Cuba. He claimed, "If to think as I do is to be a Communist, they can call me a Communist because I have acted as I believed and I have acted in the spirit of liberty, of justice, and of respect for others."[95] Although he intimated that he had a desire to work with and protect the rights of Communists, paradoxically, the following month, he denounced as counterrevolutionaries some members of Cuba's Communist party who refused to follow his lead.[96]

Fidel stressed the incompatibility between reform and revolution, and the majority of Cuba's nonsocialist radicals began to agree with him and realized that socialism represented the more humane choice.[97] U.S. writer Theodore Draper incorrectly saw Castroism as a retrospective theory, asserting that it was only after coming to power that the movement realized what had to be done and that, after taking control, Castro added socialist objectives to the existing anti-imperialist, populist, and nationalist ideas in Cuba.[98] Fidel had understood for quite some time what had to be done, but was not always sure how best to do it, and introduced his program somewhat gradually. Cuba moved from a bourgeois-democratic plan to a socialist one between January 1959 and October 1960 as Fidel became impatient with the pace of the Revolution and assumed a more prominent role to accelerate it. Political scientist

Max Azicri pointed out that Cuba moved toward socialism by contravening orthodox Marxist-Leninist theory. For example, a Communist party did not lead the process of social transformation; workers did not control social and political forces; nationalization of industry did not follow a known pattern; and although agrarian reform took place, cooperatives were not formed and considerable land remained in private hands.[99]

In the course of building socialism, Fidel found it difficult to alter old ideas and eradicate selfish interests.[100] He enlisted the aid of the Communist party, which he believed represented the most advanced or sophisticated elements of the working class. Although some of the Communists were not themselves from the working class, they represented its interests and had its respect.[101]

Castro stressed that the Communists did not recruit him; rather, he recruited himself after considerable reading and discussion. At the beginning of 1960, he and his Communist cohorts declared, "To be a traitor to the Revolution is to be a traitor to the country."[102] Through political education and new legislation, they turned the nation away from extreme individualism toward collectivism. They strove to get the people to work harder and sacrifice more. Law number 890, of October 14, 1960, nationalized 376 Cuban enterprises and destroyed a large segment of the bourgeoisie. Two million acres of private Cuban-held land and over 3 million acres of U.S.-owned land were nationalized,[103] which Fidel declared was compliance with the agrarian reform provisions of the 1940 constitution.

By 1961 Castro had discarded his assumptions that reforms could be implanted permanently.[104] In April of that year, prior to the Bay of Pigs invasion, Fidel called the Cuban Revolution "socialist" for the first time in public.[105] "We have effected a socialist revolution under the very nose of the United States,"[106] he stated. During the failed invasion of Cuba by CIA-supported Cuban exiles, he stressed that the Cuban forces knew they were fighting for socialism as well as for Cuba.[107] In a speech delivered on May 1, 1961, after victory at the Bay of Pigs, Castro said: "We must talk of a new constitution ... a constitution contributing to a new social system without the exploitation of man by man. That new social system is called socialism ... education, the dignity of man, civil rights for women, secure old age, artistic freedom, nationalization of monopolies, and the necessities of life ... is the program of our socialist revolution."[108]

Soon after the Bay of Pigs confrontation, Cuba accepted Soviet missiles to increase security in the face of the risk of conventional or nuclear war initiated by the United States. Fidel still believes that he acted correctly in accepting the missiles and was justifiably displeased when the Soviets withdrew them in 1962 and left Cuba, not a member of the Warsaw Defense Pact, unprotected.[109] The attempt by the United States to destroy the Revolution caused Castro to rapidly consolidate his support. Late in 1961, the 26th of July Movement, the University of Havana Students Revolutionary Directorate, and the People's Socialist party (Communist party) merged into the Integrated Revolutionary Organization (ORI). In 1963 ORI became the United Party of the Socialist Revolution (PURS), and in 1965 it became the new Communist Party of Cuba (PCC); this change signified the end of the old Moscow-oriented Communist party and represented Fidel's brand of communism.

At the time of the creation of ORI, Castro asserted: "We were like a man with a vocation for music. But a man's vocation for music does not grant him the right to call himself a musician if he has not studied musical theory. When we started our revolutionary struggle we already had some knowledge of Marxism-Leninism and we were in sympathy with it. We were apprentice revolutionaries. But by virtue of this, we could not call ourselves Marxist-Leninists."[110] Fidel correctly predicted that communism would not exist in Cuba in less than thirty years. But by early 1962, he noted that the masses had acquired a revolutionary perspective[111] and that the socialist phase of the Revolution was progressing.

The *Second Declaration of Havana,* issued on February 4, 1962, had a Marxist tone and called for revolution throughout Latin America. Castro's confidence in the future of revolution grew as he saw revolutionary consciousness developing.[112] His endeavors to inculcate collective responsibility succeeded, and he embarked upon a campaign to build collective prosperity.

Fidel's efforts to provide a model for revolution in Latin America were applauded by progressives in Latin American nations, but not always by the region's Communist parties. The Communists rejected his road to revolution because he initially assigned revolutionary leadership to the guerrillas, not party cadres. Also, he deviated from orthodox Communist practice by emphasizing the role of the peasantry, rather than the industrial proletariat, as the popular revolutionary army, and he appeared to downgrade urban political movements in favor of rural ones. He antagonized the Communist parties by denying them their self-assigned position as vanguard of the revolution.[113]

Fidel's problems with the region's Communists continued throughout 1962 and were exacerbated by the Aníbal Escalante case in Cuba. Castro denounced Escalante, a longtime Communist party functionary and national organizer of the ORI, accusing him of despotism, personalism, and opportunism, of building an elitist dominant Communist caste within ORI. According to Castro, Escalante wanted to control the party with the assistance of some of his Communist comrades.[114] By relieving Escalante of his position, Fidel undermined his own position among the hemisphere's Communists, whom he sometimes distrusted and whose dogmatism he frequently criticized, but at the same time he exhibited his independence from the ideological orthodoxy of Moscow.

During these formative years of the Revolution, Fidel trusted his instincts, disregarded standard Communist practice, and built a sometimes eclectic,

Cuban-style Revolution. He spent hours each week on television, explaining and teaching his version of socialism, an approach that had not been available to earlier revolutionaries, such as Lenin and Mao. Simultaneously, he developed a relationship or dialogue with the Cuban people and a vanguard. Under his guidance, ORI, then PURS, and eventually the PCC leadership directed the nation.[115]

A political vanguard directed Cuba, and the nation under Fidel assumed a vanguard position in Latin America in the 1960s. He criticized the Communist parties of the region, such as Venezuela's, which had given up on armed struggle and had adopted reformist postures. At the same time, he acknowledged that armed struggle existed as a last resort. Until 1968, he echoed Che Guevara's beliefs that the united masses can defeat standing armies, that it is not always necessary, as the Communists contended, to wait for revolutionary conditions to launch an insurrection, and that in underdeveloped areas, like Latin America, the primary battlefield is in the countryside.

An analysis of Castro's speeches during the 1960s reveals that he accepted Marxism in a general way. He used Marxist language liberally and often imprecisely, at times without linking ideas to specific conditions or situations.[116] As subsequent chapters illustrate, he worked to establish political institutions that would endure and to broaden social and economic change,[117] using established Marxist precepts where applicable and feasible and innovating where orthodox Marxist ideas did not suit Cuba's needs. His successes surprised many Marxists, especially the Soviets, who believed that Latin America's stratified class system made revolution unlikely and that Fidel's type of insurrection would disintegrate in nonindustrial states devoid of Communist party leadership. His success disproved some of the more rigid Communist beliefs and to some degree helped to precipitate the Soviet "revolutionary democracy theory" that the transition to socialism in the Third World might occur without Communist party guidance, that the peasantry, the petite bourgeoisie, the armed forces, and the intelligentsia might perform the functions of the vanguard party.[118]

Fidel confronted and handled many difficult problems and questions while building socialism. Included among them were the following: How can you transform the productive forces and social relations of society to enhance economic growth without preventing the development of socialist social relations? If you provide worker incentives, such as material benefits, do you hinder the socialist goal of equality? He promoted moral incentives, which often failed to live up to his expectations. Such difficulties he tended to blame on the bureaucracy, governmental supervisors, and individuals, but not the system. He wondered if you could maintain a popular democracy that favors the interests of the working classes, and whether this popular democracy primarily could stress sufficiency, full employment, literacy, access to education and health care and the government and secondarily emphasize democratic electoral processes and relative freedom of the press, without creating an image that people in electoral democracies would misconstrue as malevolent dictatorship?[119] From the last question, one discerns that Castro, throughout the early years of the revolution, cared how others perceived Cuba. He always wished to be understood and viewed as democratic and benevolent.

Throughout the 1960s and into the 1970s many of his actions were clearly paternalistic. Cubans placed a great deal of faith in his good intentions and honesty. In 1970, when the nation did not produce the 10 million–ton quota of sugar that he had set as political and economic goals, he confessed his failure, and fellow Cubans sympathized with him. He acknowledged publicly that he had not elevated the living standard or accumulated capital during the 1960s and declared that Cuba needed to increase democratic consultations at the lower levels if workers were to increase productivity.[120] His public admissions of error reinforced his charismatic hold on the people.

During the first decade and a half of the revolution, Fidel spent a great deal of time out of his office, mingling with and talking to the people. In the 1970s his public discourses reflected a number of themes. He warned against excessive centralization of government and bureaucratic decision-making. At the same time, more state apparatuses were created, which placed a few checks on his personal power.[121] He strove to prevent the old Communist party from dominating administrative functions, but he admitted spending less of his time on domestic affairs and more on foreign and world concerns and that he tended to follow the Soviet line more than during the 1960s.[122] He urged mass organizations to keep struggling for their objectives, not to become subservient to the state. To him, worker participation superseded managerial authority.[123] He pushed to build a workers' state mentality and opposed such practices as absenteeism in the workplace that decreased production and damaged collective efforts.

From the outset of taking power, Fidel urged that "the Revolution will not have reached its highest levels in morals until men do voluntarily, and as free men, the jobs that before they would have to do as slaves."[124] By the 1970s he had begun to accept the necessity for some material incentives. He continuously urged the Cuban people to analyze their problems from a perspective of world history, to understand how classes became divided and how human exploitation came about.[125] This process, he explained, began with Greece and Rome, proceeded through the Middle Ages, the Age of Discovery, the era of mercantilism, to the development of capitalism and bourgeois revolution.[126] He saw Cuban history as synonymous with moral support to other American nations that had yet to reach the revolutionary stage. He worked for the day that the Cuban revolutionary experience would occur elsewhere in Latin America.

During the initial fifteen years of the Castro era, Fidel was preoccupied with defending the nation, developing a socialist economy, building schools and hospitals, and educating, housing, and feeding the people. By the mid-1970s he believed that he had prepared Cuba for a new constitutional form of government led by the new Communist party.

Looking back over that initial phase of the Revolution, Fidel admits that he and his comrades were arrogant, idealistic, and even chauvinistic and that they failed to build and institutionalize democratic revolutionary structures, except on some local levels. He views that period as somewhat authoritarian. He acknowledges that volunteerism existed[127] and that when the appropriate conditions existed, human will wrought new changes.[128] In the new constitutional era that began in the mid-1970s, he would portray himself as an embattled defender of traditional Communist ideas, such as a centrally controlled economy and the supremacy of the party.[129]

3

Precursors, Philosophy, and Ideology

So many theories, doctrines, and beliefs, now out of date, that long ago were like bibles of science. Man has to pay dearly for human progress! Yet I never stopped wondering if it was worthwhile spending my time on such studies, if they would help me combat existing evils. Still, one can only feel a deep reverence for those men who gave their whole lives to thinking and finding ways to leave a legacy to humanity.

—Fidel Castro

While preparing for socialism and constitutionalism in Cuba, Fidel Castro drew inspiration from a series of intellectual precursors and mentors. As we shall see, he learned a great deal from the written works and political actions of José Martí, from the revolutionary deeds of Antonio Guiteras, and from extensive verbal exchanges with Ernesto "Che" Guevara. Their ideas, and those of others mentioned in this chapter, enabled him to piece together a humanistic philosophy that still guides him. This chapter demonstrates that he attributes his Marxist ideology to numerous socialist predecessors and mentors but above all views his Marxism as a logical outgrowth of his knowledge of the negative manifestations of capitalism.

Revolutionary Precursors and Mentors

Castro claims that during his youth he had no live revolutionary political mentors but primarily learned from reading:

When I read the work of a famous author, the history of a people, the doctrine of a thinker, the theories of an economist or the thesis of a social reformer, I am filled with the desire to know everything that all authors have written, the doctrines of all philosophers, the treatises of all economists, and the thesis of all apostles. I

29

want to know everything, and I even go through the bibliographies in the books treasuring the hope of reading those books someday.[1]

Reading encouraged Fidel to put into practice Simón Bolívar's ideas that Latin America could be a "representative force in world affairs,"[2] if the region were kept free of U.S. economic control. He also frequently invokes the names of other Latin Americans about whom he read, who fought for various types of independence. His speeches contain allusions to nineteenth-century Mexican liberal Benito Juárez, who made famous the dictum "respect for the rights of others is peace," twentieth-century Mexican revolutionary Emiliano Zapata, who sought land for the peasants, and Nicaraguan guerrilla chieftain Augusto Sandino, who fought against U.S. imperialism in the 1920s and 1930s. He admires Tupac Amarú, José de San Martín, and José Antonio de Sucre, who led fights for freedom against Spanish colonialism.[3] His ideological heroes include Marx, Friedrich Engels, Lenin, and Ho Chi Minh. Politicians he prizes are Abraham Lincoln, Franklin Roosevelt, Jesse Jackson, and Indira Gandhi.[4]

Castro's Revolution has been quintessentially Cuban. He has mastered the art of bringing to life Cuba's historical patriotic mythology and has created a new one based on the Revolution. He has devoted considerable time to analyses of the nation's past in order to prepare for its present and future. From Cuba's history come the individuals who have most influenced him. He speaks often about Carlos Manuel de Céspedes, who in his opinion initiated Cuba's Revolution on October 10, 1868.[5] He refers frequently to Father Félix Varela y Morales (1787–1853), who served as the precursor of Cuba's educational revolution. Varela moved away from the genuflection and fantasy of the thinking of the Middle Ages, advocated using reason to solve human problems, and pointed out errors in the prevailing body of Scholastic thought, which depended on dogma and theology. He explored the roots of dependency in Cuba. He opposed slavery, ties to the United States, foreign intervention in Cuban affairs, and he worked for Cuban independence. Varela proclaimed the right of Cubans to rebel and said that working people should benefit by what their labor produced. He represented a new departure in the ideological battle for freedom in philosophy. He opened up Cuba to modern thought, stressing the need for Cubans to develop their intellects, to fully analyze political and social problems, and tried to reconcile such analyses with the teachings of the church. He asserted that intellectuals had the responsibility to involve themselves in national matters. An early progressive, he served as a major link between philosophical thought and political thought, between social action and national liberation.[6]

Another influential thinker in the eyes of Castro was Spencerian positivist Enrique José Varona (1849–1933), who in a 1902 conference publicly denounced imperialism, which he saw as a biological and social phenomenon, not an economic one. Varona, whose anti-imperialist ideas predate those of Lenin, also advocated Cuba's liberation from Spain.[7] In addition to Varona, Fidel also appreciates the work of Cuban thinker-activist Carlos B. Baliño (1848–1926). Baliño organized the Socialist Workers Party of Cuba in 1905, based on the ideas of the First Communist International.[8] He helped found the Cuban section of the Anti-imperialist League and Cuba's original Communist party. He worked to abrogate the Platt Amendment by which the United States had, since 1901, the right to intervene in Cuba's internal affairs. Fidel admires Baliño's efforts to take the means of production out of foreign hands, to curtail discrimination against blacks, and to stop the exploitation of children in the workplace.[9]

Castro also extols the worth of the political thought of Julio Antonio Mella (1903–1929).[10] While attending the University of Havana, Fidel had encountered Mella's ideas on cooperation between intellectual and manual workers. Mella, who organized Cuba's first revolutionary student movement in 1927, encouraged university students to advance the cause of the working class. He wanted physical workers to understand the value of cerebral labor, to realize that it was a mistake to always identify intellectuals with the bourgeoisie and the prevailing social system. He stressed that both manual and mental workers were vital to the struggle for socialism. From Mella's writings Castro learned that Cubans would be emancipated only when they understood their own society. Mella's essays enabled Fidel to comprehend how workers' love for Cuba fit into the scheme of international solidarity. In other words, his ideas helped Fidel reconcile Cuban nationalism with internationalism. From him Fidel learned that the quest for social revolution was not an idealistic dream but a fight to advance history. Mella's thoughts pervade the current Cuban constitution (1976), especially aspects pertaining to limitations on property rights, anti-imperialism, agrarian reform, marriage and divorce, the elimination of illiteracy, and equal rights for people of both sexes and all colors. In addition, Mella warned of the dangers of the Monroe Doctrine, which he viewed as a self-proclaimed justification for U.S. expansion.[11]

Antonio Guiteras

Not only did the thinking of Mella, Baliño, Varona, and Varela influence Castro, but he also patterned his thought and actions after those of another revolutionary precursor, Antonio Guiteras (1906–1935). "Tony" Guiteras, guided by the thinking of Julio Antonio Mella, became a student leader at the University of Havana in the late 1920s and organized opposition to dictator Machado, U.S. imperialism, and social injustice. In April 1933, Guiteras and his followers attempted to instigate a popular uprising against Machado by attacking and capturing a military barracks at San Luis, near Santiago de Cuba. They then took refuge in the nearby hills and used guerrilla tactics to hold off

Machado's forces for a few weeks before being captured. They established a precedent for Castro's assault on the Moncada barracks two decades later.[12]

Guiteras subsequently served the progressive, but short-lived, administration of Ramón Grau San Martín (September 1933 to January 1934) as minister of war, interior and the navy. Castro views him as the leader of the anti-imperialist wing of that nationalist government,[13] which sponsored significant social legislation, including a minimum wage, legalization of trade unions, workers' compensation, and social security and retirement pay. Guiteras put the U.S.-owned Cuban Electric Company under state direction, lowered rates to consumers, and urged greater Cuban control over all foreign companies. After the fall of the Grau government, Guiteras went underground and founded TNT, a secret insurrectionary and terrorist organization designed to create support for a revolution in the country by showing that the government could not maintain stability. He also founded Joven Cuba (Young Cuba), a populist-oriented militant organization with nationalist and social-democratic tendencies.

Guiteras and Joven Cuba extracted the anti-imperialist component, but not internationalism, from Marxism and blamed the majority of the nation's problems on foreign control of the economic and political processes. They believed in liberation of the oppressed classes, not single-class rule. They advocated equal rights for women, confiscation of property obtained via corruption, abolition of monopolies, and nationalization of subsoil resources, public services, and large landholdings. They valued work as the highest calling and struggled for workers' rights and full employment. They also spread culture and revolutionary ideas among the masses. Guiteras and Joven Cuba wanted to convert Cuban diplomacy from a class-oriented courtesan operation to one reflecting the cultural interests of the masses. They proposed the creation of a parliament composed of all progressive Latin American organizations, united to nurture common cultural values and to oppose tyranny and imperialism.

Guiteras wanted to initiate a campaign against economic imperialism and the managerial class and to build a social and political revolution led by a popular vanguard. He refrained from talk about class struggle and dictatorship of the proletariat but advocated a form of socialism extrapolated from Lenin's *Imperialism: The Highest Stage of Capitalism* and *The State and Revolution.* He believed, as did Castro, that a small, well-organized force could successfully engage in armed struggle to obtain political ends. To him, violence was a viable way to achieve change. He introduced the concept of urban guerrilla warfare to Cuba. Guiteras and Joven Cuba eventually armed to overthrow the Batista government and failed. In May 1935, while trying to flee into exile, Tony Guiteras was shot and killed by Batista's forces, and his movement fell apart.

Cuba's Communist party of the 1930s regarded Guiteras as a socialist demagogue, but subsequently Castro held him in high esteem; Fidel's *History*

Will Absolve Me speech reflects his precursor's thinking. Castro and the contemporary Communist Party of Cuba frequently point out Guiteras's contributions to their Revolution.[14] From him they learned that a revolutionary administration, in order to implant change, had to neutralize the existing military and could best do so by building an equally vital force, perhaps by arming the people. Maurice Halperin, who taught at the University of Havana and initially supported, then turned against, the Revolution, claimed that the thinking of Guiteras led to Castro's ideas on the nationalization of subsoil rights, agrarian reforms, expropriation of large estates, public service, and the creation of agricultural cooperatives.[15] The thinking of Guiteras, who contributed significantly to Cuba's nationalist revolutionary tradition, represents an important link in Cuba's revolutionary chain. His ability to put ideas into action inspired the next generation of intellectuals and activists, who succeeded where he failed. Above all, he helped convince future revolutionaries that Cuba possessed the elements of nationhood but would not become sovereign until it controlled its economic and domestic policies and the means of production—conditions that could not exist under the capitalist system.

José Martí

Fidel Castro invokes the name of José Martí more often than that of any other Cuban. He feels a special kinship to Martí. Both of them were sons of Spanish immigrants, were imprisoned on the Isle of Pines, and raised funds abroad for the struggles they led for independence. He cherishes the memory of Martí, who succeeded in his mission to liberate his country from colonialism. To Castro, Cuba has no greater hero than the poet, essayist, and journalist who believed in the power of ideas accompanied by action and who died fighting against the Spanish in 1895 in the war for independence that he helped organize.[16] So profound is Fidel's admiration for Martí that his essays mentioning him are collected under the title *José Martí: El autor intelectual*. Throughout the country, Fidel has erected busts and statues of Martí, not Marx and Lenin, as revolutionary symbols that relate to Cuban culture.

To Fidel, Martí's greatest feat was uniting his people for struggle.[17] He uses Martí as his link to an earlier heroic epoch in Cuban history. From this revolutionary precursor he learned to love freedom and dignity, to repudiate despotism, and to have unbounded faith in the people.[18] Martí taught him that patriotism is not chauvinism but humanity.[19] Martí demonstrated how to assail cultural and spiritual oppression, how to make commitments and sacrifice, and how to prepare for "the inevitable war, the necessary war."[20]

Castro reveres Martí as a universal man devoted to culture, knowledge, and analysis that elevates humanity. Like Martí, he deplores ethnic and racial categorizing as divisive and contrary to the idea of progress. From Martí he learned the value of fighting for others, not oneself.[21] Castro believes, as did

Martí, that a genuinely independent Cuba would help sustain the desire for freedom in the rest of Latin America. Like Martí, Castro rejects the mentality that has evoked social conservatism and political inferiority and ineptitude in Latin America and has retarded progress for the majority of the area's citizens.

Fidel refers to Martí as the intellectual author of Moncada[22] and of the July 26th Movement.[23] To him, the ideas of Martí are the foundation to which he added the thoughts of Marx and built the Cuban Revolution. He maintains that by combining their ideas he can forge Cuban socialism. He believes, as did Martí, that Cuba's Revolution must be founded on flexibility and education, not ideological rigidity or ignorance. He agrees with Martí that education should teach one to think critically, to cultivate the intellect, not just to memorize information. They both realized that the educated people who make the revolution need a sense of history to enable them to look at the past in order to prepare for the future.

Castro shares Martí's contention that organized religion abused its power and the Cuban people. They both detested spiritual oppression but felt it necessary to struggle against political and economic imperialism, not religion. Believing in the unity of all fighters in the armed struggle, they concluded that a political party should prepare, coordinate, and lead the revolution.[24] Castro points out that before Lenin, in 1895, Martí formed a revolutionary party to unite all sectors of society for revolution. He also notes that Lenin and Martí saw the Cuban-Spanish-American conflict as the first anti-imperialist war. Fidel adds, however, that the war did not liberate Cuba, as Martí had hoped it would, but only broke its bonds to Spain. Neocolonialism under U.S. hegemony replaced Spanish colonialism, and Cuba's liberation did not occur until the establishment of socialism.[25]

Martí advanced political and social programs for Cuba. He knew that politics and economics were inseparable but postulated no economic program for an independent Cuba. Fidel added to Martí's political and social plans an economic base, ideas derived from Antonio Guiteras, and a modicum of scientific rigor. Castro contends that Martí did not understand the necessity of eliminating intolerable capitalism in order to achieve genuine social and political progress.[26] However, Martí did object to the exploitation of labor and considered the workers indispensable to the accumulation of capital necessary for prosperity.[27]

Castro continuously draws parallels between Marx's and Martí's thought, which he considers the essential building blocks of the Cuban Revolution.[28] For example, he calls the idea of combining study and work a fundamental precept of both schools of thought. Cuba, according to Fidel, is the first nation to implement those ideas.[29] He claims that if Martí had lived in the same environment as Marx, he would have had the same ideas and have acted similarly but that conditions were not ripe for socialist revolution in Cuba during Martí's lifetime.[30]

Although Fidel credits Martí with respect for Marx because the latter sided with the poor and the weak, nowhere does he discuss fully why Martí rejected Marx's ideas, which the former did not understand completely.[31] Martí disliked the concepts of class struggle and historical materialism. He believed that no single class in Cuba had sufficient strength to rebel successfully, and he opposed government control by one class. Understanding the value of the proletariat as a vehicle for social change, he admired Marx as a major interpreter of the anger of the workers but contended that workers could attain their objectives without class conflict.[32] Unlike Fidel, he stated that Marx went too fast and that his followers advocated excessive violence. He erroneously portrayed Marx as a critic without a program for change, one who located the injury but had no remedy for it. Martí, as did Marx, wanted individuals subordinate to the state, but Martí feared a socialist state.[33]

Martí referred to socialism as slavery of man serving the state. He viewed the United States as a country pervaded by capitalist values where the entrepreneurs and the industrial proletariat engaged in a basic social conflict. But to him the fundamental struggle in Latin America pitted the landed gentry against the peasants.[34] Somehow he neglected to make the connections between the two conflicts.

Basically, Fidel views Martí as an anti-imperialist reformer, some of whose ideas epitomize the Cuban ethos and must be incorporated into Cuban socialism. Fidel, according to Carlos Rafael Rodríguez, changed the direction of Martí's bourgeois-democratic anti-imperialist movement because he knew that historically reform processes only temporarily ousted the dominant political powers.[35] Castro did carry out Martí's secular revolution, his quests for change and freedom.[36] He expanded Martí's hemispheric search for independence to a global level.

Castro admires the fact that Martí fought for independence but never hated the Spanish, only Spanish colonialism. Similarly, Fidel fought the U.S. government but never initiated a hate campaign against the country or its people.[37] Martí and Fidel both knew that capitalist governments frequently conduct policies not supported by their citizens. Consequently, one never sees a bumper sticker or billboard in Cuba with slogans analogous to those that appear in the United States condemning the people of a foreign country, such as the "Fuck Iranians" signs of the 1970s.

Martí, Fidel explains, was the first person to refer to the United States as "the empire," employing the term before Lenin used it.[38] From Martí, Fidel learned to differentiate between "Our America" (Latin America) and the "Other America" (the United States), designations that remind the arrogant Yankees that they are not the only Americans. In the face of U.S. designs on the Americas, Martí taught Fidel the value of Latin American unity to Cuban sovereignty.

Ernesto "Che" Guevara

From José Martí, Fidel learned how to blend humanism and *"Cubanidad"* into a revolutionary package. Argentine physician Ernesto "Che" Guevara helped him to approach revolution theoretically. Castro does not mention Che by name as often as he does Martí, but the ideas of his comrade-in-arms constantly appear in his speeches and motivate his actions. Fidel had read Marx and Lenin before he met Che and claims that the Argentine was not his ideological mentor.[39] But Che, with his more-developed theoretical background, assisted Fidel in organizing the theory he had read and in fashioning a more coherent Marxist philosophy.

To Fidel, Che symbolized the most extraordinarily high human valor.[40] Che described Castro in a poem as "dawn's captain." Mutual respect and admiration pervaded their relationship. Fidel believed that Che's political thoughts would be of permanent value to Latin America's quest for change, as they "brought the ideas of Marxism-Leninism to their freshest, purest, most revolutionary expression."[41] Fidel and Che shared basic humanist-socialist ideas. Both admitted that the preconditions for a totally democratic socialist state did not exist in Cuba. They extrapolated from orthodox socialist theory and built the uniquely Cuban socialism explained on subsequent pages.[42] They, like Frantz Fanón and Antonio Gramsci, thought it necessary to get on with the revolution in order to create correct conditions for it if they did not exist. Fidel followed Che's lead and agreed that one does not have to wait for the inevitable revolution, that one can use the party to build revolutionary awareness among the masses, and that out of struggle will come political consciousness.

They concurred that the peasantry, as a class, because of the uncultured and isolated state in which it was kept, needed the revolutionary and political leadership of the working class and the intellectuals to defeat the army and the ruling class.[43] However, Che saw no revolutionary potential in the national bourgeoisie, the petite bourgeoisie, and student movements, which Fidel used to achieve victory in Cuba.[44]

Castro agreed with Che's contention that the most efficient way to build communism in Cuba was by combining the development of the material base with the development of the superstructure, rather than by having them develop in successive stages. This contradicts the Soviet assumption that communist political relationships depended on the proper development of modern technological foundations.[45] Fidel and Che believed that technology could be improved as they constructed communism in Cuba.

Che imparted to Fidel Lenin's belief that violence is a bestial means of settling human conflicts but that as long as society has class divisions and humans exploit humans, wars are inevitable. Exploitation cannot be eliminated without conflict. Che also taught Fidel that socialism is a system based as much on economics as on political consciousness. For example, using personal interest to increase production encourages capitalist ideology.[46] Che knew that a new socialist consciousness would result from a steady transformation of the social structure. He had learned from Antonio Gramsci the value of the role of the intellectual in building a new consciousness by fostering historical awareness and interpreting it for others, lessons imparted to Fidel.

Some of Che's ideas on the "new socialist person" were also derived from Gramsci and passed on to Castro.[47] Over the past three decades Fidel has worked to construct the consciousness necessary to mold the "new socialist person." One of the characteristics of the new socialist person is a lack of egoism, an ideal that Fidel has never completely achieved. He claims, "We still do not have the new man, and we no longer have the old one."[48] Che was obsessed by the idea of replacing corrupt material incentives with morality. Like Che, Castro eschews material incentives and defends value according to moral and social, or human, worth, not supply and demand. He too pictures economic man as a monster created by capitalism and believes that money is worth no part of human life. Although he prefers moral incentives, Fidel realizes that they can be motivated by ego and people can compete for them. Cuban specialist Jean Stubbs added that you can argue in pure Marxist terms that ideas and attitudes are basically determined by material and economic reality, not vice versa, and that in Cuba economic reasons exist for emphasis on the moral aspects of work incentives.[49]

Fidel followed Che's suggestion that material and moral incentives should be balanced and used intelligently, a process that leads to the withering away of material incentives.[50] He understands that through political and ideological education, not government edicts, you reduce the necessity for material incentives. To him, the existence of some material incentives is not synonymous with a loss of revolutionary idealism.

Che, although basically impatient, stressed that the conversion of Cuban society to moral incentives would take considerable time. Fidel agreed that the transition period would be protracted and that slow and complex ideological transformation posed a contradiction between production and consciousness. For instance, during the transition years the habits of capitalist thinking, like personal ambition and selfishness, affect production negatively. He understood that change in the ownership of the means of production could be quick but that a long adjustment period is required for people's consciousness to adjust to the new socialist order.[51]

Castro viewed Che's economic thought as superior and adopted his belief in the effectiveness of voluntary work. He agreed with Guevara's assessment of the problem of unequal exchange in a world capitalist market that siphons off an excessive amount of the value created by the labor of workers and peasants in the Third World. Because of this situation, Che and Fidel concluded, Cuba as a socialist nation had to assume extraordinary internationalist responsibilities. Che also convinced Fidel of the need to construct new social attitudes toward work, related this objective to the wage system, and implored him to encourage workers to improve their skills and educational levels.

Che helped Fidel lay the theoretical base for the transition to socialism. From him Fidel learned to what degree market and commodity relations carried over from capitalism and how much they continue to operate as aspects of production and distribution during the transition period.[52] Che denounced the injustices of unequal exchange and advocated basic revision of the international economic system, ideas that Fidel championed and that led to his campaign to cancel foreign debts and establish a new international economic order, explained in Chapter 6.[53] Initially, Fidel wanted to concentrate on building Cuban communism, but Che disagreed and convinced him of the necessity of opening new revolutionary fronts in the Third World to sustain efforts at home. When Che departed from Cuba in 1965 to open new revolutionary fronts, his dream of industrializing the nation appeared to evaporate for the time being. So did his unique approach to Marxism, as Cuba began to adhere to a more orthodox Soviet system. Internal debate diminished in Cuba after Che left the country. For instance, three newspapers, *Hoy,* the organ of the Communist party, *El Mundo,* a paper without political affiliation, and *Revolución,* the journal of the 26th of July Movement, were all replaced by *Granma,* the official party newspaper. Eventually Che's concept of simultaneously building external and internal revolution prevailed. When Che died while trying to stimulate a revolution in Bolivia in 1967, Castro felt a deep personal loss and grieved for quite a while for his *compañero.*

Philosophy

Although Fidel acknowledges his debts to revolutionary precursors and Che, he contends that his political ideas, for the most part, result from reflection. He does not regard himself as a philosopher. Whereas philosophers formalize or explain the relations between ideas, Fidel informally interprets ideas. He very rarely puts pen to paper, as a thinker such as Mao Zedong would have, to map out strategies or, for example, to theorize about the correct course for the peasant in the Revolution. He is more concerned with mobilizing forces around ideas, thereby giving the latter legitimacy. He also has the ability to blend his ideas with those of others. For example, after coming to power, he merged the native ideas of the 26th of July Movement, the populist views of Antonio Guiteras and José Martí, and Marxist ideology to form Fidelismo or Castroism. He found no insurmountable contradictions between Martí's dream of a just society free of racism, foreign domination, and the power of the propertied interests, on the one hand, and the socioeconomic teachings of Karl Marx, on the other.[54]

Historicism pervades Castro's thinking. He proceeds on the premise that all sociological phenomena are historically determined, all truths are relative, no absolute values exist, and all events are influenced by the past. He believes in a moral imperative in politics. The latter he calls "an ugly animal" and a "fabulous stimulating activity."[55] He feels that only when politics works to terminate the exploitation of human by human will prehistory end.[56] To him, political events often determine governments and governmental forms, and he does not believe that each nation has the government it deserves. In other words, Fidel does not blame the colonized for colonization. Geographical and historical conditions determine a society's form.[57] In his ideal society, initiative flows up from the bottom and down from the top.

In directing Cuba from above, Castro adheres to the Marxist concept of praxis. The Greek word *praxis* means action. In contrast to theory, the goal of which is knowledge or wisdom, praxis is oriented to doing. To Marx, it meant the ability to put theory into action while confronting problems. The German thinker believed that theoretical contradictions could be resolved only through practical action. He construed as praxis only objective activity designed to transform the social and natural world and satisfy human needs. He sought liberation through praxis. To Marx, by examining past praxis one could see what new praxis could foster revolution. Lenin reiterated Marx's notion of the unity of thought and action. Gramsci argued that the thinker understands historical contradictions, sees himself or herself as an element of them, and works to acquire knowledge and institute revolutionary action.[58] Fidel understands the need to blend theory with action and knows how to get the masses to utilize the former in order to implement the latter. From time to time, he has severely criticized purely philosophical Marxists, who ignore praxis.

When asked to describe his philosophy, Fidel repeatedly invokes the term *humanism,* meaning that he considers human beings, not God, responsible for society's conditions. He sees people, as did Aristotle, as essentially social animals, capable of evaluating and solving their problems.[59] To him, human behavior is learned and can be unlearned, as people are malleable. Castro, like Marx and Engels, does not have an exalted opinion of human nature but expects the superior morality of communism to elevate humanity. He believes that if a person has superior intelligence, it should be put at the service of humanity, but that individual should receive the same benefits as one with lesser intelligence. All owe society their maximum effort.[60]

Like Marx, Castro identifies human beings with their surroundings, institutions, ideas, and the mode of production. To him, no concept of human nature exists. People are shaped by class experience, personal involvements, and strivings. He sees no need for competition to urge people to do their best: The social responsibility of the individual provides sufficient motivation.[61] He rejects the idea that "man is like a little animal who only moves when you dangle a carrot in front of him or whip him with a stick."[62] Fidel considers those who share his beliefs to be his family.

He believes that individuals interpret events and develop ideas and allows that individuals can affect conditions.[63] Basically, he agrees with Marx, who stated in the *Third Thesis on Feuerbach* that circumstances change men, just as circumstances are changed by men.[64] Fidel relies upon Marx's axiom found in the *Critique of Political Economy* that life is not determined by consciousness, but consciousness by life. Thus people recognize only problems they can solve. The problem is not recognized until the basis for solving it begins to emerge. Marx thought that human emancipation, in the widest sense, depended upon human control over the forces of nature, or the advance of science. He felt that this would lead to progress, not as a gradual process, but as a result of class conflict and societal description. Fidel concurs.

Fidel, as did Marx, believes in ultimate human perfectibility, that "man is the product of struggle and difficulties, that problems gradually mold him in the same way a lathe shapes a piece of material, in this case, the matter and spirit of a human being."[65] He contends that in their innermost souls, people are warriors who respond to a premature urge to fight, even though it gains them nothing. In his estimation, it will take generations to overcome such irrational responses.[66] However, according to Fidel, people possess a revolutionary core and work through a process that prepares them for objectives that are possible.[67]

Castro thinks that if you can halt the philosophy of plunder, the concept of war will be eliminated.[68] He distinguishes between war for profit and revolutionary struggle. Whereas traditional orthodox Communists have viewed revolutionary force as the last step in the struggle, Fidel has at times advocated the reverse. He claims, "I do not know what pleasure oppressors find in using a whip against human backs, but I know that there is infinite happiness in fighting against oppression, in raising a strong hand and saying, I do not want to be a slave."[69]

To him, struggle can initiate the awareness that builds revolution. It is history that creates the objective conditions for revolution, but it is people that create the subjective conditions. Revolution is part of the creative process, according to Marx, who stated that he "who has a Raphael in him should be afforded the opportunity to develop freely,"[70] a philosophy adopted by Fidel.

Marx and Martí believed that labor played a major role shaping the person and could be used to develop revolutionary tendencies and create new societies. Fidel agrees, claiming that the jobs people perform should contribute to their revolutionary development and that of society as a whole. To him, if work is merely a way to earn a living, it loses its mobility and becomes vulgar, and workers should not be an instrument for human exploitation but a tool for the "redemption of man, for the elevation of man, for the progress of man."[71] Fidel condemns those who do not work and praises the workers who understand that their efforts contribute to the collectivity. Work and the collective consciousness it builds have been a cornerstone of the Cuban Revolution. Through work one also learns the elements of socialist democracy, where officials elected directly by the workers and those appointed by the administration represent the same class interests.

Ideology

Like Marx and Hegel, Fidel views history as progressive. To achieve progress, upon assuming power, he strove to eliminate what Gramsci called bourgeois-ideological hegemony, which in Cuba had led to popular acceptance of the fundamental precepts of capitalism. While pursuing social revolution, he made the pursuit of socialist ideology and theory patriotic. As noted previously, he claims that the study of capitalist political economy led him to socialist conclusions. For over three decades he has encouraged all Cubans to study capitalism and socialism.

Only after seizing power did Castro begin to offer an ideological explanation of his movement. Once in control, he referred to his doctrine as revolutionary and dialectic, a guide to action. To him, dogmatic theory that functions like a catechism is anti-Marxist.[72] Castro asserts that he is more interested in how Lenin created a successful revolution than in whether Marxism-Leninism has a valid theoretical base on which to run a nation.[73] He understands that "had we been willing to follow stereotypes, theory had it that no revolution could have been made here."[74]

Scholars have interpreted Castro's actions according to various Marxist principles. For the sake of examining the Cuban Revolution in an organized fashion, this is a valid technique. A categorization of the stages of the Cuban Revolution according to the thinking of Marx would indicate that the bourgeois-democratic phase began in January 1959. It lasted until the state nationalized the means of production between October 1960 and April 16, 1961, at which time Fidel proclaimed the socialist revolution. The socialist stage has endured from then until now.[75]

Although Castro does not want the Cuban Revolution to be judged by dogmatic theories or categories, he concedes, "There is room only for ecological coexistence with the spiritual creation of the revolutionary peoples, with socialist culture, with the forms of expression of Marxist-Leninist ideology."[76] He means that flexibility exists within socialism but that counterrevolutionary ideology will not be tolerated.[77]

Fidel equates progress with the affirmation of the role of human consciousness and will in changing society. To him, human will is not subordinate to material forces but a coequal force, and revolutionary consciousness emanates from thought and analysis, not indoctrination. He stresses: "Do not allow anyone to believe anything that he does not understand. That is the way fantasies are made and mystic, dogmatic fanatical minds are developed."[78] Consciousness prepares people for revolutionary ideology, develops a collective judgment, a societal consensus, and a desire for equality. Cubanness is a part of political consciousness and creates new loyalties and unity and reduces alienation. Castro's brand of revolutionary consciousness and nationalism has allied middle-class reformers, radicals, idealists, and communists in support of Cuba's independence from foreign domination.[79]

An integral part of Castro's revolutionary ideology is the aforementioned rejection of materialism. He claims, "We have something more powerful than money and that is conscience," and "a communist is more powerful than a capitalist, because a communist is not for sale."[80] He avers that "we will never create socialist consciousness, and much less communist consciousness with a shopkeeper mentality."[81] Fidel constantly explores and reevaluates revolutionary consciousness and claims that every year, through the dialectical process, he develops new ideas and adds to the revolutionary ideological nucleus.[82]

Once Cubans buy into Fidel's ideology, they become more than socialists. Loyalty to him makes them *fidelistas*.[83] The new Cuban person, a *fidelista*, has a developed revolutionary consciousness, which means being more than a soldier in the class struggle. It connotes altruism, caring for others, and an internationalist perspective.[84] To Castro, ideology encompasses a fighting spirit, dignity, revolutionary morale, and high principles. For the revolutionary, ideological struggle is the "front line of combat,"[85] an effective weapon against misconduct, weakness, privileges, and immorality.[86]

To Castro, socialist ideology is not automatically produced by structural transformation. It must be molded out of class struggle and political education based on national and international information.[87] He believes that "to give man participation in more collective wealth because he does his duty and produces more and creates more for society is to turn political awareness into wealth."[88] Fidel fears that material wealth alone can diminish consciousness and contends that the material base must grow concomitantly with revolutionary consciousness.[89] Socialist awareness must develop at the same rate as the production forces, and consciousness must accompany each step forward in the development of those productive forces.[90] Perhaps Fidel best explains his own ideology when he praises Che, who he feels continuously stressed the inseparable social relations of production and the transformation of the social and political consciousness of the workers involved in the revolutionary process.[91]

Capitalism

As noted above, Fidel considers a critique of capitalism an indispensable socialist tool. He agrees with Marx that 10 percent of capitalist society lives on the back of the other 90 percent and that capitalism "left remaining no other nexus between man and man, than naked self-interest, than callous 'cash payment.' It has drowned the most heavenly ecstasies of religious fervor of chivalrous enthusiasm, of philistine sentimentalism, in the icy waters of egotistical calculation."[92] Fidel related Marx's thinking to Cuba, where most people lived in poverty, while a few held the wealth. Before 1959, he explained, Cuba experienced a nine-month season between the harvests when 600,000 out of 1,500,000 workers were unemployed. One-quarter of those who worked the land owned some of it, less than 0.1 percent of the landowners held 20 percent of it, 8 percent of them owned 70 percent of it, and 70 percent of them held only 11 percent of it.[93] This specter led Fidel to comment, "The prospect of a world without capitalism is not too frightening for us revolutionaries."[94]

Castro likes to generalize about economic conditions in the capitalist world, in the past and the present, and his facts are usually accurate. To him, only during the era of the French Revolution did the bourgeoisie represent the most advanced class and speak in the name of society as a whole. In subsequent years, in capitalist society there existed two groups, the exploiters and the exploited, and little equality.[95] He credits capitalism with technological and organizational successes[96] but, as did Marx, expresses skepticism about the permanence of reform under capitalism. At a 1987 economic conference in Havana he noted that capitalists organized production better than socialists and had better methods that you can learn from but that you cannot learn from their ideology.[97]

According to Castro, capitalists take better care of their factories and their money than of their employees. However, he acknowledges that they compete with other capitalists, go bankrupt, and are sued and lose their property. Socialism, he insists, must be efficient without competition, without the abuses and risks of capitalism. He believes that socialists must guarantee employment and pay salaries commensurate with the quantity and quality of goods produced and that this will benefit the state as long as workers hold revolutionary ideas.[98]

Fidel regards capitalism as corrupt and harmful to humanity, as the "twisted" legacy of centuries of colonialism, imperialism, and unequal social relations.[99] It is responsible for underdevelopment, hunger for billions, the arms race, and the danger of nuclear war.[100] He views the resources that enabled the developed states to accumulate investment capital to be a result of the efforts of exploited workers in colonies.[101] He refers to capitalism as "a pyramid of exploitation … where those on the top exploited those below them, who in turn exploited those below them."[102] He sees in capitalism a negative freedom, the freedom to exploit, and believes that positive freedom cannot exist in a society where exploitation exists.[103] Socialism, in contrast, teaches the idea of laboring for the spiritual and material well-being of humanity.[104]

Castro stresses the idea that competitive capitalism engenders repressive nondemocratic governments. Under capitalism employed people compete against the unemployed, and discipline is maintained through a person's needs, whereas under socialism it is dependent on one's conscience. Capitalists dismiss workers from jobs for protesting or striking, but under socialism, with workers' justice, labor tribunals, and legislation, strikes are unnecessary.[105]

He notes that in capitalist bureaucracies government functionaries consider their work professional and removed from politics; however, in reality they are intermediaries subordinate to the will of the bourgeoisie. With the transition to socialism, bureaucracy assumes a new character relative to the means of production, becoming more active in the political process. He warns of the dangers of a special stratum of privileged citizens who tend to become insensitive to the political and human aspects of their work. He says that you should not venerate special ministries of government and must constantly struggle to keep the administrators committed to the masses, not the hierarchy.[106]

Fidel believes that capitalism deforms individuals and entangles them in egotistical struggles for existence. Capitalism motivates people exclusively by material incentives, and in such a system profit-oriented behavior is considered correct. Marxists feel that people can act uprightly out of moral character and love for fellow humans.[107] When capitalists talk about liberty, equality, and fraternity, they mean, according to Castro, liberty for the bourgeoisie and the white elites. Capitalist equality connotes some vague form of metaphysical egalitarianism, not financial or material parity. Finally, he says, fraternity between the rich and poor, or blacks and whites, is a fantasy.[108] He regards capitalism as unjust, as it requires for its maintenance a continuous maldistribution of wealth. He points out that the more equitable socialist system regards use value as more important than exchange value.[109] Why produce a diamond-studded wristwatch with great exchange value but no more usefulness than an inexpensive quartz watch, which performs the same function? Also, the difference in price between the $30 watch and the $6,000 watch can feed thousands of starving children.

To Castro, socialism is inherently more democratic than capitalism. The capitalist state supports the interests of the capitalist class, whereas the socialist state serves the majority. He thinks the latter is what democracy is about, not merely holding elections. He considers capitalist elections "auctions for the highest bidder among those with the most money for propaganda and vote buying."[110] People submit to capitalist electoral laws devised by those who own the means of production and delude themselves into thinking that they participate in a democratic process.

Similarly, the masses submit to economic systems that favor the holders of capital. For example, under capitalism prices are set in an arbitrary fashion according to profit value. Under socialism, in Cuba, essential products are produced according to the needs of the populace, and simultaneously, the state assumes most of the cost of education, health care, lodging, and food.[111] In market economies food is sold at the highest price the market will bear. Cuba rejects a price policy to compensate for the imbalance between supply and demand, which hurts those with the lowest incomes. Fidel believes that such a policy is acceptable for luxury goods, but not for staples; thus Cuba employs a rationing system.[112]

On the international scale, Castro has demanded an end to unequal trade, to dumping and protectionism, and to abusive financial policies, such as excessive interest charges and overvaluation of the dollar, to which Third World currencies are pegged.[113] He blames these capitalist practices for causing disintegration of the masses and the formation of an underclass. Fidel refers to the lumpenproletariat, the vagabonds, discharged soldiers, ex-convicts, thieves, brothel keepers, and beggars, who drag down capitalist society and who become receptive to reactionary ideologies and movements. Such elements, he contends, are necessary to keep capitalism afloat but rarely exist under most forms of socialism. He maintains that everyone in a society should share in its production, not just the producers. Public health or military personnel, for instance, do not produce capital goods, yet they contribute to society and should benefit by its production.[114]

The worst excesses of capitalism are synonymous with the United States to Fidel. He fears the reassertion of Yankee influence in Cuba. While working assiduously to prevent the rise of capitalist sentiment in Cuba, he asserts, tongue-in-cheek, that he has no intention of fomenting socialism in the United States. When that occurs, he says, it will be led by the U.S. working classes.[115]

Fidel views Third World economic cooperation as a threat to the U.S. neo-colonial mechanisms. The United States fights diligently, often covertly, to prevent nations such as Cuba from working out advantageous economic arrangements with other underdeveloped nations.[116] He repeatedly notes how the world capitalist crisis devastates the other nations of Latin America more than Cuba.[117] In today's world, neocolonialism places the underdeveloped nations in a more difficult position than Cuba's. Big capital has replaced direct ownership of colonies and uses sophisticated and worse methods of exploitation. Fidel likes to point out that in the Third World more than 14 million children under five years of age die annually of curable diseases.[118]

Capitalism goes where it can earn the most, and the Third World suffers as a result.[119] Yet, Fidel distinguishes between the capitalism of the Third World and that of the developed world, with the former being more exploitative than the latter.[120] He sees no future for Latin America in terms of capitalist development. England, Germany, France, Japan, and the United States initiated industrialization when it was less expensive to do. Today there is no alternative but to plan economies, centralize, and pool raw materials. Poor states do not have sufficient money to permit the waste created by free competition. He thinks that only socialism can prevent waste and provide for adequate technological development to overcome underdevelopment.[121]

The Third World, as a result of terms of trade imposed on it by capitalist powers, now pays three times more for goods than it did thirty years ago.[122] By the early 1970s private capitalists' direct investments in Third World states had decreased, whereas funds from transnational commercial banks had increased. Thus underdeveloped nations acquired huge interest payments on external debts. Growth in trade took place primarily among the developed nations, not between developed and underdeveloped states. Non-oil-exporting nations' share of world exports fell from about 25 percent in 1955 to slightly over 11 percent in 1970–1980. Thus the underdeveloped countries—with most of the world's population—were responsible for just over one-tenth of the world's trade.[123]

By 1983, according to Castro, the world economic crisis, which originated in major capitalist nations, had brutally affected the Third World countries, and the latter experienced the sharpest economic deterioration in the post–World War II era. They were plagued by enormous balance-of-payments problems, and giant conglomerates controlled 40–50 percent of the major commodities they exported.[124] Currently, the developed market-economy nations absorb more than 85 percent of the world's manufacturing and control over 83 percent of all industrial exports, 26 percent of which go to developing nations. Fidel states that the most serious aspect of this dependency is that Third World imports, consumer items, and capital goods are manufactured according to the demands and technology of the most advanced industrial states. This affects trade and contaminates values in Third World nations.[125] Fidel admits that, of late, capitalist countries have been compelled to make some reforms to stave off social revolutionary and socialist movements, but more often than not the latter have provoked takeovers in Latin American capitalist states by right-wing militaries in order to prevent change in their social relations of production.

4

Foundations of
Cuba's Marxist State

Karl Marx says in his Communist Manifesto *that capitalism digs its own grave. But capitalism digs two graves—one for itself and the other for the society which comes after capitalism. What we must do is to fill in the hole quickly, so that the heritage of capitalism may not also destroy and bury socialism.*

—Fidel Castro

Every civilization considers its worldview eternal, but it is always superseded by another. Karl Marx believed that worldviews constantly work to ascend to another stage. The transition period between stages he referred to as revolutionary. This chapter illustrates how Fidel Castro's worldview evolved to include Marxist beliefs as well as the ideas of Lenin and how it transcended various stages. It delves into the Cuban leader's thinking on revolution, which he opted for in pursuit of a Marxist-Leninist state. It examines his insights into socialism and revolutionary nationalism and details, generally in his words, how the Cuban socialist state emerged and why it was necessary to build a vanguard party to guide it.

Marxism

To Fidel, Marx and Lenin stand out "among the most transcendental men in the history of humanity for ideas, intellect and activity."[1] Castro learned from Marx and Engels's *Communist Manifesto* that a small segment of the ruling class breaks away from it and joins the revolutionary class.[2] From Lenin he learned how to blend theory with praxis. With the thoughts of these two predecessors in mind, he fashioned for Cuba a pragmatic, not theoretical, form of Third World Marxism. As the Cuban Revolution unfolded, he has indicated that Marxism means more than theory and philosophy, that it serves as a guide to daily life, to solving the practical problems that humanity has faced since classical times.[3] He has operated on the premise that every bourgeois politician understands that class problems exist and has used this as a starting point to spread Marxist ideas.[4]

Asserting that "nothing is more anti-Marxist than dogma and thought which are petrified," Fidel has continuously searched Marxist literature for new ideas. He uses Marxism as "a map of the forest," seeing it as a flexible theory that coincided with the humanist goals of the 26th of July Movement.[5] Like George Lukács, he sees Marxism as a logical ideological expression of an embattled proletariat.

Since December 1, 1961, when he declared, "I must say with full satisfaction and full confidence, I am a Marxist-Leninist, and I shall be a Marxist-Leninist until the last day of my life,"[6] he has sprinkled his speeches and writings with allusions to classical Marxism. After almost ten years of revolutionary struggle, he admitted that he had no doubts about Marxist-Leninist interpretations. He now acknowledges that his appreciation and understanding of Marxism has grown over the decades and that during the earlier years of the Revolution he was influenced by a lifetime of exposure to imperialist and reactionary propaganda against communism.[7]

By the time that he announced that Cuba would pursue Marxism-Leninism, he assumed that its people had acquired socialist spirit and morality,[8] that they were ready to accept his belief that "Marxism is a living science, a developing science."[9] He urged Cubans to follow Marx and write history as they observe it, not as they wish it to be.[10] He rejected theory that exists outside of the world and is then applied. He told his people that to be a Marxist-Leninist they must first study its principles and then apply them to real situations, that theory and praxis are necessary to construct socialism, then communism.[11] He maintained that Marxism has to keep growing, to constantly reinterpret, with honest scientific objectivity. "It must behave like a revolutionary force and not like some pseudo revolutionary church."[12]

To Castro, Marxism does not represent a total explanation of life. He sees Marxism as "a revolutionary and dialectical doctrine, not a philosophical doctrine."[13] Like Marx, he is more concerned with the historical self-consciousness of humanity than with pure theory, with understanding what action is required for change. He believes that Marx never prepared a blueprint for all cultures and countries nor devised a universal formula for revolution. Marx never explained how things are but rather explained developments: He proposed but did not predict. Fidel follows suit. He views the theory of Marx as a science, one that applies to each concrete case, but he indicates that no two cases are identical.[14]

Naturally, says Castro, Marx made errors and warrants criticism on specific points. But the Cuban leader points out that those who do not use Marxist scientific analyses are prone to make more mistakes. Mistakes, he asserts, generally emanate from lack of serious in-depth or collective analysis, which he calls a fundamental part of Marxism-Leninism.[15] To him, the Marxist idea of class struggle permits us to understand the society in which we live[16] and thus plot out a revolutionary and liberating course. He favors a brand of Marxism that can accommodate to diverse tendencies, one that is constantly brought up to date to meet existing conditions.

In the preface to his *Critique of Political Economy,* Marx argued that knowledge as a passive observation of reality can effect nothing. Only the active critical handling, constant change, and improvement of facts and ideas can recreate the world. When you add action to knowledge, said Marx, you initiate a dialectical process in both organized production and social relations.[17] It is this process, thinks Fidel, that enables utopians to become revolutionaries.[18] To him, Marx's and Engels's ideas added the concreteness that made utopian idealists look unsophisticated by comparison.[19] Castro agrees with Marx's rejection of the utopian views of humanity, or the idea of voluntarism—that individual will has primacy in the historical process. Fidel allows for individual will, but not as a primary factor.[20]

Marx in his *Theses on Feuerbach* explained that philosophers have only interpreted the world, but the point is to change it. To the German master, understanding laid the foundation for change. He rejected understanding for its own sake. Castro interprets this as meaning lip service is cheap: Do something. He followed Marx's course of establishing in Cuba a new cultural level, a greater love for reading, sharing, and implementing social and political ideas. He promotes popular comprehension of political and social theory so that every citizen can understand a modicum of socialist thinking and offer constructive criticism.[21] Like Marx, he strives to raise reality to the level of thought. He sees ideas growing out of immediate circumstances. He states that Marx noted that when an idea penetrated the masses it was transformed into material force. For example, says Fidel, the idea of work for the benefit of all becomes a material force to strengthen society by increasing production.[22]

Castro contends that "Marx never posed as the prophet."[23] Like Marx, Fidel presents no absolutes that are valid for all times and places or solve all problems. He concurs with Marx's idea that people make their own history. They do not make it under circumstances they choose but under circumstances transmitted from the past. Cuban history, in his estimation, has led the country to socialism.

In a speech of July 26, 1958, Fidel said that no society has ever achieved communism. He noted that Marx believed communist societies must be based on mastery of technology and the full development of productive forces, which would enable people to create sufficient material goods to satisfy the needs of everyone. To attain communism, stated Castro, you need to emerge from underdevelopment. You must build communist consciousness at the same rate as you develop the forces of production.[24] He realized that

Marx expected people to attain communism in different ways, that tradition and native character help make diverse types of Marxism.[25] Fidel concurs with Marx that history is a process of development determined by the material conditions of production.[26] But he realizes that Marx never offered a doctrine of economic determinism. To the latter, economic determinism belonged to capitalism, under which economic laws could be ascertained. Fidel often refers to Marx's stages of production, the Asiatic, ancient, feudal, and modern bourgeois, as preludes to socialism.

Castro borrows Marx's theory of human labor as enunciated in the latter's *Economic and Philosophical Manuscripts of 1844*. Fidel too views labor as a human activity in which material and intellectual production go together. People produce for their physical, spiritual, and cultural existence simultaneously, but the economic importance of labor serves as a foundation for all social life. Thus Castro, as did Marx, views Marxism as political economy.[27]

Marx taught that people should be free to form their own lives and attain their potential and understood that under capitalism such freedoms are linked by the decisions of a few. In other words, under capitalism the availability of commodities that are essential to live is regulated by those who control their production.[28] According to Marx, labor is the fundamental interchange between man and nature—it transforms society. Labor has a progressive character, as it constantly moves toward increasing people's control over nature. In *Capital* (Volume 3) Marx indicated that the relationship between the controllers of the conditions of production and the direct producers reveals how the social system and the state works and the degree to which there exists popular sovereignty.[29] With this in mind, Castro hoped to place Cuban production in the hands of people, thus creating more individual freedom.

Fidel learned from Marx that the working class has the greater power, for the capitalists cannot produce without it.[30] When the working people take over, they can make the decisions. From the German thinker Castro picked up the idea that capitalism is run by egoists whose acts are aimed at personal gain. The Cuban chief sees revolution as a means to equalize incomes from the bottom up so that eventually money as life's primary incentive and cause of alienation will be eliminated.[31]

Communists, according to Fidel and Marx, rather than dominating the workers, should teach them the value of the abolition of private property, which causes greed and exploitation. Without the leadership of communists, the workers, not knowing better, might settle for capitalist reforms. Moreover, workers must live in a world where the natural resources are at the service of humanity, where science and technology benefit all people, not just the wealthy.[32] Engels predicted that the takeover of the means of production by the people would end commodity production. But Castro understands that has not occurred anywhere in the socialist world, including Cuba. The market still exists, but Fidel believes that it must not control the economy.[33]

He contends that the means of production are controlled scientifically under Marxism-Leninism and that situation differs greatly from the U.S. government's distorted view of socialism as designed to precipitate international revolution in order to destroy different governmental and economic systems.[34] He also points out that the Marxism that evolved in the Soviet Union and Eastern Europe deviated from Marx's concepts. It dealt with the economy separately from the social superstructure. In essence, it put forth a "socialist" distribution of wealth but did not change the relations of production in accord with the type of equality Marx envisioned in a classless state. Che Guevara brought this deviation to Fidel's attention and convinced him that a different, more human-oriented, egalitarian social order should accompany Cuban socialism.

The social and political aspects of Marx's thought intrigue Castro. In particular, the Cuban leader admires the German's emphasis on the social theory of the working-class movement, exactly the aspect of his thought that Marx hoped would be recognized as significant. Marx referred to his system of ideas concerning the social order as ideology. Fidel does too, noting that the *Communist Manifesto* "was a revelation. It was so persuasive that I was absolutely amazed. I was converted to those ideas."[35] Fidel contends that Marx did not invent classes or class struggle but merely studied and demonstrated how they functioned. Marx did not preach class hatred but noted that class struggle gives rise to class hatred.[36]

Castro follows the standard Marxist view that class struggle existed in ancient Rome and Greece with slavery and that the feudal system added a bit more humanity to civilization. He sees capitalism as superior to feudalism but believes that the drive for more productive forces and private wealth caused greater insensitivity to human needs. Thus, capitalism divides people, causes egoism, inequality, and privilege.[37]

Marx, Castro knows, did not see an automatic transition to socialism through the dialectical process. For Marx the dialectic meant people learning how to control their world through knowledge of natural law, by making technological progress, and by adapting economic institutions, systems, and ideas to the changing industrial base.[38] Fidel operates on Marx's premise that a theory of universal historical development does not exist, that it varies according to how people master their respective external environments.

He also realizes that "no political process, none, follows any pattern."[39] For example, he asserts that under certain circumstances some nations can achieve peaceful change. But historically, most major social changes have resulted from revolutions. He says that armed struggle is not one of his original ideas but the invention of oppressors who have protected their vested interests by force.[40]

Once a transition to a workers' state is accomplished, Marx believed, democracy would increase. Fidel brings up this point frequently and notes that Marx concluded that the dictatorship of the proletariat was a transitory phase en route to socialism and the dissolution of the state.[41] To them both, dictatorship of the proletariat theoretically means political power for, and democratic rule by, the majority, not some harsh form of authoritarianism, as it is generally construed by cold war mongers. Fidel likes to insert into his speeches Marx and Engels's admonition: "Let the ruling classes tremble at a communist revolution. The proletarians have nothing to lose but their chains. They have a world to win. Working men of all countries unite."[42]

However, Castro understands that Marx underestimated the capacity of capitalist states to co-opt mass and working-class parties and make them allies of the state. Fidel realizes that despite class conflict, people do not dive right into revolution. Instead, they first attempt to exhaust all ways of working within the system. For instance, he is aware of the fact that prior to the Revolution, especially during the 1930s and 1940s, Cuba's Communist party's labor unions contained 400,000 to 500,000 members. Not all were Communists, but most were sympathetic to the Communist cause. Yet during World War II, Communist party leaders Juan Marinello and Carlos Rafael Rodríquez served in dictator Batista's cabinet, and the party allied with the Cuban state.

Leninism

According to Fidel, Lenin's ideas have endured and have helped change the world. They led to the emergence of the first socialist state, a state that helped save humanity from fascism. He invokes the name of Lenin almost as often as that of Marx. Lenin's books *The State and Revolution* and *Imperialism: The Highest Stage of Capitalism* made an enormous impression on him and helped him prepare for change in Cuba. He frequently acknowledges his debt to them for clarifying his thinking. French philosopher Régis Debray, who knew Fidel fairly well during the 1960s, referred to him as a Leninist, or an opportunist with principles.[43] Just as Lenin seized the opportunity to turn the chaos and disruption of 1917 in Russia into stability, Fidel knew that after his takeover he could best establish order in Cuba through a benevolent authoritarian system, which he felt would subsequently give way to a more democratic state.

Fidel also realizes that many analogies between the Russian and Cuban revolutions break down. For example, he recalls that Lenin said that Russia under the czar was the weakest link in the capitalist world and the revolution could be started there. Although Cuba was one of the strongest capitalist links in Latin America during the 1950s, revolution worked there,[44] partially because Fidel learned from Lenin the need to abandon old schemes for new ones more compatible with contemporary life.[45] He understood that Lenin, although he believed in the inevitability of socialism, stated that all nations would attain it differently and that each would reach it with another form of democracy or a variation of the dictatorship of the proletariat.

Castro saw how Lenin successfully organized a revolution[46] and defended Marxist doctrine against mystifications and distortions.[47] But he disagreed with Lenin's dictum that there could not be a revolution without revolutionary theory. In 1960, Fidel adopted the antithetical position, which he followed until 1971, that is, that every revolutionary, versed in theory or not, had the duty to make the revolution. He criticized the Latin American Communist parties that awaited propitious conditions to begin a revolution. He exclaimed, "It is not for revolutionaries to sit in the doorways of their houses waiting for the corpse of imperialism to pass by."[48] Simultaneously, he followed Lenin's precept that the professional revolutionary is the one who teaches the masses to struggle and guides the transformation of their thinking. The Russian leader believed that the workers, if left to their own devices, might never understand their revolutionary role in freeing themselves from capitalism.

To Lenin, a proletarian vanguard party was essential for revolution. Marx and Engels opposed guerrilla warfare as a valid form of popular struggle but, unlike the Cubans, did not link it to proletarian tactics for gaining power. Castro and his *compañeros* proved Engels, Marx, and Lenin wrong by successfully winning a guerrilla war that was not guided by a vanguard party. But Fidel acknowledges that you can never regard guerrilla warfare as the only, or even the primary, method of struggle. He knows that although it worked in Cuba, it might not elsewhere.

Castro paid attention to Lenin's contention that one learns more rapidly and thoroughly during revolution than in peacetime. The Russian theorist also impressed Fidel with the idea that revolution needed the capability of defending itself.[49] To do so, Castro concluded, ultimately a party had to be built in Cuba (after the military phase of the Revolution). His critics today claim that he is too tied to the Leninist theory of party control to permit a more relaxed political atmosphere in Cuba. He likes to quote Lenin that "the seriousness of purpose of a revolutionary party is measured basically by the attitude it takes toward its own errors."[50] The Leninist party, described in fuller detail later in this chapter, engages in politics, which Castro construes as a social science and an art—the science of evaluating situations and devising appropriate programs and the art of applying them while teaching the masses.[51]

Of course, those who engage effectively in politics must understand, as did Lenin, that "politics is a concentrated expression of economics" and that politics must take precedence over economics.[52] By no means is understanding society and economics easy, and Fidel constantly encourages more research in the area of Marxist-Leninist theory, especially to link vital topics to the needs of the people.[53]

Lenin, according to Castro, made a great contribution when he conceived of the possibility of building socialism in an economically backward nation, one that was not an industrial power.[54] He agrees with Lenin that socialism cannot be constructed with illiterates, and he concurs with Chile's Luis Emilio Recabarren (1876–1924), whose works have been reprinted in Cuba, who insisted that the first step toward socialism was to educate the working masses.[55] Castro's Cuba has emphasized the development of worker-intellectuals. Cuban socialism places more emphasis on the practical aspects of revolutionary thought than on strict adherence to dogma, such as obtained in the Soviet Union.[56] Fidel agrees with Lenin that underdeveloped states do not have to pass through the capitalist stage en route to socialism;[57] the Soviets, however, maintained that the material base for socialism had to exist or state ownership of the means of production had to be developed before attaining socialism. Fidel and Che felt that by developing ideology and social and political consciousness before the material base, the transitional stage from capitalism to communism could be omitted. Thus Cuba and Fidel have departed from conventional Leninism, which declares that life is not determined by ideology, but ideology by life.[58]

Lenin believed that it was far more important to create a paradise on earth than to prepare for one in heaven. Thus he would not permit people to escape the responsibility for the suffering of others.[59] Fidel shares Lenin's humanistic vision. He also credits Lenin with defending Marx's belief in combating revisionism while pursuing his revolutionary dream. Fidel agrees that there exists an ever-present danger of revisionism, or bourgeois ideas that corrupt the proletariat. He is preoccupied by the fact that revisionists might kill the spirit of revolution, negate the principles of internationalism, and turn the democratic centralist party into a discussion club.[60]

To Castro, Lenin armed Marx with the concept of the party, interpreted Marx, and put his ideas into action. Lenin knew how to build a socialist society; Marx did not.[61] Castro concurs with Lenin's vehement objections to intransigent "left," or sectarian, Marxism, which does not permit compromise. He refers to Lenin's belief in the possibility of peaceful coexistence between capitalist and socialist states. Cuba is willing to cooperate with capitalists, and Fidel notes that the recent development of tourism in Cuba would not have been possible without money and technology from capitalist countries.[62]

Revolution

The theories of Marx and Lenin alone do not create revolution. According to Fidel: "There cannot be a revolution in the first place unless there are objective circumstances that at a given time in history facilitate the revolution and make it possible. That is, revolution cannot spring from men's minds."[63] But he believes that the Cuban Revolution disproved the idea of Marx that revolution could succeed only when the objective conditions were ideal. Fidel defied the Communists' strategy of waiting for "ideal conditions,"[64] having perceived that conditions favored initiating a guerrilla movement in the Sierra.[65] To him, what occurred in Cuba could happen only there and then. He reminds us that if Lenin had been born at the end of the eighteenth century, he could not have developed the theories he did or interpret Marx. He could not have been the intellectual of a nonexistent class or of a revolutionary doctrine that could not be realized.[66] Thus Castro infers that Cuba's Revolution could not have occurred at an earlier time.

Revolution, Fidel says, presupposes a series of conditions including: a struggle, the masses voluntarily joining the process, a spirit of sacrifice or willingness to relinquish privileges, and the disposition of the people to advance and develop.[67] Marxism, combined with his intuition, taught him that power had to be seized to make a revolution. Nothing could be accomplished through traditional political methods. Even before Batista took power in 1952, Fidel believed that workers, peasants, students, teachers, professionals, soldiers, and part of the middle class would, because of discontent, join his revolutionary movement.[68]

Marx had warned that there could be no real revolution until there was a world revolution. Fidel asserted, "We are not stupid enough to believe that we can build a brave little Communist state in splendid isolation."[69] In the wake of events in Eastern Europe and China and progressive currents elsewhere in Latin America, Asia, and Africa during the late 1940s and 1950s, Fidel considered the Cuban experience part of the larger picture. He added to progressive currents the romantic belief that revolutionary goals can be attained through hard work and an awareness of the primary importance of the worker in the world to be changed.[70] Like a work of art, revolution, if refined constantly, can be improved.[71] Thus, after the tyrant Batista was deposed, Castro believed, forces could be united to radically restructure class and property relations in Cuba.

Since coming to power, Fidel has continuously emphasized that a revolution is not the work of a person or of a group but of an entire people. It expresses the will of the people every day, not every four years.[72] It involves citizens in the revolutionary process and permits them to replace tyranny, with no chance for reform, with a new state that makes change possible.

According to Fidel, no one is born a revolutionary. To become revolutionaries people must undo centuries of ingrained ideas, and that cannot be done by verbal persuasion. Revolutionaries are forged by engaging people in the revolutionary process. A person who is dissatisfied with the prevailing injustice of society, wants change, and has fighting instincts begins to be a revolutionary and never stops. Day by day, the revolutionary's ideas are enriched and knowledge expands.[73] The revolutionary might identify with the spirit of Don Quixote[74] and be a dreamer, as long as he or she knows how to learn from the facts. The revolutionary embraces thought and action: "Whoever stops to wait for ideas to triumph among the majority of the masses before initiating revolutionary action will never be a revolutionary."[75]

Although Castro does not state that you must go out and grab a rifle to be a revolutionary, he understands the likelihood of having to use force to make a revolution.[76] Force, he believes, is justified when tyranny prevents social justice. While being a fighter, the revolutionary must also be a politician in the highest and purest sense. According to Castro, "Those who aren't aware of political realities have no right to even undertake a revolutionary program, because they couldn't lead their people to victory and carry out their program."[77] He claims that "the role of Job doesn't suit a revolutionary. Each year that the liberation of America is speeded up will mean the lives of millions of intelligences saved for culture, an infinite quantity of pain spared the people."[78]

Fidel views the Cuban Revolution as part of history showing the way to liberation, particularly for the Third World.[79] He believes that history will ultimately applaud his actions and understand them as part of Marx's larger concept of revolution. He feels that he has contributed the idea of a tactic for insurrection and the seizure of power adjusted to the specific contradictions of each Latin American state and in that way has furthered Marxist-Leninist theory.

In other ways, the Revolution has operated within a uniquely Cuban mythology. Almost every Cuban can relate to Fidel in uniform and to tales of the Moncada insurrection, the *Granma* crossing, the *History Will Absolve Me* speech, the slogans *venceremos* (we shall overcome) and *patria o muerte* (homeland or death), and to the *barbudos* (bearded ones). Cuba's revolutionary ethos includes the idea of the rebel army representing the Cuban people in the battle against Batista and Yankee imperialism. From the overthrow of the dictator to the present day, Fidel has perpetuated the idea of national redemption through sacrifice.[80] He built a revolutionary spirit that was the antithesis of the Soviet Union's bureaucratic and more repressive communism.[81] For over three decades Fidel has sustained the myths of the Revolution and its spirit; however, that is not to say that the process has gone unchanged since 1959.

Marx called a democratic revolution bourgeois and declared socialist revolution to be proletarian in nature. As we have seen, the initial phase of the Cuban Revolution represented neither a bourgeois-democratic nor a proletarian movement. Castro made some bourgeois-democratic promises, which he failed, and possibly never intended, to keep. In a sense, he was simultaneously Cuba's counterpart of Russia's Aleksandr Kerensky and Lenin.[82] Since taking over from Batista, Fidel has reportedly reiterated, "Workers and peasants, comrades, this is a socialist and democratic revolution for the poor, by the poor."[83] He has identified with the poor, working-class sector, which he unconvincingly maintains is in charge of the Revolution. He points with pride to the fact that in Cuba the symbols of power have changed. He claims: "We also destroyed the philoimperialistic bourgeois state apparatus, the bureaucracy, the police and mercenary army. We abolished privilege, annihilated the great landowners, threw out the foreign monopolies for good, nationalized almost every industry, and collectivized the land. We are ... fighting to build a completely new society, with a new class content."[84]

How did Fidel accomplish this feat? Some have said he followed Blanquism, whereby a small number of well-organized, dedicated people seize the state and retain power by energy and action that attracts mass support.[85] He contends that although he had Marxism-Leninism in mind, no totally coherent plan for carrying out the Revolution existed in 1959. By 1961, his theoretical framework clarified. He then realized that his 1959 efforts were not a revolution but part of the classical stage building toward the Revolution. Through experience and trial and error, he found out that revolution is not made overnight.[86] From then on, he became obsessed with ensuring the Revolution's permanence as an institution and a process.

Through the mid-1960s, part of Castro's plan to ensure the permanence of the Revolution was to ignite and maintain similar movements elsewhere in the Americas. His inability to do so perhaps helped convince him of the value of theory as a guide to revolution,[87] that is, theory that could be adapted to different national conditions. He now feels that "revolution cannot be imported or exported, a socialist state cannot be founded through artificial insemination or by means of an embryo implant."[88] The Castro of the 1990s prefers to encourage revolution by making Cuba a model socialist nation and showing solidarity with states endeavoring to cast off the bonds of neocolonialism. The message of Fidel, in his new role as Third World statesman rather than guerrilla leader, is more sophisticated. He points out the links between the scientific and technological revolution and the destructive capacity of the modern military in capitalist nations, which keeps the world on the edge of thermonuclear destruction. He asks what the same technological and scientific revolution could do if aimed at improving human well-being. The enormous production of goods—much of it superfluous—in capitalist societies could, if better directed, provide necessities for hundreds of millions of people. Why can we put people on the moon but not feed ourselves?[89]

Socialism

Castro likes to tell audiences,

We are the first socialist country in the western hemisphere, the first socialist country in Latin America, the last one to free itself from Spain, the first one to free itself from U.S. imperialism, the first one to establish full control over its own wealth, the first one to disobey their orders, the first one to carry out the most all-encompassing of revolutions on the bases of new concepts, new ideas, new values.[90]

Cuban socialism did not evolve out of a vacuum. From 1956 on, Castro calculated how his national liberation process, if successful, could be transformed into socialism[91] and how he could encourage his fellow citizens to freely select this new social system. Today, he revels in the fact that Cubans chose socialism, that unlike the case in Eastern Europe, it was not imposed from without.

Fidel rejects the claims of antirevolutionary propagandists who assert that in the transition to socialism humanism was sacrificed. To him, socialism encompasses humanism, which it seeks to improve upon. He acknowledges that "every socialist country is like a laboratory experimenting on how to achieve its political, economic and social goals."[92]

Castro had the power to select socialism for Cuba and imposed it from above.[93] By no means was it the result of a spontaneous grass-roots movement capturing the fancy of a whole society. He clarified his views in the Second Declaration of Havana, issued on February 4, 1962, after the United States had engineered the expulsion of Cuba from the Organization of American States (OAS). In that declaration he noted that capitalism's industrialization process was spurred on by economic, not moral, motives and that the discovery of the Americas resulted from a search for shorter trade routes to the Orient. He asserted that a new social class, the merchants and producers of manufactured commercial articles, arose from feudal society to pursue gold. New political and philosophical ideas emanated from the bourgeoisie and affected the consciousness of the exploited masses. Revolutionary ideas opposed feudal ones. Peasants, workers, and artisans, led by the bourgeoisie, overthrew feudalism. The latter considered revolution necessary and did not see the feudal order as eternal, as it now thinks of capitalism. To be liberal then constituted a serious crime in the eyes of the ruling class, similar to how today's bourgeoisie perceives socialism.[94]

When Cuba entered the socialist stage, Fidel followed Gramsci's suggestion that socialist changes could not await the collapse of the capitalist economy, that socialists must intervene in capitalism and assert a leadership role in restructuring its institutions. For the first time in Cuban history, the political participation and consciousness of the working-class majority became the key to the economic organization of society.[95] Socialism endeavored to eliminate self-centered "individualism," not the individual. It represented a new type of social regime, one alien to the ambitions of encroaching upon the sources of raw materials, conquering the markets, dominating the strategic areas, and exploiting the labor and resources of other people.[96] Development in Cuba implied a socialist economy and progress for the majority.[97]

Cuba's socialist phase, according to Castro, is far from perfect but holds great possibilities for improvement. It does not settle all conflicts, invariably creates some new ones, but ends the idea of production for profit and the state's oppression for the benefit of the bourgeoisie. It presents an opportunity to work for the community, to protect against illnesses and accidents, to allow all to study,[98] to plan the economy, and simultaneously to help liberate the international working class.[99] Castro views socialism in Cuba, not as a conjunctural option or a passing game, but as an undeniable historical necessity.[100] Buttressing Fidel's thinking, economist James O'Connor argued that for Cuba socialism is an inevitable way to rescue the nation from permanent social and economic stagnation, degradation, and political corruption.[101] Without socialism, Fidel reminds us, after his takeover the nation would still have suffered from the same ills.

The first step toward socialism for Karl Marx was a theoretical one—a mind change, what Thomas Kuhn called a paradigm shift, or an alteration in worldview. Fidel could no longer accept the old system or conditions and moved into the socialist orbit politically, ideologically, and morally. Building on the consciousness provided by the 26th of July Movement, he pushed the Revolution forward, assuming responsibility for it himself and placing an obligation on the people to foster it. He worked to equalize society from the bottom up and the top down.

In the new Cuban society, everyone had something.[102] Castro rejected the capitalist principle of a surplus labor force, under which it is easier to organize production and maintain labor discipline, in favor of full employment, thereby involving society as a whole in the Revolution.[103] Theoretically, one had to contribute according to one's capacity and one received in accord with work. Fidel realized that complete fairness did not exist in the transitional, or socialist, stage where, for example, if one person could carry more sacks because he was stronger, he received more in return. Material incentives existed in the socialist stage, as society developed the necessary resources for distribution. At the same time, Fidel endeavored to keep the people aware that some socialist formulas militated against the communist goal of a society where everyone contributes according to his or her capacity and receives according to needs.[104]

Fidel believes that you cannot have a society where everyone has a car and that if many do without one, everyone can eat well and have adequate housing and free education. He realized that he could not build this philosophy alone from above. In order to institutionalize it, a Marxist-Leninist organization had to function within the national revolutionary or reformist movement. Non-communists toppled the capitalist state, but to build and sustain a revolution you need theory and discipline. Thus in October 1965 Fidel announced that the United Party of the Socialist Revolution was being transformed into the Communist Party of Cuba (PCC). He pursued a socialist path by working to eliminate all barriers to the development of productive forces, with revolutionary, not capitalist, methods.[105] He mandated that during this transformation process, no matter how long it took, former bourgeois exploiters had no right to govern or even to publish their views. A quarter of a century later this mandate still prevails.

He diverged from the Soviet belief that one must wait to build communism until after the consolidation of socialism. Castro knew that during the socialist period remnants of material incentives, production for profit, and the role of money still often linked the new system to market relations. But he believed that during the socialist era, you could replace the aforementioned remnants of capitalist society with aspects of communism. In particular, he wanted voluntary labor and new values concerning work. He felt that the eradication of poverty depended on sacrifice and communist attitudes.[106] During the socialist transition, people such as the ill, aged, and students could receive in accord with their needs, a communist precept, rather than in accord with their work, the socialist credo.[107] Castro admitted that it would be an error for Cuba to completely bypass the socialist stage but saw nothing wrong with combining aspects of socialism and communism.

In May 1966, he announced that Cuba would undertake a parallel building of socialism and communism. Orthodox Communists declared this heresy. Some saw it as a tilt in the direction of Trotsky's theory of permanent revolution, although Castro ascribes none of his beliefs directly to that Russian thinker. Meanwhile, Fidel saw no reason why you could not curtail the role of the market and that of money in the distribution of goods and services. For instance, cultural events, medical care, and education could be provided free. He felt it only fair that those who had bigger needs should receive more, that those with greater intelligence should make larger intellectual contributions, and that all should work to capacity to strengthen society. Castro claimed that aspects of communism could be constructed in Cuba without an advanced standard of living because social relations are more significant than wealth. For a brief time during the 1960s, he advocated using the communist formula of paying salaries on an egalitarian basis, the same for all workers in a field, whether they loaded three tons of sugar a day or one. Subsequently, he realized that he had committed an idealistic error. During the 1970s Cuba reverted to a more orthodox idea of first passing through a socialist stage. The nation went back to the socialist formula of payment according to quantity and quality of work.[108] In the 1990s, Cuba still utilizes this socialist practice, but at the same time it stresses the virtues of voluntary work.

Although Cuba hopes to enter the communist stage eventually, its leadership realizes that communism is a formula of absolute abundance and that in an underdeveloped world you cannot have one nation with abundance or equal trade relations with a rich country trading with the impoverished ones. Fidel asks how you can live in superabundance when you see poverty elsewhere[109] and concludes that Cuba must support parallel struggles for national liberation, socialism, and communism elsewhere in the world.

While extending solidarity abroad, Cuba concentrates on building social-ism at home. In its current socialist stage it has many benefits, including some that resemble those of communism.[110] Besides socialist principles such as state ownership of the means of production, Cuba also employs capitalist ideas such as responding to supply and demand. Fidel worries about letting compe-tition for production create unhealthy values for workers, and every so often he has moved to eliminate or tone down these vestiges of capitalism and re-place them with less competitive socialist institutions. He has operated on the premise that you must simultaneously develop the material base and institu-tions that eliminate individualism and selfishness.

In Castro's ideal socialist world the worker identifies totally with the soci-ety, the state, and the means of production and covets complete harmony be-tween his work and himself.[111] All resources are used in a rational fashion, and people become socialists by experiencing social change. For example, when the government cut rents, the people supported the measure and realized that the state no longer sided with the rich.[112]

Fidel considers the Cuban peasant the most privileged in the world, an ally of the Revolution and the working class. He views the worker-peasant alliance as a permanent arrangement that will "advance the revolutionary process un-til all, absolutely, belong to a society without classes, a society of workers with equal rights."[113] He believes that this alliance would have been more difficult to effect if Cuba had divided up the land and given each peasant a parcel. Then, each person would have built a hut on his or her own land; schools would have been far away; it would have been difficult to establish roads, sew-age systems, and recreation sites;[114] and people would not have developed a collective consciousness. Fidel notes that agrarian reform in Cuba differed from that implemented elsewhere in the world. Cuba did not break up large landholdings, which historically reduces production. Instead, it kept the large holdings intact and developed them as big production enterprises.[115] Also, Cuba united little plots into large collective enterprises. Some land remained in the hands of individual farmers. As recently as 1989, 650,000 hectares were held by 71,000 farmers for their lifetimes.[116]

To accomplish land reform, Fidel had to overcome years of conditioned reflexes against socialism. He tells about a conversation with a hypothetical person. Castro asks, do you agree with the agrarian reforms and that all land-holdings should be turned into cooperatives and land distributed? Yes! Should peasants be freed from paying rent or a sharecropper's portion? Yes! Should foreign businesses be nationalized and funds kept in the nation to be used for the entire population? Yes! Should banks be run by the government and de-voted to national development? Yes! After the respondent concurred with a total socialist program, he was asked, Do you agree with socialism? No![117]

Once the Cuban people were reconditioned to accept socialism, they then had to understand its limitations. Fidel points out that it is not realistic for all people in the Third World to have the consumer patterns of the First World. If in India there existed one car per family, the population would be poisoned by carbon monoxide. Socialist programs must combat such ecological disasters. Fidel notes that capitalists keep on producing, not stopping to think about the consequences of their actions, but socialists plans for the human environment.[118] Cubans now understand the concept of exporting one ton of lobster, leaving none at home, to permit purchases of twenty tons of powdered milk to produce 200,000 liters of milk for many formerly malnourished children. To them the sacrifice is worthwhile.[119]

Castro claims that socialism is a relatively new system in human history. Since its inception it has been threatened by imperialism. Fascism attempted to destroy the first socialist state only twenty-four years after it was founded.[120] He says, "Nowhere is it written that socialism is irreversible";[121] thus, he strives to prevent counterrevolution. He asserts that the present generation of Cubans must consolidate the Revolution and make it depend less on him.[122]

To date Cuba, compared to other Third World states, has made spectacular social gains through socialism. While this was being accomplished, Castro has continuously agonized over the degree to which material incentives should be used to increase productivity. He has deviated from orthodox Marxist practices, where moral incentives come into play only when sufficiency exists for everyone. He sees moral incentives as a political necessity, one that must be employed before achieving sufficiency. Thus, Cuba has reduced the monetary wage in favor of the social wage. It has increased and improved social services for all rather than providing individual wage raises. Fidel stresses that Cuba does not function like capitalist consumer societies ruled by the spirit of profits instead of the desire to solve human problems; he rejects the capitalist contention that profit-motivated interests correspond to the interests of society.[123]

Material incentives tend to raise a person's consumption level according to his or her productivity.[124] Thus, Castro feels, material incentives corrupt workers and dilute their revolutionary fervor. He prefers a moral incentives imperative that encourages all Cubans to emulate the revolutionary vanguard, whose members exemplify the socialist ethic in terms of productivity, job quality, and professional excellence.

Fidel employs moral incentives to construct socialism and communism simultaneously. He, as did Che, calls it using consciousness to create wealth. This differs from what existed in the USSR, which endeavored to create wealth to build consciousness, an effort that Fidel deemed destructive of the latter.[125] Early in the 1960s, the Cuban position on incentives moved toward morality. Fidel chose to view wages as giving "a man participation in more collective wealth, because he does his duty and produces more and creates more for society."[126] However, during the 1960s, moral incentives alone failed to stimulate a sufficient number of people to work primarily to develop society. Absenteeism was excessive and productivity dropped below expectations. Therefore, in the 1970s, the Cuban government instituted material incentives, which caused some economic inequalities. One scholar insisted that this system of material incentives undermined the building of the new socialist person, as it encouraged workers' absenteeism. Since there were no goods to buy, workers exchanged money for leisure time. Tensions increased among workers, and trade union effectiveness waned.[127] Fidel reluctantly accepted material incentives and subscribed to the principle of "to each according to his or her work" as a means to develop the forces of production. The use of material incentives increased in the 1980s. Free markets for farmers were established, authors received royalties, and, subsequently, even banks paid a small amount of interest on deposits.

Castro detected harmful flaws in these material incentives. According to him, they violated the socialist distribution formula of payment according to work. Too many bonuses based on quantity rather than quality of work were distributed. Workers received too many excused days off from work and unwarranted sick leaves. At the second session of the Third Party Congress in December 1986, Castro referred to the dangers of "filling people's heads with material aspiration" and embarked upon a "rectification" process to revitalize the concept of voluntary work[128] and to streamline material incentives. Fidel understands that, to date, Cuba has not used moral or material incentives efficiently enough to increase productivity significantly.

Nationalism

As Castro wrestled with the question of material versus moral incentives in building socialism and communism, he simultaneously confronted the problem of how to buttress Cuban nationalism while forging a viable revolution. He believed that nationalism would strengthen revolution in Cuba. Other Cuban thinkers, Jorge Mañach for example, felt that the diffusion of national consciousness, because of narrow individualism, militated against Fidel's ideal.[129] But freedom from foreign control provided a strong central theme for Cuban nationalists. A large sector of the nation's lower and middle classes possessed a strong sense of nationalism, predicated on anger with U.S. imperialism and the rampant corruption that it caused in Cuba's body politic.[130] Cuban reformers, idealists, and revolutionaries found a haven in the Cuban Revolution, which provided a victory for those who had long striven for national independence.

Fidel capitalized upon Cuban nationalism. In his writings and speeches he tells audiences that nationalism was initially as important as Marxism in fostering the Revolution. He has opposed narrow-minded nationalism but has strongly supported Cubanidad (Cubanness).[131] The epitome for him is to be

Cuban and communist. He declares: "The Cuban people ... have achieved a source of national independence that they never had before. They enjoy a personal dignity that has always been denied them. For the first time, Cubans are masters of their own country."[132]

At no task has Fidel worked harder than building a national consensus or a sense of community. By encouraging nationalism, he expands political consciousness and identification and creates new loyalties and revolutionary resolve, while eliminating prerevolutionary political alienation. To him, "old-style" chauvinistic nationalism exemplifies ambition and ego for those for whom national interests take precedence over international interests. He maintains that the interests of Cuban workers do not have to conflict with those of workers of other nations.[133] Fidel construes nationalism negatively if it defends national interests to the detriment of other countries. Nationalism, by strengthening Cuba and enhancing its potential for making international contributions, becomes a positive force.[134] He constantly works to temper the egocentrism inherent in nationalism. Because of Castro's achievement in this regard, Cuba has become a socialist model among nonaligned and Third World states.[135]

One way that he sustains nationalism is by railing against a common enemy, the United States. The latter has cooperated by its persistent and intransigent belligerence toward the Cuban Revolution. Not only does Fidel gloat over Cuba's independence from the Colossus of the North, but he also periodically declares his nation's independence from all foreign states.

Castro would prefer a socialist world without national boundaries but views nationalism as a reality that will forever preclude such a situation. He understands the historical role played by countries, which supplanted tribes, and does not believe that the concept of the nation, with all it entails culturally and ethnically, will disappear.[136] He believes in the ability of Cubans to subordinate their national interests to the higher objectives of socialist and communist progress and in the elimination of the imperialism, colonialism, and neo-colonialism caused by chauvinistic nationalism.

The Cuban State

Fidel's interpretation of the Cuban state partially illustrates how he construes revolutionary nationalism. Until the Revolution, he contends that the Cuban state was basically authoritarian, and democratic civil and political liberties never existed. "The ruling classes ... organized the state in such a way as to maintain themselves in power ... they used not only physical instruments, ... but all possible instruments to influence, to deceive, to confuse."[137]

To Castro, bourgeois revolution in postcolonial Cuba never achieved the French Revolution's tenets of liberty, equality, and fraternity because of class differences. By nature, he insists, true fraternity cannot exist in a bourgeois society, although some degree of camaraderie can. Workers can be fraternal, but some high-salaried workers and industrialists cannot, nor can peasants and landlords.[138]

Under the 1940 constitution, capitalist dictatorship passed for representative democracy in Cuba.[139] Cuba's constitution proclaimed legal and political equality but tolerated, even encouraged, social, economic, and religious servitude, which existed as part of the superstructure and protected the ruling class. Existing law, to use Marx's terms, constituted a form of alienation, as the modern Cuban state was run by a committee that managed the common affairs of the bourgeoisie and defended their property interests.

Fidel concurred with Marx and Engels's idea expressed in *The German Ideology* that social organization flows directly from production and commercial life and with Lenin's belief that the bourgeois state cannot be reformed. He concluded that the 1940 constitution had to be abolished. Lenin's call in *The State and Revolution* for the abolition of the old state apparatus and its repressive instruments became a revolutionary axiom to Castro. Lenin's thinking demonstrated to Fidel the difference between genuine revolution with societal restructuring and the typical superficial Latin American "military putsch." From Lenin he learned how to take state power and transform it into a vehicle to serve the formerly exploited.[140]

Castro's concept of the state, like that of Marx, is that it can only be comprehended by understanding the material conditions of life. The relationship of the rulers to the ruled derives from the form in which labor is paid. The state as an institution is exceedingly sensitive to the mode of production and the class that regulates it and benefits most by it. The capitalist state in Cuba was organized to protect the possessor class against those who did not possess.

Marx understood that a modern state requires planning, organizing, and authority. So does Fidel. They share the belief that once a communist (not socialist) society is established, the state as a coercive institution will disappear. Castro contends that his government did not come to power by a coup d'état but with the support of the masses;[141] thus although the socialist phase of the revolution necessitates direction from the top, the authority to direct has been vested in him by the people. During the early phase of the Revolution, in the 1960s, he referred to his regime interchangeably as "a proletarian dictatorship or a proletarian democracy."[142] He claimed that his goal was the absorption of the state by society, not the absorption of society by the state. Between 1966 and 1970, the era of Che Guevara's "new man" supplanted the Soviet model in Cuba. During this period, Fidel emphasized capital accumulation, mass mobilization, and egalitarianism. He endeavored to abolish crass materialism and gave equal weight to cultural and economic revolution.

In 1970, when the above measures failed to yield significant advances, Fidel returned to a more pragmatic approach to development and moved, once again, closer to the Soviet model for revolution. He complained that Cuban theorists, like those in the USSR, could not quite comprehend the Marxist precept that one day the state would wither away. He justified the imposition of greater state control by noting that historically states have maintained social systems, that even under Athenian democracy, slavery existed and only a few had the right to assemble and assess current problems, and that Rome's Senate maintained privileges for the ruling class. The United States maintains capitalism by force throughout the world and at home preserves its system through elite-made laws, biased judges, and the Federal Bureau of Investigation (FBI). He acknowledged that Cuba initially needed force to mold the collective ownership of the means of production. But he insisted that Cuba's laws and state institutions strove to create a new society, one not maintained by force but supported by the masses. He viewed Cuba as a society struggling to make class differences disappear and to build a general consensus.[143]

At the time of this writing, Fidel cannot predict when the Cuban state will wither away or will be able to function without his direction. Some foreign and U.S. progressives who once supported Castro now resent him because he has not created the state of their dreams or has not conformed to their idealized versions of constitutionality.

Since his university days, Castro has distrusted Cuba's constitutional system, with its electoral process that repeatedly perpetrated frauds. He waited over a decade and a half to promulgate a new Cuban constitution and to institute a different electoral process. He justifies these actions on the grounds that before Cuba could pursue a more democratic course it had to resist aggression in the form of U.S.-instigated counterrevolution and be in a position to continue social and economic advancement.[144] He confided that Cuba had not rushed into establishing new political and legal institutions "because we would like them to conform to [social] reality, and not the other way around." He believed that new institutions had to emanate from Cuba's Marxist revolutionary ideology and that time was needed for new beliefs to take hold and generate new social and political forms.[145]

The constitution issued on February 24, 1976, established three levels of governmental power, the Council of Ministers, the Communist party, and the Organs of People's Power. It did not give the people leadership but provided greater access for their ideas to reach those in leadership capacities. It also granted all Cubans the right to work free of exploitation, gave peasants access to land, eliminated high rents, made as much education as they desired available to all children and adults, initiated free medical care and hospitalization, provided access to physical education and sports facilities, gave everyone the right to rest and vacation from work, established universal accident and sickness insurance, guaranteed maternity leaves and job retention for women, provided equal pay for equal work, promoted racial equality, defended the right to organize unions and Committees for the Defense of the Revolution, and gave all citizens over sixteen years of age the right to participate in political life.[146] Fidel concluded that the new constitution institutionalized the Revolution. He saw it as the child of the party, not its mother.[147] However, some Cuba watchers feel that the Revolution will not be institutionalized until Castro's personalism is gone.

Under the 1976 system, one person serves as both head of state and head of government. This follows Latin America's tradition of a strong executive. Despite his legal claim to multiple offices, Fidel has continuously contended that "revolutionary justice is based not on legal precepts but on moral conviction."[148] Cuba currently contains approximately 11,000 voting districts, each with about 1,500 citizens in large cities and 1,000 in rural areas. Under the 1976 constitution one delegate was elected for every 910 citizens in each voting district. Neighborhood assemblies, not political parties, nominated delegates. Each district had to run two to eight candidates for every office. To win, a candidate needed 50 percent plus one, and runoffs decided elections. Elected delegates exercised state power. They elected the members of the Municipal Bodies of People's Power, which elected members of the Provincial (State) Bodies of People's Power, which elected members of the National Assembly, which has deliberative but no executive and few legislative functions, but which chooses the Council of State and national executives. At the Fourth Congress of the Communist party in October 1991 it was decided to henceforth elect delegates of the provincial assemblies and deputies of the National Assembly by direct vote and to restructure party leadership bodies. At that time, almost all provincial delegates and about one-quarter of all municipal delegates and national delegates were Communist party members. In addition, the party had the right to approve the candidates for the presidency of the Council of State and the National Assembly.[149]

Under the 1976 system the municipality of Santiago de Cuba elected Castro,[150] who ascended the electoral ladder to the National Assembly, which elected him president of the Council of State, the nation's top political organ, and head of the Council of Ministers, its highest administrative post. Despite his dominant role, Fidel claims that the Revolution will continue under collective leadership when he can no longer carry out his duties or when the people feel that he no longer functions in their best interests.[151]

We know that Cuba pursued revolutionary policies aimed at the radical transformation of society before it became a constitutional state. We do not know precisely how decisions were made prior to the enactment of the 1976 constitution or after its implementation. The final chapter of this book contains a fuller discussion of the decision-making process and of whether power lies primarily in Castro's hands or in those of the bureaucracy.

Castro has frequently warned against bureaucracy, which has grown rapidly. For instance, from 1973 to 1984 it grew from 90,000 people to over 250,000. He views the struggle against it as almost as difficult as that against imperialism, and he strives to remove the petit bourgeois mentality from the state apparatus. He despises governmental or bureaucratic inertia and red tape and sees bureaucracy as the most negative product of the division between intellectual and manual labor.[152] He says that "bureaucracy engenders bureaucracy" and leads to a brake on revolutionary action.[153] Fidel is reluctant to let Cuba's bureaucracy assume the proportions that its counterparts have had in other socialist nations.

He is excessively paternalistic about aspects of Cuban socialism that he finds unique. He points out that unlike other socialist revolutions, Cuba's was not planned by a communist party. Its education programs correspond strictly to Cuba's needs and desires, not to a master plan or a "little red book." The highly original Committees for the Defense of the Revolution, examined below, provide greater strength and unity to the Cuban Revolution than what has existed elsewhere in the socialist world. He maintains that the state involves itself in a less intrusive fashion in people's daily lives in Cuba than in other socialist nations. Cubans, more than other socialists, feel like participants in the Revolution. Fidel reiterates that Cuba has not had internal states of siege, highway inspections, or armed soldiers patrolling the streets. Bloody conflicts have not existed between the government and the workers. Greater unity exists in Cuba than elsewhere in the socialist world.[154]

Castro states that Cuba, the first Latin American state to make classes disappear and eliminate conflicting interests, has no need to coerce its citizens. Nevertheless, he admits that an administrative body will always be necessary to run what belongs to the people, who are not to be thought of as a group of owners.[155] He explains that Cuba's security apparatus, run out of the Ministry of Interior, exists to prevent ideological laxity and counterrevolution, primarily encouraged by the United States and Cuban exiles.[156] Until the security of the regime is established, he acknowledges, he will use some harsh measures for its protection.

To some extent, the internal security of the Revolution is left in the hands of the aforementioned Committees for the Defense of the Revolution (CDRs), originally organized in 1960 as a system of collective vigilance designed to keep the Revolution pure and to disseminate information. Castro initially supported the CDRs to supervise the Revolution "because anything that happens anywhere, in any block, on any public service center, from a distribution center to a school, a bakery, any service of any kind—if those function poorly, it is bound to affect directly the people living within its boundaries and receiving these services."[157] The CDRs exist in every neighborhood in Cuba to disclose counterrevolutionary behavior in workplaces and residential areas and to guard against lack of bureaucratic restraint. They do public health work, organize urban reforms and cultural and athletic programs, and integrate revolutionary activities. By the 1980s, almost 80 percent of Cubans belonged to CDRs. By the 1990s, the CDRs had lost some political clout but retained a vital mass organizational function, especially in community projects such as blood donation drives.[158]

The CDRs represent a part of what Castro calls *poder popular* (people's power), designed to institutionalize political organization. *Poder popular* emphasizes mass organizations and gives all citizens some say in local enterprises. Mass organizations, such as the CDRs, answer a democratic demand for consent. They provide a mechanism for popular participation in government and help develop community spirit. Fidel explains that sending an administrative official from the top to solve a problem involving 15,000 to 20,000 local people is not the same as involving those people in the problem-solving process.[159] *Poder popular* makes the people a part of the political system and helps curtail alienation. It represents what Fidel refers to as an aspect of "participatory democracy," or "consultative democracy," as opposed to U.S.-style "electoral democracy," from which most people feel disassociated.

The Vanguard Party

No discussion of Castro's views on Cuba's socialist state would be complete without looking more specifically into his thoughts on the vanguard party. As we have seen, the Cuban Revolution triumphed without a Leninist party leading the way. Initially, Fidel governed by virtue of his dynamic personality and strong leadership skills and the commitment of the masses to social and political change. In the 1950s, he believed that many of the objective conditions for revolution did not exist in Cuba. He created his leadership group, the 26th of July Movement, not to effect proper revolutionary conditions, but to accelerate growth in mass awareness of Cuba's need for radical change. Anti-Castro scholars as well as some orthodox Marxists have erroneously called the July 26th Movement voluntarist and claimed that it erred by trying precipitously to create conditions for revolution in Cuba.[160] Fidel knew that revolutionary ideas would not simply spring forth from the minds of the general public. From the days of the Moncada uprising, he acted on the premise that the people were generally not revolutionary and needed intellectually prepared leaders. "Do you know how many real revolutionaries there were in Cuba at the moment of the revolution," he asked rhetorically. "Well, there weren't even one percent," he responded, referring to himself and his followers.[161]

From the outset, Castro knew that revolution could not exist without a vanguard, but he did not always equate it with a Marxist-Leninist party. He subsequently came to understand that "socialism is not created by spontaneous generation. Socialism must be built, and the basic builder is the party."[162] He thought of the pre-Revolution Cuban Communist party as a sect in spirit, a group apart from the rest of society.[163] In 1959, he viewed the old party members as honest, loyal, well organized, and trained, characteristics needed by the Revolution.[164] But he rejected the old party's reliance on a class coalition to build toward revolution, an idea he saw discredited by Communist party failures elsewhere in Latin America.

Rather than becoming subservient to an organization he thought clung to retrograde and unrealistic ideas, Fidel determined to reverse the process and put the Communists under his control. He rejected the old party's willingness to participate in a multiparty system. Such systems generally talk about majority rule and practice rule by an elite, and Fidel had great concern for Cuba's forgotten minorities. Multiparty systems speak about one person, one vote, which is not equivalent, in Castro's mind, to the will of the majority prevailing. Under the 1940 constitution, Cuba had constitutional guarantees, a multiparty system, and exploited masses.

Fidel did not want political pluralism wherein interest groups sell their support to candidates in exchange for favors. He preferred a form of democratic centralism where the party theoretically assumes a higher position with respect to the people and their mass organizations and does not permit divisive factionalism. He felt in 1959, and still does, that Martí's idea that Cuba needed just one party to win and preserve independence was right.[165] To Castro, the single party does not represent an authoritarian device; rather, it is the successful unification of the majority (the revolutionary people) of Cuba.

Responding to a student's question about the feasibility of the theory of a single revolutionary party in all of Latin America, Castro stated: "Look, from our point-of-view, the ideal is one thing, and reality is another. Very often we have to take reality as it comes, and not hope for the ideal, very often we have to get along with what we have, not seek perfection."[166]

Fidel embraced the concept of a Leninist organization for Cuba. When the new Communist party formed in 1965, he made it clear that it would function according to Cuban ideas and methods.[167]

The Communist Party of Cuba (PCC), with 611,000 members as of spring 1992, along with Castro, controls the Revolution and has come to occupy the majority of seats in the National Assembly even though it does not run candidates for office and is not a political party in the middle-class sense used in the United States. Technically, it should guide and serve as a counterbalance to the state, but in reality it governs or controls state institutions. Fidel construes it as an association of free revolutionaries who follow policies predicated on principles and methods that provide equal guarantees to whoever works and fulfills responsibilities to society.[168] Under the 1976 constitution the party represents the "organized Marxist-Leninist vanguard of the working class," the "highest leading force of the society and the state."[169] In theory, the workers control the party; in fact, they do not. But to Castro the party embodies the visions of all of the revolutionaries in Cuban history.

Members are admitted through democratic consultations and must accept the party's program, which is theoretically derived by a constant dialogue with the masses.[170] The party operates on the basis of democratic centralism, which to Fidel means that the leaders organize the state, using Marxist-Leninist methods; in reality sometimes it serves to limit debate in popular assemblies. Castro stresses that professionals should help prepare and scrutinize governmental programs but leave the decisions to the leadership. In other words, he has not encouraged middle-level professionals to question the leadership's decisions.[171]

According to Fidel, the party is composed of model workers who accept the socialist revolution and its ideology. One must cherish the responsibility of party membership.[172] The party selects the best people in the working class, those who will devote themselves to the work of society.[173] It exists as a vehicle of merit.[174] To enter one must be elected by members from one's workplace or mass organization. Although the nonparty masses do not directly choose party members, their opinion must be considered.[175] In 1992 almost 6 percent of all Cubans held party membership, and Fidel took pride in the fact that the newly selected Central Committee and Political Bureau contained a larger percentage of proletarian and female leaders and internationalist fighters that its predecessor. He concluded that the party had become more Marxist-Leninist and revolutionary.

In theory, the party constitutes the heart of the Revolution.[176] It has the power to define the boundaries of revolutionary policy.[177] Its internal organs are elected, the minority subordinates itself to the will of the majority, all organs agree on methodology, and all decisions are collective. It encourages free democratic discussion among members, but all must follow its discipline and decisions,[178] and, frequently, ordinary party members are afraid to criticize their leaders. Under Castro's aegis, the party's Central Committee has been elected fairly, with special weight given to women and blacks. Only comrades Blas Roca, who served as secretary general of the Communist party (CP) from 1934 to 1961 and helped to organize the new party, Fábio Grobart, a founder of the original CP in 1925 and former president of the Institute for the History of the Communist Movement and Social Revolution of Cuba, and Nicolás Guillén, Cuba's most famous poet and president of the National Union of Writers and Artists, have received continuous membership on the Central Committee because of their long-standing contributions to Cuba and the party.[179]

The party supervises the administration of the state and provides society with ideological and political unity. It functions to orient, not to govern.[180] It serves as a link to the masses and educates them about socialism and communism. The party has no army, police force, or judges. Its authority is ideological and political. It leads by education and persuasion.[181] It points out deficiencies but theoretically cannot tell the administration how to do its job.[182] It monitors performance, provides direction, and keeps the machinery of state oiled. It does not substitute for the state or the mass organizations but guides them by moral authority.[183]

The party supersedes even the unions in the role of transforming the nation into a working-class society, according to Fidel. The Communist party will never subordinate the working class to the influence of a political bourgeoisie.[184] It explains to workers the laws of development and distribution. It operates on the premise that workers with a voice in production, expressed through mass organizations, will be more reliable than those without a voice. The party builds workers' support while it leads the masses and wields power on their behalf, factors that it claims enhance equality and democracy.[185]

The Communist party has integrated society by promising and delivering equal abundance for all, giving some cohesion to planning and policies, implanting a philosophy and an identity in the country, making work respectable, defending classlessness, and creating national consensus by providing participation for most citizens.[186] Fidel asserts that "the party must be the great instrument of merit, the great instrument of revolutionary vocation, the great instrument of revolutionary intelligence."[187] Nevertheless, he points out, Cuba has channels for nonparty participation in the body politic, especially at the provincial and local levels. The party also functions to ensure that the governmental bureaucracy does not become a supreme entity.[188] Cuba's Communist party clearly has an inherent dislike or fear of institutional factionalism or domestic disunity, which would cause or expose vulnerability. This partially explains its aversion to dissent.[189]

Internationally, the party emphasizes the subordination of Cuban interests to the global struggle for communism and socialism and the fight against all facets of imperialism. It urges solidarity with all socialist states, the international communist movement, and all forces for national liberation. It condemns opportunism, stresses peaceful coexistence and world peace, and pursues relations with all nations, based on equality, sovereignty, and national and territorial integrity. It endorses the right of all countries to economic and social independence and to freely choose their economic and social systems.[190]

Fidel has studied the history and operations of vanguard parties elsewhere in the world. He finds that nowhere but Cuba "are candidates nominated for election by the people, without party intervention."[191] He considers Cuba's party a modest representative of the international communist movement, one with a particular penchant for peace.[192] Rejecting the idea that the international communist movement insists on an immutable line that all parties must follow,[193] he believes that each party should pursue independent methods and actions[194] after applying Marxist-Leninist analysis to unique national conditions.[195] He views the communist movement as divided and subdivided, with each country confronting different problems.[196]

Fidel has implied that Cuba's party holds legal power as opposed to the Soviet party that was created "in the struggle for power and under conditions of secrecy and illegality."[197] In essence, he has said that the Soviet party, unlike that of Cuba, ruled over, not with, the masses. He acknowledges that history demonstrates that some revolutions acquire extraordinary power, especially during their early years. But after processes are institutionalized, when a party exists and standards are established and become a culture for the community, there is no longer any danger from excessive power.[198] Thus he explains his long tenure and why not to fear it. He notes that neither Marx nor Engels ever said that the party would disappear, that only the state would wither away, and the latter is a long way off in Cuba.[199]

Fidel declares that "men die but the party is immortal," and founders such as he always command a lot of personal authority and prestige; but when the generation of founders disappears, there will be many better-trained party member replacements. He proclaims that he does not feel at ease with the idea of being supplanted by a *caudillo* and implies that the party, which has produced the highest degree of politicization of the masses in Latin America, will not permit that to occur.[200] Chapter 9 in this book contains evidence to support his contention.

5

International Concerns

My family is very large. My family is not only Cuba. My family is Angola. My family is the liberation movement in southern Africa. My family is made up of the progressive, revolutionary peoples of the world.

—Fidel Castro

Cuba's vanguard Communist party adheres to a theme of proletarian internationalism. In keeping with that orientation, the nation, under party guidance, gears its foreign policy to the international struggle for national liberation.[1] Fidel stresses that international activism is an integral part of a revolutionary's thought and praxis. His political and moral support for other underdeveloped countries has gained him enormous respect, especially in the Third World. In this chapter we see that he has demonstrated how a socialist state can successfully reconcile nationalism with internationalism. We examine his reactions to and dealings with imperialism, his attitudes toward and interactions with the Soviet Union and its successors, and why he has emphasized strong ties to Africa.

Internationalism

Under Castro's direction, Cuba has become a significant player on the world field and a role model for other developing nations. He explained, in a 1979 speech to the General Assembly of the United Nations:

> History has taught us that when a people that frees itself from a colonial or neocolonial system obtains access to independence, that is, at one and the same time, the last action in a long struggle and the first one in another difficult battle, for the independence, sovereignty and freedom of our apparently free peoples are continuously threatened by external control of their national resources, financial imposition by official international bodies, and the precarious situation of their economies, which reduces their full sovereignty.[2]

Castro views international solidarity as a way to buttress nations in similar positions to Cuba and, in return, gain their support for his Revolution. As the first socialist revolutionary nation in the Americas, Cuba, says Fidel, is "a symbol, we are the road to freedom and independence."[3] The Cuban model demonstrates that every country has the right to peaceful coexistence, to self-determination, to independence, to sovereignty, to territorial integrity, to be free of foreign occupation, and to choose its own social, economic, and political system.

Castro believes that the more-advanced developing nations, such as Cuba, should, in accord with their means, contribute to less-developed states. Thus Cuba has sent tens of thousands of technicians, engineers, physicians, teachers, agronomists, and middle-level skilled workers to other countries.[4] By so doing, Cuba has shown its continual willingness to sacrifice to further internationalist solidarity. Fidel points out that even during the late 1970s when domestic volunteerism fell off in Cuba, the nation dispatched tens of thousands of Cubans to Ethiopia, Angola, Nicaragua, and Grenada.[5]

Castro sees a natural alliance between socialist states and the Third World. To him, bourgeois-imperialist nations are enemies of both.[6] Engaging in solidarity with socialist and capitalist Third World countries does not, in his opinion, impede Cuba's independence. Each side gains from the relationship. Also, he warns that not every socialist state practices internationalism. During the 1970s, for example, he referred to China as internally socialist but not so internationally, as it supported reactionary regimes such as Chile under dictator Augusto Pinochet.[7]

Fidel realized soon after taking power that total economic independence could be brought about in Cuba only if a greater number of developed socialist nations were available as trade partners. The more socialist states there were in Latin America, he reasoned, the greater the ease of equitable trade for Cuba. Thus he has pushed solidarity as a means of enhancing and strengthening trade between his and like-minded regimes. Until recently, Cuba exported nickel, citrus, and sugar to socialist nations and in return purchased their manufactured goods and energy sources. Cuba's trade relations with socialist states included long-term credits and low-interest rates, refinancing of debts without interest, and fair prices for products. He repeatedly claimed that Cuba had solved many of its problems by building new international economic relationships within the socialist community, where nations did not try to outdo each other financially.[8] Without this solidarity, he believes, Cuba could not have remained intact. By the mid-1980s, 85 percent of Cuba's trade took place with socialist states, and the nation was on its way to achieving the economic development Marx had predicted for socialism.[9] When the socialist community in Eastern Europe disintegrated in 1989 and 1990, Cuba's economy suffered greatly.

Although Cuba operated predominantly within the international socialist economic community until the 1990s, Fidel never intended to give the impression that what he called "collective self-reliance" meant that there existed a self-contained formal system or economic bloc. On the contrary, he worked to broaden international economic cooperation, to develop untapped potential, and to increase Cuba's bargaining power in both the socialist and capitalist worlds.[10] As "a small underdeveloped country, with limited natural resources" and no energy sources in the 1970s, and few thereafter, Cuba could ill afford to detach itself completely from capitalist trading partners.[11] The U.S. economic blockade never created a feeling of isolation for Cuba because it traded with socialist nations, nonaligned countries, and capitalist allies of Washington. The blockade, however, which did cause problems for Cuba, served as a major focus of Castro's diatribes against U.S. imperialism.

Meanwhile, Castro reasoned that developing and nonaligned nations could not solve their trade deficits and balance-of-payments problems within the framework of the neocolonial system of trade relations between the developed capitalist states and the underdeveloped world. In 1974, through the Movement of Non-Aligned Countries, he introduced in the United Nations the idea of establishing a new international economic order under which nations could defend their sovereignty over natural resources, maintain the right of national self-determination, and implement reforms in the international monetary system.[12] Basically, Castro proposed to strengthen the cohesion of underdeveloped nations in the pursuit of a world without exploitation. He sought a more equitable world, one devoid of colonialism, dependency, and backwardness, for over a hundred countries, which contained three-fourths of the world's population and most of its poverty, hunger, and hopelessness.[13]

By 1990 Cuba had diplomatic relations with 120 nations, twice the number it had in 1959. Castro believed that in a nuclear age, problems had to be solved through dialogue, not war, that the latter risked world destruction. He was delighted by the Soviet-U.S. mutual nuclear disarmament agreements of 1991 but believed that the moves toward peaceful coexistence also signified Moscow's capitulation to Washington, which would prove detrimental to nations pursuing revolution or national liberation. Cuba's foreign policy, under his direction, has aimed at survival, furthering the Revolution, and averting global conflict. Only through peace can Cuba develop. Without development, he thinks, the nation cannot maintain peace.

Most perceptive observers of Cuban foreign policy view Fidel as the key to relations with the world and believe that Cuban policy has generally adhered to an established set of principles and goals, but that over the years the nation's foreign policies have changed as the Revolution has matured.[14] Castro views foreign relations as interpersonal, not intergovernmental.[15] He uses public speeches to conduct some foreign policy. Since 1959, he has delivered over two thousand talks on foreign policy, many of them excruciatingly long.

Most of them exemplify his Third World views and commitment to national liberation. He tries hard to gain the ear of the Latin American republics and maintains active relationships with all of their left-wing and popular organizations.[16] Fidel emphasizes that he does not believe in closing off Cuba from the rest of the world. He welcomes visitors and especially encourages foreign scholars and government officials to explore the island. So open is Cuba that upon landing at Havana's José Martí Airport, I have been told by immigration officials, aware that the United States can fine and imprison its citizens for visiting the country, that I could enter and leave the country without having my passport stamped.

In terms of specific foreign policies, Cuba primarily pursues an activist course, one designed to maintain security and not run the risk of war with the United States. It endeavors to normalize relations with as many socialist, liberal, and moderate states as possible, to pave the way for economic exchanges. It retains a prominent position in the nonaligned movement. For years it urged the Soviet Union to aid leftist insurgencies in the world without attempting to control them.[17] Cuba also advocates the Panama Canal for Panama, supports Puerto Rican independence, opposes colonialism, condemns the U.S. overthrow of Chile, Grenada, and Panama, rails against U.S. intervention in the Third World, claims that the Malvinas (Falkland Islands) belong to Argentina, favors negotiated settlements of Central America's conflicts, refers to Zionism as racist, and demands a homeland for the Palestinians.[18]

Castro also worries a great deal about the future of the Third World under the domination of the capitalist system.

> We can't go on being selfish as nations, we can't go on being selfish as human beings. We must give up individualism that makes people want to have everything for themselves, while others starve. I even think that, unless we have economic development planning on a world-wide scale, we are going to deplete all natural resources and poison the environment ... in [the year] 2000 there will be 7,000 million people in the world. I ask myself, what will mankind live on?[19]

He promotes industrialization that responds to Third World interests and that can be integrated with the economies of developing states and pave the way for more development. To begin to accomplish this, he asks that nations exercise sovereignty over their own natural resources and have the right to nationalize them. He wants to keep transnational corporations from instituting models of technology, investment, consumption, and profit remittance that harm the underdeveloped nations.[20] He dreams of a new, equitable, and stable universal monetary system, where credit and voting rights reflect the needs of all nations rather than the power of its strongest members, a multilateral operation, not manipulated by banks or the major capitalist powers.[21]

Asserting that over a billion people in the underdeveloped world suffer from malnutrition, he calls this a manifestation of poor international distribution, not a production problem.[22] By the year 2000 the situation will worsen. By then, 40 percent of the forest lands will be gone in the underdeveloped world, but only 0.5 percent will have disappeared from the developed nations.[23] If forests in countries like Costa Rica continue to be cut down to make rangeland for cattle to provide beef for U.S. fast-food hamburger chains, soon no firewood will exist for the 2 billion Third World people who rely on it exclusively for heating and cooking. He points out that during the final two decades of the twentieth century, the world's population will grow more than it did through all history until 1900. More than 90 percent of the world's population growth will occur in underdeveloped countries. Third World people are poor, hungry, disease ridden, or illiterate not solely as a result of biological factors, he emphasizes, but also as a result of social and economic conditions arising from centuries of oppression and exploitation.[24]

How can Cuban foreign policy best contribute to the rectification of the problems mentioned above and simultaneously sustain the Revolution? From the inception of his regime, Fidel has been preoccupied with these questions. He fears a duplication of the defeat of the Paris Commune, whose supporters paid in blood.[25] He knows that Marxism-Leninism does not impose a duty to support revolution but feels that a triumphant revolution bears a responsibility to support, at least morally, revolution elsewhere, and doing so enhances Cuba's security.

On February 4, 1962, in the Second Declaration of Havana, he marked the transition from the period of consolidation of power to one of radical and militant action in foreign policy.

> The duty of every revolutionary is to make the revolution. ... Now the anonymous mass, the America of color, somber, taciturn America, which all over the continent stings with the same sadness and disillusionment, now the mass is beginning to enter conclusively into its own history, is beginning to write it with its own blood, is beginning to suffer and die for it. ... And their great march will not be halted until they conquer true independence.[26]

Initially, Cuban foreign policy reflected Fidel's desire to start revolutions throughout Latin America as a means to combat the U.S. drive for world capitalist domination. After the death of Che Guevara in Bolivia in 1967, revolutionary fervor in Latin America ebbed. By 1968 Fidel announced his willingness to wait for national historic conditions conducive to revolution to evolve elsewhere. He now believes it impossible to export the conditions that foster revolution.[27] When asked if Cuba exports revolution, he replies facetiously, "Cuba is above all an exporter of sugar."[28] Nevertheless, he contends that "revolution cannot be prevented"[29] and cites Cuba as an example of genuine revolution in a neocolonial situation.[30] Although solidarity with popular and revolutionary movements remains a focal point of Cuban foreign policy, he believes it a mistake to support revolutionary movements in countries whose governments have solid diplomatic relations with Cuba. For example, he retained cordial diplomatic and trade relations with the Spanish government of dictator Francisco Franco, refrained from supporting movements to overthrow him, did not condone his form of government, and ultimately applauded his fall from power. Castro has learned how, for the sake of vital trade, to deal with ideological opponents, such as Spain, and to refrain from interfering in their internal politics.

In order to resolve disputes, implement foreign policies, foster better relations with other states, support internationalism, and increase its prestige, Cuba maintains a strong presence in the United Nations. Fidel sees the UN as a place to unite Third World and nonaligned countries against the vested interests of the powerful nations.[31] He seeks to democratize the organization's Security Council by allowing Third World and nonaligned states to rotate through it.[32] Cuba's representatives at the UN strive to get countries to channel their material resources into economic and social development and not the arms race. Castro views arms expenditures as irrational when people need food, housing, medical care, education, and other social services. He blames the world's most serious problem, the international economic crisis, which causes rampant inflation, unequal trade relations, and the plunder of natural resources in the Third World, primarily on cold war policies and the arms buildup it generated.[33]

A major thrust of Cuba's UN policy has been to garner support to protect the nation from the ravages of capitalism, imperialism, and the United States. Cuba has continuously pressed in the UN for dismantling of U.S. bases in Guam, the Philippines, the Indian Ocean, Malta, Cypress, Panama, Puerto Rico, and at Guantánamo, in Cuba.[34] At the same time, Cuba assiduously campaigned to negate the U.S. contention that it served as a Soviet surrogate and that its presence in the UN somehow undermined efforts at détente between the superpowers. Castro asserts that Cuban foreign policy led the Soviet Union to offer assistance to Angola, Nicaragua, and Grenada, not the other way around.

Cuba conducts the preponderance of its Middle East diplomacy through the UN, and Castro devotes a proportionately small amount of his verbal and written comments to that region of the world. Fidel maintains that the Middle East conflict between the Arab states and Israel cannot be worked out unilaterally by the United States and Israel through something as unfair and exclusionary as the Camp David Accords. Prior to the 1993 Arab-Israeli peace pact, he insisted that a solution must involve the international community, including the Palestine Liberation Organization (PLO), and be processed through the United Nations.[35] Although he has condemned the PLO's various vows to destroy the entire Israeli people, he recognizes the PLO as the legitimate representative of the Palestinian people and calls for the creation of a Palestinian state.[36] He condemns Israel, with which Cuba broke diplomatic relations in 1973, for aligning itself with the United States and doing Washington's bidding by collaborating with right-wing dictators in Latin America, selling them arms, and training their death squads. He once said, "From the bottom of our heart, we repudiate the merciless persecution and genocide that Nazis once visited on the Jews, but there is nothing in recent history that parallels it more than the dispossession, persecution and genocide that imperialism and the Zionists are currently practicing against the Palestinian people."[37]

In the United Nations, Cuba supports most Arab efforts against Israel, does not take sides in disputes between Arab nations, endeavors to create a Middle Eastern front against capitalism and imperialism, and maintains close ties to all radical and conservative Arab states,[38] with the hope of purchasing oil there in the future. Cuba has maintained close diplomatic ties with Iraq since the early 1960s and has sent military advisers to Baghdad since 1976. Castro denounced Iraq's takeover of Kuwait in 1990 but opposed sanctions against Iraq that would cause hunger and deprive it of medicine.[39] He opposed the UN resolution condoning force to expel Iraq from Kuwait and preferred to solve the problem by the use of diplomatic sanctions.[40] He called the 1991 U.S. and allied air strikes on Iraq a massacre, as tens of thousands died, but did not criticize the Soviet Union, which could have vetoed the UN resolution for the use of force and thereby possibly prevent the war.[41] He viewed the UN and Soviet handling of the matter as capitulation to the Bush government, which sought to control Middle Eastern oil,[42] and felt that it signified a return to U.S. control over the United Nations.

Within and outside of the UN, Cuba seeks normal relations on the basis of mutual respect with capitalist nations, especially those which adopt an independent stance vis-à-vis the United States. In recent years, Fidel has sought better relations with members of the European Economic Community and has encouraged them to invest in joint ventures with Cuba, particularly in the tourist business, which he feels compromises socialist principles but is a necessary expedient to economic survival, as it improves Cuba's hard-currency deficiency.

To advance the anti-imperialist cause and counter the "Soviet surrogate" label, Cuba became a charter member of the Movement of Non-Aligned Countries in 1961, the first Latin American republic to join the organization. Within that body of recently independent nations, he immediately began to campaign for a new international economic order to eliminate the old colonial order and dependency. Castro feels a strong bond to the nonaligned nations, which have never questioned Cuba as a valid member; he has been a major presence in the movement since its fourth summit meeting, which took place in September 1973 in Algeria. He believed that the stronger Cuba was in the nonaligned movement, the less it was restrained by its ties to the USSR. In other words, relations with the nonaligned states could help break Cuba's reliance on the Soviet Union. Also, relations with the movement have impeded Washington's campaign to isolate Cuba. A high point in Cuba's Third World prestige came about in 1979 when Fidel chaired the nonaligned summit meeting in Havana.

Within the Movement of Non-Aligned Countries, Castro has, in addition to the economic measures noted previously, struggled to end protectionism, which raises tariffs and other barriers, hinders Third World exports' access to markets, reduces the competitiveness of products, and acts as a powerful coercive mechanism against the underdeveloped nations.[43]

Fidel has increasingly drawn closer to anti-Western Third World revolutionary states, with which he felt greater kinship than with the Soviet Union. For example, at the meeting of the Organization for the Solidarity of the People of Asia, Africa and Latin America, also known as the Tricontinental Conference of 1966, he worked to reduce the influence of both China and the USSR and to build Cuba's power base for anti-imperialism among nations that no longer saw the USSR as a beacon of socialism and were willing to pursue armed struggle as a means to liberation. In August 1967, Cuba founded the Organization for Latin American Solidarity (OLAS) to further the policy of guerrilla warfare. The group's enthusiasm waned, as a result of U.S. pressures, and OLAS went out of existence after two years.[44]

When dealing with the Third World states, Castro frequently speaks with pride about Cuba's health care system. He brags that no one goes untreated medically in Cuba and notes that Cubans have a sense of security about health care and freedom from fears of incurring financial obligations for it. He wants to alleviate the world's health crisis, to mobilize national and international resources, human and financial, to promote mother-and-child-care programs, control communicable diseases, provide potable water, train technical medical personnel, and guarantee everybody access to basic medicine.[45] He claims that Cuba's model health care system reveals the humanitarian nature of socialism and proves that a Third World state can have First World care. He calls Cuba's 51,000 doctors "symbols of the Revolution."[46] Since the late 1970s, he has referred to Cuba as "the bulwark of Third World Medicine."[47]

He fervently hopes that someday Cuban scientists will find the final cure for cancer.[48] Although not a global medical power, Cuba provides a model for training physicians, biomedical research, and the delivery of health care.[49] He tells everyone that Cuba sends more doctors to all parts of the earth to help out than does the World Health Organization. He says that the United States "steals" brains by bringing so many foreign physicians to its shores.[50] Fidel calls them greedy money seekers. To his way of thinking, medical people should be idealistic and want to work in impoverished countries where they are most needed. Also, Cuba sends many doctors abroad in exchange for hard currency.

During 1989 and 1990 the Eastern European socialist-bloc states became profit oriented. Although devastated by the prospect of the end of socialism in Europe, Fidel maintained that Cuba must respect the right of socialist nations to build capitalism. To him, unrestricted respect for the sovereign will of each people and country is a golden rule of Marxism-Leninism.[51] But he lamented the euphoria in the capitalist world that existed as a result of the European turn of events.[52]

Castro blames the situation in Eastern Europe on the long-term cold war strategy of undermining socialism from within, precisely what he fears will occur in Cuba. As the Eastern European socialist states disintegrated, Fidel said that they talked about socialism while raising the banner of anticommunism. He believes that anticommunism equals antisocialism, that you cannot have socialism and a market economy.[53]

By 1990, Cuba had been deprived of essential resources,[54] as the socialist common market (Council for Mutual Economic Assistance [COMECON]) nations, to which it had belonged since 1972, moved to a free market. Cuba paid higher prices for goods. In the spring of 1990, when the Eastern European nations broke with the Soviet Union, Castro agreed that they should be free of interference from the USSR.[55] He applauded the elimination of the Berlin Wall, which he saw as a nationalist barrier, and drew an analogy between it and the "electronic wall between the United States and Mexico or that between Cuba and Guantánamo."[56]

Speaking in Havana on December 6, 1989, Castro said: "If destiny assigns us the role of one day being among the last defenders of socialism in a world in which the Yankee empire has succeeded in embodying Hitler's dream of world domination, we will know how to defend this bulwark to the last drop of blood."[57] He complained that people were slandering socialism, destroying its values, discrediting the party, eliminating social discipline, and sowing chaos in Europe. He admitted that as socialism unraveled in Europe, it became more difficult to build a communist state in Cuba.[58] He reminded his people that Vietnam taught all oppressed nations that no force can defeat a people determined to fight for its freedom.

As the Soviet model disappeared, Fidel insisted that the Cuban model became more viable. He renewed his opposition to Soviet-style reforms, which he believed would tear apart the fabric of Cuban socialism. His refusal to follow the Soviet reforms intensified the U.S. desire to see Cuban socialism destroyed. When told that even China had altered its approach to the world and especially improved its relations with the United States, he accused the Chinese, not of moving toward capitalism, but of left extremism. He stated that China, which he does not mention frequently, had not lost its socialist goals, but he rejected its willingness to capitulate to U.S. demands and reiterated that countries must develop through their own experience.[59] By 1991, as relations improved between China and the Soviet Union, Fidel stopped accusing the Chinese of allying with imperialists; instead, he sought greater trade ties with them.

Imperialism

Cuba predicates its foreign policies and actions on the idea that imperialism exists as a part of the world capitalist system of domination and must be resisted. Fidel argues that "for Cuban revolutionaries the battleground against imperialism encompasses the whole world."[60] To him, imperialism represents the chief cause of war, and socialism can guarantee peace. In other words, by halting the doctrine of plunder, you terminate the philosophy of war. He views humanity dialectically: On one side is socialism; on the opposite, imperialism.[61] He defines imperialism as the exportation of capitalism, the investment of surplus capital in underdeveloped states where labor receives low pay and corporate earnings are large.[62] He claims that "imperialist circles dream of 1,000 year empires just as Adolf Hitler dreamed in his time of a 1,000 year reich."[63] He equates imperialism with declining social and economic conditions and shows that the overall quality of life improves for the majority when the native working-class interests take control over institutions formerly run by the upper and middle classes and foreigners.

According to Castro, in Marx's era modern imperialism did not exist. It is a relatively new phenomenon, which Lenin researched and analyzed to guide the revolutionary struggle under new conditions.[64] Marx rarely used the term *imperialism* and generally did so only to refer to facets of empire. Lenin, however, in his 1916 pamphlet *Imperialism: The Highest Stage of Capitalism*, delineated its five characteristics: (1) the export of capital, (2) production and distribution centralized by great cartels, (3) the merger of industrial capital and banking, (4) capitalist powers dividing the world into spheres of influence, and (5) the subsequent struggle (implied by the fourth characteristic) to divide the world and its wealth.[65] Castro's concept of imperialism also includes the ideas of cultural and spiritual domination articulated by José Martí and later by the Anti-Imperialist League, which worked in the early decades of the twentieth century against the spread of multifaceted U.S. colonialism in the Americas. Fidel sees cultural imperialism and neocolonial dependency lingering after the removal of colonialism.[66]

He repudiates the Chinese theory that two imperialisms exist, the U.S. capitalist variety motivated by money, and the Soviet type, which inflicted its ideology upon others. He asks where the USSR's monopoly corporations were. What mines, oil fields, and factories did it own in the industrialized world? What workers did it exploit in the Third World?[67] He refrains from delving into the question of ideological subversion. He directs his venom primarily against various U.S. modes of intervention in the Americas, which he says can be combated only through revolution.[68] He finds Yankee imperialism so threatening that he cites the lack of political opposition in Cuba as a safeguard against it. "The only really important enemy we have has been the North American imperialism, a powerful enemy who would have liked to have opposition parties here against the Revolution—newspapers, radio stations speaking out against the Revolution. ... Look at the Chilean example, Allende respected these rights. The opposition press conspired. There were newspapers clamoring for a coup d'état every day, and they finally gave a coup."[69]

He believes—and he has good evidence to support the contention—that U.S. imperialism will never be resigned to the existence of the Cuban Revolution. He construes the battle with the United States as critical. It represents David versus Goliath, the little, underdeveloped state against the developed colossus. If Cuba fails, he reasons, so will all the victims of imperialism, and the resolve of the other socialist nations to continue to fight will wither. The battle is ideological, military, and waged in "our conscience." The United States, he says, continuously presents an idyllic image of its consumer society and portrays socialism as on the wane. He points out that Cuban society ranks among the top in the world in terms of health, education, social security, employment, and daily consumption of calories.[70] For thirty years he has questioned how the imperialists could present socialism as a failure, as a system with no future.[71] Ever the realist, after what transpired in Eastern Europe in 1990, he proclaimed: "Imperialism's enemy no longer is the socialist camp. Now that the Soviet Union is no longer the enemy, we are the enemy of the empire. It's as if it has no enemies left but us: Cuba."[72]

The Soviet Union

Historically, the Soviet Union was a Eurasian power with weak political, ideological, and economic ties to Latin America and Cuba. Prior to the Cuban Revolution, the Soviets generally thought of Castro's type of movement as "adventurism," likely to fail. In the late 1950s Moscow endeavored to support newly independent and emerging nations. After Fidel's triumph, the Soviet Union would have aided Cuba because it exhibited a desire to be independent of the United States, even if Castro had not announced his socialism.

Fidel declares that it would be absurd to blame the Soviets for the Cuban Revolution or for the ones in Nicaragua or El Salvador, which emanated from indigenous historical circumstances.[73] Cuba selected the socialist path without Soviet help or interference. Wayne S. Smith, a former U.S. diplomat in Cuba, noted cogently that Fidel decided to undercut U.S. influence in Latin America and that only the USSR had the power and the will to do so. This concurs with the thinking of former U.S. ambassador to Cuba Philip W. Bonsal, who told me that when Castro visited the United States in the spring of 1959, Acting Secretary of State Christian Herter asked what the United States could do for him. Fidel replied that if he took from the hand that had fed Batista, in six months he would be just like him. A few weeks later Castro turned to the Soviet Union for economic assistance.[74]

Smith believed that when the Soviet Union failed to enter into a bilateral military pact with Cuba (but provided it with defense guarantees) and explained that certain obligations were reserved for socialist countries, Fidel proclaimed himself a Marxist-Leninist.[75] (I prefer to believe that he revealed himself to be a Marxist-Leninist.) Once Castro lined up with the Soviets and decided to convert Cuba into a Marxist-Leninist state, according to Smith, the Cuban leader had to suggest that this had been his original intention.[76] Fidel's testimony contradicts Smith's conclusions. Castro insists that he was a Marxist-Leninist, with socialist goals for Cuba from the outset. He has never indicated that he always intended to become a close ally of the USSR, nor has he denied thinking that his allying with the USSR would make the United States reluctant to attack Cuba. One might ask, if the Soviet Union only entered into military alliances with socialist nations, why it never did so with Cuba? Clearly, the Soviet Union always realized the enormous expense and possible futility of fighting a war in the Americas against the United States.

Fidel denies ever having been a puppet of the Soviet Union. Those who know him assert that he is not the type to be anybody's puppet or surrogate. He points to the fact that he had no personal contact with the Soviet Union when he took over in 1959 and that Cuba had no diplomatic relations with the USSR for the next two years. This situation existed because Castro insisted upon independence from close allies and also because he hesitated to antagonize the United States. He says, however, that the USSR became a trusted ally and that Cuba could not have survived without the Soviet markets and subsidies for sugar and access to its inexpensive petroleum.[77] To questions of whether Cuba traded dependence on the United States for similar reliance on the Soviet Union, Fidel answers that we live in an interdependent world and will always have to depend on others for energy sources. Until 1990, he pointed out that Cuba's economy did not generally respond directly to developments in the Soviet economy as it used to do with that of the United States.[78] He reiterates that the United States owned or controlled Cuba's economic infrastructure, whereas the Soviets, who did not practice economic imperialism, owned and controlled nothing in Cuba,[79] not even the factories they helped to finance. Also, unlike previous debts to the United States, those to the USSR were automatically rescheduled at ten, fifteen, and twenty years without interest.

When questioned whether Cuba was a Soviet satellite, Castro asserted that the Eastern European states were satellites, not his nation. He then asked why the United States paid proportionately more attention to the Caribbean island than to the Soviet Union?[80] He states unequivocally that the Soviet

Union never told Cuba how to act or with whom to have diplomatic, economic, or cultural intercourse.[81] He does not hesitate to credit the Soviet Union with influencing certain Cuban policies. For example, he is proud of following the Soviet policy of subsidization of the arts and never fails to note that in the area of classical ballet the Cuban National Company compares most favorably with the Bolshoi Ballet.

Fidel stressed how much Cuba differed from the Soviet Union by analyzing their respective revolutions. In agrarian reform, he noted, Cuba modernized but did not break up large landholdings as did the Soviets. Cuba at one time produced food for 40 million people in the world, whereas the Soviet Union imported grain. The electoral systems differed. In Cuba, unlike the former Soviet Union, the Communist party does not nominate primary election candidates. Fidel mentioned that he and former president Mikhail Gorbachev both liked to ask, "Why must we do things the same way?"[82] However, when the "same way" proves beneficial, why not emulate it? Thus, Cuba, as did the Bolsheviks, established councils of workers, peasants, and the military as a means of getting democracy to the masses.[83] Most reputable scholars reject the Sovietization theory that Cuban domestic and foreign policy decisions emanated from the Kremlin and see them springing from the dynamics of the Cuban Revolution.[84]

Castro assures interviewers that a Stalinist "closed society" has never existed in Cuba. Cuba, unlike the USSR, has always welcomed contacts from abroad, especially from the Third World. Fidel admits that Cuba played the cold war game on the side of the Soviets to gain assistance in the struggle against the United States. Even at the height of the cold war, he denied that the Soviets sought to control the world. He contended that "the world is a mountain of problems, and you would have to be really crazy to want to take over the world." He asserted that the capitalist powers want to regulate the world's raw materials, natural resources, and cheap labor, whereas socialist nations do not have to be subservient to transnational corporations and would not want to control foreign resources, or exploit foreign workers.[85] From the Cuban experience, the USSR learned how costly it was to support allies lavishly without making huge profits in return and backed off from repeating the situation elsewhere in Latin America. In fact, to reduce its financial assistance to Cuba, the USSR by the 1980s favored the reestablishment of economic and diplomatic relations between the United States and Cuba.

Fidel scorns leftists who, spurred on by the capitalists, exhibited a frenzied hatred for the Soviet Union. He loudly condemned the "anti-Soviet left."[86] For those on the left and the right who blamed the Soviets for intervening militarily in wars of national liberation in Latin America, Fidel suggests that such behavior would have jeopardized the peaceful coexistence the USSR long pursued with the United States.

Castro offers no apologies for Cuba's alliance with the Soviet Union and openly identified with many of its policies. One scholar referred to this relationship as "mutually acceptable hegemony" by the Soviets. By this he meant that Cuba agreed to work within the Soviet orbit.[87] The Havana government contends that the nation has to exist in a world with others and subscribes to a foreign policy based on a balance-of-power system. Within that system, economic and political security had, until recently, been ensured by international principles followed by a major world power, the Soviet Union. Castro knows that all states cannot reach accord on ideology and foreign policy and allied with the Soviet Union, whose anti-imperialist position he respected. He emphasized that Cuba had a close working arrangement with the Soviet Union while following an independent course.

During the early years of Fidel's tenure, the USSR had little choice but to accept many of Cuba's unorthodox Marxist policies in order to keep Latin America's first self-proclaimed socialist state as an ally. The nations quickly worked out a beneficial coexistence policy. As the Revolution progressed, Fidel adopted more-orthodox positions, especially during the 1970s. Simultaneously, the Soviets encouraged him to play a major role in the nonaligned movement to win over Third World states[88] and were willing to tolerate some of his ideological deviations in order to gain that objective. Over the years, the Soviet Union tried to convince Castro to support its policy of fostering the process of international détente. Fidel complied when he could do so without jeopardizing his plan to restructure North/South relations. This eventually included such nonrevolutionary policies as working toward a negotiated settlement of Central American conflicts. The détente process brought the USSR and the United States closer together and logically should do the same for Cuba and the United States. But Castro knows that emotions rather than logic often govern U.S.-Cuban relations, as Washington has been obsessed with eliminating socialism in what it erroneously calls "its backyard."

Since the inception of the Revolution, Cuba disagreed with the Soviet Union on numerous major issues and agreed with it on others. For instance, a high-ranking Cuban official confided to me that his government condemned Poland's Solidarity Movement as antirevolutionary and considered the extended Soviet presence in Afghanistan as objectionable as that of the United States in El Salvador. He related that Fidel initially praised the Soviet action in Afghanistan but subsequently communicated, privately, negative sentiments about it to the Kremlin.[89] Also, Cuba constantly criticized the USSR, as well as the United States, for wasting valuable resources on nuclear weapons, which are in oversupply.[90] During the 1960s, Fidel castigated the Soviet Union for maintaining relations with Latin American states where Cuba supported antigovernment guerrillas. He added, "The least we expect of any state of the socialist camp is that it will lend no financial or technical assistance of any type to these governments."[91] When the Sino-Soviet split occurred, the Soviets, trying to keep Cuba on its side, overlooked Fidel's criticisms, including his statement that he favored the unity of all socialists.[92]

Castro has never hesitated to discuss Stalin, whom he credits with industrializing the USSR, thus fulfilling a socialist goal, and for helping defeat the Nazis in World War II. But he reproaches Stalin for abusing his power and developing a harmful cult of personality.[93] He has long maintained that Stalinism has never existed in Cuba, "unless I am considered ... a Stalin, and in that case I would say that all my victims in our country are in excellent health."[94]

On the Soviet invasion of Czechoslovakia in 1968, Castro commented: "The Czechoslovak regime was marching toward capitalism and was marching inexorably toward imperialism. We don't have the slightest doubt of that. ... And our point-of-view is that is not permissible, and that the socialist camp has the right to stop it one way or another."[95] In essence, Fidel defended the actions of the Soviet socialist system the same way he tried to justify his hard line at home, on the basis of fear of liberalism, counterrevolution, and destabilization. Paradoxically, he deplored the USSR's violation of Czechoslovakia's sovereignty, while maintaining that socialist states have the right to intervene to preserve their security.[96] If Czechoslovakia successfully broke from the Soviet Union, Castro feared the breakup of the socialist bloc, which would damage Cuba's economy and security. Events of the 1990s proved him correct. What he defended in 1968 was essentially the same behavior for which he condemned the United States in Guatemala in 1954, the Dominican Republic in 1965, Grenada in 1983, Panama in 1989, and Iraq in 1991. Consistency is not Fidel's strong point. It sometimes takes a backseat to political expediency.

During the early years of Castro's regime, his personality often clashed with the Soviet Union's institutionalized concept of internationalist leadership. In recent years, his increasingly institutionalized leadership led to disagreement with Soviet attempts to reform and liberalize. Leonid Brezhnev viewed Cuba's aggressive anti-imperialist course with trepidation, and Fidel questioned that Soviet leader's commitment to Marxist revolution.[97] Over the years, Fidel bridled at the suggestion of the USSR's discussing Cuba with the United States without consulting him. I recall that in 1962, Nikita Khrushchev infuriated Castro by pulling Soviet missiles out of Cuba without his permission. Fidel responded similarly in 1989, while Mikhail Gorbachev was in Cuba, when a reporter intimated that the Soviet president might engage in discussions with the United States about Cuba's role in Central America without consulting the *jefe máximo*. Castro also voiced displeasure with the Soviets in the late 1980s when they announced the abandonment of the policy of universal class struggle and support for national liberation movements.

The Soviet Union, basically interested in superpower politics, tried to retain its preeminent position in the world in the face of internal upheaval. It regarded Cuba as an observer in its struggle to maintain its international influence. Fidel, never one to be taken for granted, endeavored to garner for Cuba some of the respect that the USSR once received for championing progressive movements in the Third World. Castro reiterated his support for class struggle and national liberation and reviewed his dedication to proletarian internationalism. Despite the aforementioned disputes with the Soviet Union and countless other disagreements that he has not seen fit to air in public, Castro for years managed not to antagonize that country to the point of losing vast amounts of aid from it.

Fidel rejected Gorbachev's *perestroika* (restructuring), or willingness to move toward privatization, and *glasnost* (public openness). He believed that *perestroika* and *glasnost* could not increase national productivity, which can best be accomplished under the guidance of the central government. Although he and Gorbachev both wanted to increase productivity in their respective countries, he claimed that *perestroika* and the concept of using capitalist relations of production to build socialism were inappropriate for Cuba.[98] It "is another man's wife, I don't want to get involved."[99] "We shall always obstinately refuse to be servile copies of other people's recipes"; to do so would show lack of confidence.[100] Fidel says that Cuba does not need Soviet-style *glasnost* because its Revolution never resembled anything like Stalinism and, unlike in the Soviet Union, the Cuban Communist party has never become alienated from the people.[101]

Latin America's critical press called Fidel's objection to Gorbachev's reforms "*Castroika*," which the Cuban leader believes misses the point by implying that he expects others to do things his way. When Gorbachev visited Cuba in April 1989, Fidel referred to 1975–1985 as the "lost years," when Cuba tried to implement a Soviet model[102] and erred in doing so. But he, like Che, believes that capitalists who think that socialists have no choice but to adopt capitalist methods and motivations engage in wishful thinking. He asserts that Cuba cannot be primarily oriented to economic profitability. His critics, even some on the left, say that it must be so oriented for the sake of development. He believes that emulating Soviet economic moves would risk turning more Cuban dissenters toward market reforms and U.S.-style politics. He says that those who criticized Cuba for not doing things the Soviet way attempted to pit the nations against each other. Moreover, he pointed out, the Soviets did not expect Cuba to copy its methods.[103]

Fidel told the visiting Gorbachev that whereas the Soviets fostered restructuring and looser state controls, Cuba pursued a policy of "rectification," meaning more centralization and greater sacrifices and moral commitment to the Revolution, a process that he believed could be implemented successfully in a small country, where the leadership could mobilize the masses more easily than in the Soviet Union.[104] He thanked the Soviet leader for the USSR's world peace initiative, including the reduction of nuclear weapons. Castro also commented that the Soviet president had never assumed a paternalistic stance toward Cuba.[105]

When informed in 1990 that the Soviet Union wanted to pursue aspects of a market economy, Fidel took the opportunity to indicate that the Soviet interpretation of Marxism had long been incorrect, as it claimed that the means of production in a communist country should be held either by the state or collectively. Castro, taking off from Marx and Engels's *The German Ideology*, insists that in communism private as well as public property is abolished.

When the Soviet Union's publications *Sputnik* and *Moscow News*, in August 1989, proposed revising the terms of trade with Cuba, he banned those periodicals on the grounds that they undermined the Revolution by justifying bourgeois democracy. The ban demonstrated that Cuba did not take orders from the Soviet Union and also that censorship intensifies when Fidel feels threatened. Castro reflected, sadly, that capitalist nations urged the Soviet Union to begin to practice unequal trade with Cuba, to sell products at higher prices, buy goods at low prices, and eventually join the U.S. economic blockade.[106] Perhaps paranoia motivated Fidel's actions, as the Soviet Union primarily sought balanced trade relations with Cuba, which could be accomplished by eliminating some of its subsidies. For example, Cuba uses approximately 13 million tons of oil annually and produces less than 1 million tons. The Soviets supplied most of Cuba's oil needs until 1990 and also sold it surplus oil at low prices, which the Cubans exchanged on the world market for higher prices paid in hard currency.

When the Soviets raised prices for some exports to Cuba, Fidel, early in 1990, said we live in uncertain times and expressed doubt about how long the USSR would strongly support the Cuban Revolution. He predicted correctly that the Soviet Union might undergo a civil war or the disintegration of its union.[107] He counseled that Cuba should remain vigilant and not relent if the Soviet Union entered a crisis and curtailed its support. Fidel understood that the Soviets could not guarantee aid and that internal strife might deplete its resources. If the Cuban leader ever pursued an extensive investigation of why the Soviet Union collapsed, in order to preclude a similar occurrence in Cuba, he never communicated the results to the public. Castro told his people that he objected to the way that *Sputnik* and *Moscow News* were telling how the USSR was changing and giving the impression that the Soviet Union had been left without a history, that work there had to start from zero to overcome years of error. He resented the fact that the past was, to some extent, negated in the Soviet Union in order to advance new concepts not compromised by Marxist ideology.[108] These publications not only poisoned the USSR against itself but also set a dangerous precedent for Cuba.[109]

By the summer of 1991 the United States had convinced the Soviet Union to pull its troops out of Cuba. When Gorbachev agreed to remove Soviet forces from Cuba, Castro suggested, in reference to the Guantánamo base, that the United States do likewise. The Soviet-U.S. détente clearly dealt a severe blow to revolutionary movements throughout Latin America. It also meant the end of considerable Soviet influence in Cuba, where henceforth Russian technology, training manuals, and advisers would be gone. At the time of this writing, Fidel admitted that he did not know what the future held for Cuban relations with the newly independent countries that were formerly members of the Soviet Union.

Africa

Contrary to a common assumption, Cuba and the Soviet Union at times differed on policies toward Africa. They sometimes worked as partners in ventures on that continent, but Cuba was not a surrogate for the USSR there. For example, although the Soviet Union had long supported anticolonial movements in Angola, it was Cuba that drew the USSR into the conflict there, rather than vice versa. Fidel denies that Cuba's activities in Africa, which he refers to frequently, brought additional Soviet aid to Cuba. With regard to Cuba's motives vis-à-vis Africa, Castro explains: "We are a Latin-African nation. ... African blood flows through our veins. ... Without proletarian internationalism the Cuban Revolution would never have existed, and without proletarian internationalism we would cease to be revolutionaries."[110]

He believes that Cuba has an obligation to extend proletarian internationalist solidarity and assistance to the African nations, which have experienced colonial and neocolonial circumstances. To him, Cubans and Africans are linked by historical bonds that extend from the early slave trade to the contemporary realities of underdevelopment. Cuba feels duty bound to help protect Africa from imperialism and to support Africans who struggle against it. As Cuba backs Africa, it also enhances its own independence and wins friends in the black Caribbean.

In Castro's mind, Africa represents the weakest link in the chain of imperialism. He thinks that because enormous crimes have been committed against the African peoples, there exist excellent prospects for a transition from tribalism to socialism without going through traditional stages. He perceives weaker imperialist doctrine in Africa than in Latin America and believes that genuine possibilities for fundamental change exist there. He claims that in Latin America the bourgeoisie controls the economy, education, the press, and all facets of life. But "that phenomenon doesn't really exist in Africa where, properly speaking, there is no bourgeoisie."[111]

Fundamentally, Fidel sees his views on the region as validating Pan-Africanism. Pan-Africanists often disagree. They contend that the mere presence of people of African descent in Cuba does not give it a right to intervene in African affairs. Castro responds that Cuba has a national interest in Africa but never involves itself in the area without a specific invitation. Fidel reminds the critics of Cuba's various African policies that the nation has no economic or strategic interests in Africa, that it has been active in the region only to help combat apartheid and its ally, the U.S. government, and to eliminate racism, colonialism, and fascism, which he views as manifestations of capitalism.[112] He adds that as Cuba's involvement in the region has grown, his nation has become more aware of its Africanness and has developed new insights into African identity. Also, Fidel has used Cuba's forays into Africa to strengthen nationalism among Cuba's black population and thereby foster racial cohesion at home.

In 1960, within a year after Batista was toppled, Cuba began to send medical supplies and military advisers to the Algerian National Liberation Front (FLN)[113] to assist in its war against French colonialism. Cuba dispatched troops to Algeria in 1963 to help in the border conflict with Morocco and gained access to oil in return. Cuba subsequently expressed its support for the Popular Movement for the Liberation of Angola (MPLA), the Front for the Liberation of Mozambique (FRELIMO), the African Party for the Liberation of Portuguese Guinea and the Cape Verde Islands (PAIGC),[114] Zimbabwe's Patriotic Front, and the Southwest African People's Organization (SWAPO), representing the citizens of Namibia.[115] Fidel contends that he supported revolutionary movements, which he hoped would pursue socialism, and that he did so to reciprocate for the assistance he had received from Europe's socialist states.

Castro believes that one need not be a Marxist-Leninist to be a revolutionary.[116] He cites Libya's Muammar Qaddafi as one who holds some anti-socialist ideas. Nevertheless, Fidel considers the man who liberated Libya from colonialism as an anti-imperialist revolutionary who has helped his people enormously and given them dignity.[117] Cuba's political support for Libya has also given it access to much-needed oil.

Fidel also has high regard for South African Nelson Mandela, leader of the African National Congress (ANC). He looks upon Mandela as a courageous comrade who has spent a half century opposing South African apartheid and other forms of racial discrimination long known in Cuba. Mandela sees Fidel in the same light and appreciates Cuba's no-strings-attached assistance to his movement. Not only does Castro condemn the racist government of South Africa, but he also casts blame for the situation in that country on the United States and major European nations, especially Great Britain, which have enabled apartheid to survive by collaborating with the Johannesburg government economically and technologically and by supplying it with weapons. He believes war to attain racial equality in South Africa can be avoided, that its government can be brought down by international pressures.[118]

When the Soviet Union pulled out of Angola, a former Portuguese colony, in 1974 and ignored it, Cuba extended aid to it. The following year, at the request of the MPLA, Cuba's Communist party leadership, without consulting the Soviet Union, decided to send a battalion to Angola to resist invasion by CIA-supported South African forces[119] and to help establish an independent Marxist state governed by a democratic working-people's administration.[120] Under Operation Carlotta, approximately 35,000 Cuban troops helped the anti-imperialist, prosocialist MPLA secure power in 1975 and 1976. At that time, Fidel also believed it advantageous for his troops to receive some battle-field experience, in case the United States decided to invade Cuba. Ironically, the presence of Cuban troops in Angola made the Caribbean nation—in the eyes of the United States—a greater threat to the Third World. Repeatedly, Castro has stated that Cuba has no intention of intervening in the internal affairs of Angola, that primarily it wants to help the nation prepare to fend for itself.[121] The Angolans were delighted to have the assistance of a country like Cuba that stressed its own blackness. Cuba's solidarity also enabled it to purchase some petroleum in Angola and to fish its waters.

Fidel refers over and over to the 1988 battle at Cuito Cuanavale, where Angolan forces, with the aid of Cuban and SWAPO troops, defeated South African forces decisively for the first time. At the end of that year South Africa agreed to respect the sovereignty of Angola, and all foreign parties, including Cuba, consented to withdraw from the nation, under UN supervision. Fidel (who personally checked on the smallest details of the Angolan operation), when no longer guaranteed Soviet support for his ventures in the region, pursued a negotiated settlement and announced that he would remove 50,000 troops over a two-and-a-half-year period in return for a guarantee that Namibia, a buffer state bordering on Angola and South Africa, would be independent. Moreover, he thought that the Angolan settlement would weaken Jonas Savimbi's U.S.-supported National Union for the Total Independence of Angola (UNITA). Cuba's long-term presence in Angola helped secure the possibility of peace in southwest Africa. Unfortunately, the victory at Cuito Cuanavale did not terminate apartheid in Namibia, nor did it abolish all racially discriminatory laws there.

In Africa, in addition to Angola, Cuba has been heavily involved in Ethiopia. According to Fidel, when a 1974 popular revolution ousted the decadent regime of Emperor Haile Selassie and freed Ethiopia from feudalism, its people needed to prevent counterrevolution, a situation the Cubans understood well.[122] To Castro, Ethiopia had an opportunity to set an example for the rest of Africa.[123] Also, to some extent, the Ethiopian revolution showed that the African continent could be a decisive place to confront imperialism. Fidel felt compelled to extend solidarity to the emerging state, where Lt. Col. Mengistu Haile Mariam instituted radical reforms. When the United States aided neighboring Somalia in invading Ethiopia, Castro, in 1977 and 1978, sent 15,000 troops to help repel the Somalians. He justified backing a Marxist African government in a conflict with a socialist African nation by claiming that Somalia, which called itself an Arab-Semitic country, not black and African, did not work to preserve black Africa. When Cuba helped to destroy the Somalian force, most black African states approved.[124] But Cuba's support for the Ethiopian military cost it some loss of prestige in the nonaligned and Third World movements.

Cuba's internationalist involvement in Africa, primarily to assist the region's progressive forces, has generally brought it closer to the nonaligned nations and to Third World states in the Middle East and Asia. It also has caused some anxiety among Cubans, who fear for the lives of their loved ones in far-off military forays. However, it has stimulated national pride in Cuba's international solidarity. But despite the African involvements, Cuba's major international thrusts have been toward Afro-American states and Latin American countries, which Castro longs to mold into a community of socialist nations that will work together to offset the power of the United States and thereby enhance the security of his Revolution.

6

The Americas

The role of Job doesn't suit a revolutionary. Each year that the liberation of America is speeded up will mean the lives of millions of children saved, millions of intelligences saved for culture, an infinite quantity of pain spared the people.

—Fidel Castro

Prior to the Revolution, Cuba was, after Panama, the most neocolonial state in Latin America. The United States had maintained a continuous economic, political, and social presence in the country since its independence from Spain. This chapter explores Fidel Castro's attitudes toward and relations with the United States. It shows that he conceives of himself as a patriot of all Latin America and strives to build solid opposition there to the political, economic, social, and cultural incursions of "the empire," as he calls the United States. Space does not permit an examination of the Cuban leader's views on all of the nations and problems of the Americas. This chapter deals with the countries (Mexico, Chile, Grenada, El Salvador, Nicaragua, and Panama) that have attracted a great deal of Fidel's attention. It also delves into his thinking on the seemingly unsolvable debt problems that plague the Latin American states.

The United States

Castro exploited anti-Yankee sentiment in Cuba from the moment he gained power. He explained: "We are a sovereign country. The United States has no rights over Cuba, no privileges, no jurisdiction. Cuba is not property of the United States. Latin America is not property of the United States."[1] The Cuban Revolution, only ninety miles from "the most powerful empire on earth, and 10,000 miles from the socialist camp,"[2] was a prime target for Castro's neighbor to the north, which hoped to liquidate the revolutionary spirit in Latin America. Until 1990, Washington blamed all revolutionary, national

97

liberation, and progressive processes in the Americas on Soviet interference and expansionism. The United States promoted militarism in the region to stop the—mostly imaginary—actions of the USSR. Meanwhile, Castro depicted U.S. militarism and arms development as a lucrative business.[3]

Fidel insists that the United States detests him because he dares to expose the venal nature of its version of capitalism. He finds the Yankee hatred of socialist Cuba obsessive,[4] feels that it emanates from racist contempt for Latins, about whose culture and geography the average U.S. citizen, who according to Castro confuses Mexico with Brazil, knows nothing.[5] He accuses the United States of chauvinism, which differs from patriotism based on conscience. Chauvinism, in Castro's view, is predicated on disdain, the aversion of one nation for another.

Fidel believes that the majority in the United States do not understand genuine democracy, only the skewed version of it they see. He knows that the people of the United States are manipulated into certain prejudices and false ideas about life in Cuba.[6] Yankees, because they do not question what they are told, believe in good faith that their government fights to defend freedom elsewhere in the world. But nobody outside of the United States believes it.[7]

He thinks that most Yankees do not want war but have been educated to perceive socialist Cuba as a military threat. For over thirty-one years he has tried to convince the U.S. Department of Defense of the costliness of an invasion of Cuba.[8] He doubts that he has succeeded and questions the desire for peace of a country that exterminated its Indians[9] and oppresses its blacks. Incidentally, he visualizes the blacks as the future revolutionary vanguard in the United States.[10]

Part of Castro's strategy to combat the influence of the United States entails frequent castigating of the Colossus of the North publicly. He refers to the U.S. system as a dictatorship of the owning class.[11] He says that U.S. policy has historically been based on intervention and aggression, and thus Cuba is always subject to invasion.[12] To him, the United States conceived of peace as harmony with the Soviet Union, which it deemed feasible, and the right to intervene and wage war against any Third World nation,[13] such as Nicaragua.[14] Fidel says that the United States, England, and the Occidental world share the responsibility for the rise of fascism because of their anticommunist campaign, which Hitler emulated.[15] After World War II, he says, the United States, with its industrial potential intact and its treasury full, assumed Germany's mantle of counterrevolutionary crusader and international gendarme.[16] Under this version of Pax Romana, peace is based on world domination.[17]

Fidel maintains that fundamentally the U.S. institutions and people are not fascist, but that at times those running the government have harbored fascist tendencies. They arrogantly reject human rights policies, display contempt for world peace, refuse to seek a formula for honorable coexistence, pursue the quest for military superiority at all costs, and even ally with terrorist governments such as South Africa and Chile under Pinochet.[18] From history, Fidel discerns that these forms of fascism can only be eliminated by strong resistance.

Although the United States has occasionally searched for pretexts to conduct a military campaign against Cuba,[19] Fidel clings to a hope for détente. Realistically, he says that as long as "the empire" exists alongside a revolutionary Cuban people, his homeland will be in danger.[20] He often asks rhetorically how anyone can be safe from the country that dropped atomic bombs on Hiroshima and Nagasaki after victory in World War II was virtually assured for the Allies.

He thinks that the United States gambles that it can conduct aggression without danger of nuclear retaliation because of nuclear equilibrium. By the same token, he deduces that nuclear equilibrium, or stalemate, leaves revolutionaries free to conduct their conventional warfare.[21] Moreover, he says that when the United States talks about "limited nuclear war" and preventive nuclear strikes for demonstration purposes, it plays a dangerous game.[22] He finds ideas such as military superiority and Star Wars incompatible with solutions to the world's serious problems.[23] He advocates the elimination of all chemical weapons and notes that even though the United States manufactures them, it hypocritically claimed the right to bomb a Libyan chemical weapons plant. He asks how any Third World nation can be secure when the United States adheres to the law of the jungle.[24] He is puzzled by the fact that U.S. figures show that spending $1 billion generates 76,000 military or 112,000 civilian jobs and questions his neighbor's priorities.[25] He says that Cuba calls into question all whom it finds guilty of unnecessary loss of life.[26]

Fidel's condemnation of the United States goes beyond the problems examined above. Long before he rose to political prominence, he viewed the United States as a sworn enemy of Cuba. Beginning early in the nineteenth century, he says, elements in the United States allied with Cuba's powerful white landowners and its annexationists, who wanted to preserve slavery more than they desired independence. He explains that, even after independence, the annexationists in a sense got their way, as the United States virtually took control of Cuba under the 1901 Platt Amendment,[27] which enabled the United States to legally infringe upon Cuban sovereignty. Even after the abrogation of the Platt Amendment in 1934, Cuba and the United States entered into a reciprocal trade agreement that allocated a sugar quota to Cuba in return for preferential treatment for U.S. exports. This tied Cuba's economy to the United States. As a result of the Platt Amendment, U.S. ideology, culture, prejudices, and vices became a part of Cuba's neocolonial dependent way of life.[28] U.S. entrepreneurs owned Cuba's mines, electrical plants, telephone and transportation companies, lands, sugar mills, and banks and controlled its foreign trade.[29]

During the preliminary stages of the Revolution, Castro promised that the United States would eventually pay dearly for its past interference in Cuba.[30] With deep-rooted hostility, he stated in the late 1950s that he was destined to wage war on the United States or, at least, to vigorously oppose its influence on Cuba.[31] When he assumed power in 1959, despite his steady stream of vitriol toward the Yankees, he assured the world that he would abide by all international treaties, including the 1934 pact granting the United States the perpetual right to operate the Guantánamo naval base. He hoped to resolve the Guantánamo issue peacefully over time.[32] "Never has anyone in Cuba had the idea of recovering Guantánamo by the use of force," but he claimed that someday it would belong to Cuba as a result of the advance of consciousness in the world.[33] Although Fidel rejects fighting over the Guantánamo site, his law training tells him that contracts for an unreasonable length of time are invalid in international law. To make that point, he refuses to cash the annual rent checks sent to him by the United States for the Guantánamo base. On occasion, he shows the stack of uncashed checks to visitors to his office.

When Castro took control in Cuba, he did not foresee that public opinion in the United States, which initially supported the Revolution, would eventually oppose it. When it did, to his credit, he distinguished between the people, the businesses, and the government of the United States.[34] He has inculcated in the Cuban people the need to make distinctions, and they generally do not, on principle, dislike individual Yankees. He blamed the opposition to his regime primarily on the U.S. government, which turned its citizens against him by plying them with anticommunist propaganda. He blames U.S. businesspeople less because he knows that most of them prize profits above ideology and would be delighted to sell their wares in Cuba.

From the inception of his government, the United States authorized the CIA to destabilize Cuba. Within a few months after Fidel took over, the U.S. National Security Council connived to put another government into power in Havana.[35] Over the years, the CIA has conceived thirty plots to assassinate Castro. Fidel notes that Washington wanted to destroy the Revolution even before its socialist character emerged.[36] He concluded that Washington's contention that it was "fighting communism" was a manipulative ploy to win public support and to mask the fact that it wanted to remove all nationalist or reformist movements, even democratic ones, that threatened the repatriation of profits to the United States. He asserted, "Anyone who doesn't sell out or buckle under is smeared as Communist. As for me, I am not selling out to the Americans nor will I take orders from the Americans. Without economic independence there can be no political independence."[37]

After May 17, 1959, when Castro signed the Agrarian Reform Act, fear rose in the United States that he would nationalize Yankee-owned business. Although nationalization is legal in international law, Fidel realized that Washington disregarded the latter with impunity when it was in its interests to do so. He felt that the Revolution was imperiled. What would prevent the United States from launching an attack from the mainland or the Guantánamo base, which he said the United States did not need but retained as a show of strength[38] and to humiliate Cuba.[39] He wondered who would save Cuba from imperialism. Even after Cuba entered into close relations with the Soviet Union, he implied that Cuba could not rely on an ally that distant to rescue it from destruction by the United States, that if push came to shove, Cuba would have to defend itself.[40]

Fidel concluded that any nation that eliminates private property in favor of state control would become an enemy of the United States. The Eisenhower government broke diplomatic relations with Cuba on January 3, 1961, allegedly in response to Fidel's demand that it reduce the size of its embassy staff in Havana. Castro, with no alternative, decided to make the most of the rupture in diplomatic relations. The Washington government henceforth became a useful, and justifiable, whipping boy for him.

On April 16, 1961, when a group of U.S.-sponsored and CIA-trained Cuban exiles invaded Cuba's Playa Girón (Bay of Pigs), Fidel called the attack a treacherous crime.[41] He stated that the "invaders came to fight for free enterprise," which by this time the Cuban people understood as slums, unemployment, and beggary.[42] He pointed out that after the Cuban victory at the Bay of Pigs, his government treated the invaders as counterrevolutionaries and did not put them to death as traitors as might have the United States had the tables been turned.[43] He has watched with great interest the growth of political influence of the cold warrior Cuban exiles in the United States over the decades, especially with the Republican party. So violently anti-Castro are these exiles that they bomb contemporary Cuban art exhibits in Miami, murder countrymen who want to reestablish relations with the United States, and have gone to absurd lengths to discredit my own work.

A year after the Bay of Pigs fiasco, in 1962, when the United States demanded the removal of Soviet missiles from Cuba, Castro commented that for the first time the world became conscious of nuclear vulnerability. He felt that the United States would not hesitate to use missiles on Cuba. Although the decision to place missiles in Cuba had been made in Moscow, not Havana, Fidel displayed considerable irritation when the Soviets removed the missiles without consulting him. He later realized that his objections to the removal were unwise, even though he viewed the missiles as a deterrent to nuclear war.[44] In 1990, when Khrushchev's memoirs revealed that in 1961 Castro wanted a preemptive nuclear strike on the United States, Fidel admitted that the Soviet leader could have misinterpreted his signals that way.[45] But he denied the allegations and said that the Khrushchev memoirs were being used to distort Cuba's image because the nation represented the last Communist domino.[46]

Cuban-U.S. relations deteriorated rapidly during the 1960s, in light of Operation Mongoose, initiated by the Kennedy administration to undermine Cuba. Despite U.S. attempts to destabilize his country, Castro believes that Kennedy, had he lived, might have discussed better relations with Cuba. Castro even saw altruism and merit in Kennedy's Alliance for Progress (1961–1971), a plan designed to ward off socialism by offering financial support to Latin American nations' efforts to strengthen their capitalist structures. Prospects for improved relations brightened in the 1970s. Fidel acknowledges that the Jimmy Carter administration, which opened a diplomatic Interest Section in Havana and permitted Cuba to do likewise in Washington, tried to strengthen relations. The Carter government, which Fidel believed to be more compassionate than its predecessors and successors, permitted dissatisfied Cubans to enter the United States. Castro explained that Washington felt obligated to these Cuban exiles because the United States had encouraged others to conduct counterrevolutionary activities.[47] The thousands of Cubans who came to the United States via the Mariel boatlift in 1980, he says, were not basically political people. Most were "lumpen elements," those who rejected the social order, parasites, gamblers, work shirkers, and people who could not accept discipline.[48] Initially, Fidel called some of them "criminals" but later modified his claim by explaining that in Spanish a criminal is a convicted felon, and those he allowed to go to the United States were guilty of misdemeanors and thus just "delinquents."[49] He also denied the U.S. allegation that he opened mental hospitals and sent psychotics to Miami, asserting that he had too much compassion to do that.[50]

Castro speculated that if Jimmy Carter had won a second presidential term, Cuba would have overcome U.S. demands for its withdrawal from Africa, and relations between the countries would have been normalized.[51] He respected Carter as a man of principles based on a deep religious ethic, one not too proud to compromise, as shown by his willingness to negotiate the future of the Panama Canal. After Carter left office, Fidel informed the Reagan administration of his willingness to discuss all issues with the United States. Washington ignored his overtures. For example, Castro offered to remove all Cuban personnel from Nicaragua and to observe an arms embargo in Central America if the United States did likewise. Reagan, without testing the Cuban's sincerity, rejected the offer as not serious and refused to discuss the matter.[52]

On another level, it became clear during the Reagan years that the U.S. refusal to recognize Cuba represented poor capitalist practice, as business allies and competitors of the United States did not hesitate to trade with Cuba. For example, in 1990 Canada did over $300 million in business with Cuba, the lion's share of which, U.S. businesspeople believe, would have been theirs if relations between the countries existed. However, Castro has found alternative markets for Cuban products and does not think that renewal of relations would enhance Cuba's economy much. He downgrades the idea that U.S. businesses have great market potential in Cuba,[53] whereas U.S. economists estimate that their country is losing approximately $1 billion in sales annually by not trading with Cuba. This does not imply that the U.S. economic blockade has not damaged Cuban trade with the rest of the world.

The blockade has not toppled the Revolution and has failed to isolate Cuba from Latin America. But it has stood as a warning to the other Latin American republics to stay in line or suffer the same consequences as has Cuba. Space precludes enumerating all the effects of the embargo. A few samples of Castro's specific reactions to it suffice to make one aware of its impact. Fidel has shown that the United States will not import any steel or equipment containing Cuban nickel and has pressured allies, such as Italy and Japan, not to buy Cuban nickel.[54] The Cuban leader was appalled in the 1970s when a severe famine struck Bangladesh and the United States agreed to send food to it but in return required that it not export jute to Cuba.[55] He speaks continually about U.S. control of the International Monetary Fund and the World Bank, two major lending agencies from which Cuba cannot obtain loans.[56] He asserts that the embargo retards Cuba's development, increases his faith in strong centralized government, and sometimes forces him to intensify his tight control on the nation.

Fidel views the blockade as part of the North/South conflict, whereby the North wields economic power that creates great industries and has vast financial reserves through which it controls advanced technology, and the South generally has the largest amount of raw materials and cheap labor and is inordinately indebted to the North's financial institutions. Consequently, the North has undergone a massive fusion of huge monopolies with state apparatuses, and the inequality in trade relations between North and South has increased as manufactured goods flow to the Third World, where economic crises, sparked by inflation, burgeon.[57] Fidel believes that changes in the U.S. and North policies could foster economic growth in the countries of the South, thereby improving mutually beneficial international trade, and possibly leading to greater internal democracy in the underdeveloped states.

Although Castro has an extensive list of grievances against the United States and rarely hesitates to express them publicly, in recent years he has made fewer direct verbal assaults on specific U.S. officials. Also, he uses less bombastic and self-centered rhetoric. He speaks more in collective terms, replacing the first person "I" with the third person "Cuban people." He responds negatively to the statement "in our country [the United States] we think that Cuba is Fidel and Fidel is Cuba" and quickly points out that although citizens of the United States venerate George Washington, they, not he, brought independence.[58] To him, the people, not a person, make the nation, but "great men or women" lead the masses.

Fidel reads everything he can about the internal machinations of government in the United States and keeps abreast of contemporary events there via periodicals and television. In particular, he has a penchant for examining the personalities of those who govern. He notes that there always seems to be a sinister type behind the throne in the United States, one who is believed to be intelligent and wise. Presidents Nixon and Ford had Henry Kissinger, and Jimmy Carter had his national security adviser Zbigniew Brzezinski, whom Fidel characterized as unrealistic and erratic. In turn, Brzezinski, an anticommunist zealot, referred to Castro as "an ideological fanatic and brutal dictator."[59] It is true that both men have strong convictions, but at least Fidel, who dislikes bourgeois thought and action intensely, realizes that you cannot interpret it on the basis of socialist principles. Brzezinski, as well as many of Castro's critics in the United States, think that theirs is the only way and judge the Cuban leader by a capitalist set of standards.

Fidel's disdain for the cold war prejudices of those of Brzezinski's ilk hardly compares to his contempt for Richard Nixon, whom he first met in Washington in April 1959. Nixon, who immediately depicted Castro as "either incredibly naïve about Communism, or under Communist discipline,"[60] subsequently became a frequent target for Fidel, who claimed that the U.S. president tried to intervene in the Cuban Revolution.[61] He looked upon Nixon as a false person and a mediocre, untrustworthy politician.[62] In reference to Nixon's most costly indiscretion, Watergate, Castro, stretching logic a bit, said, "They hired ex-Cubans to try to overthrow the government of Cuba, and all they succeeded in doing was to overthrow the government of the United States."[63] He added that the United States prizes stable government and at the time of Watergate was less stable than Cuba. He also believed that Nixon employed members of the Mafia to assist the CIA in trying to dislodge his government and to assassinate him. The crime syndicate's extensive interests in Cuba were destroyed by the Revolution; thus it was willing to work with Nixon.[64]

Fidel found Ronald Reagan as devious as Nixon. To Castro, Reagan, who preached that Cuba constituted a "Red Menace" to peace in the region and was the "source" of its problems, was bent on regenerating McCarthyism. Fidel thought that Reagan communicated well with his people, while exploiting their frustration with the U.S. defeat in Vietnam. Castro saw him as a chauvinist nationalist who imposed a costly arms race on the world.[65] To Castro, the poorly informed Reagan represented the ultraright; he was a reactionary, not a conservative. Fidel distinguished between Carter, who lacked the capacity to see a lie, and Reagan, for whom lying was acceptable.[66] With regard to Reagan's involvement in the Iran-Contra scandal, Fidel said, "He looks for scapegoats, lets others take the blame and denies that he knew what was going on, something that no one believes."[67] He characterized the Reagan government as "fascist," operating in the style of Goebbels, Hitler's propaganda minister. Castro accused Reagan of falsely blaming Cuba for shipping arms to El Salvador's guerrillas,[68] who in fact took their weapons from the enemy or bought them on the open arms market. He also thought Reagan, who ordered the CIA to establish and maintain a Contra army, containing some Cuban exiles, to overthrow the Nicaraguan government, was a supreme hypocrite. Fidel denied Reagan's accusation that Cuba had military advisers in Nicaragua in 1982 and noted that 2,200 Cubans assisted there, 2,000 teachers and 200 physicians.[69]

Reagan exacerbated problems with Cuba by banning travel there for most U.S. citizens in 1982, blocking some of its nickel sales in Western Europe, and trying to thwart Cuba's endeavors to reschedule its international debts.[70] Reagan's secretary of state, Alexander Haig, had a great deal to do with the president's policy of using military might to prevent social and economic change in the Americas under the guise of stopping communism. When Haig declared that the United States would resume relations with Cuba when it abandoned Marxism-Leninism, Castro called the statement "arrogant and absurd" intervention. During the Reagan presidency, Castro's fear of a U.S. invasion reached an all-time high, especially after the Yankees took over Grenada and sent a Contra army to overthrow the leftist Nicaraguan government.

The replacement of Reagan by his vice president, George Bush, did not bring relief to Fidel. Castro remarked: "He was one of the directors of the CIA. When you imagine the lack of scruples, moral standards and disgracefulness of that institution, then you know who George Bush is."[71] Fidel despises the CIA and took great pleasure in announcing in July 1987 that it had been infiltrated by twenty-seven Cuban agents. As for Bush's attitude, Castro went on to say: "If he wants to come to the conclusion that he is very important because he attacks me, that's his problem. ... I never felt so important as to think that those who attack me are important."[72]

Early in 1988, the United States proposed to the UN Commission on Human Rights in Geneva that it designate Cuba a violator. The measure failed, but Castro was incensed. He noted that all U.S. administrations have slandered Cuba, but that this was the first to take such actions at Geneva. He denounced the Reagan-Bush administration as the least ethical, most reactionary, most dishonest and unprincipled ever.[73] In an NBC interview on February 24, 1988, Fidel mentioned with incredulity that former Batista policeman Armando Valladares, whom he characterized as a terrorist arrested with a bag of dynamite that was intended to destroy Cuban government buildings, had recently been made head of the U.S. delegation to the UN Commission on Human Rights.[74] Valladares, who Castro contends would have been executed for treason if he committed a similar crime in the United States, had been released from a Cuban prison as a human rights gesture. He then flew directly to Miami and, in record time through an act of Congress, received U.S. citizenship and the aforementioned political appointment. It did not surprise Fidel when, during the U.S. presidential debates in 1988, George Bush referred to the non-English-speaking Valladares as one of his heroes, or that the Bush administration refused to take action against Miami resident and Cuban exile Orlando Bosch, who in 1976, while on the CIA payroll, planted a bomb that blew up an airborne Cubana Airlines passenger plane.[75]

Castro's respect for Bush declined even further on May 30, 1989, when the U.S. president promised: "Until Fidel Castro shows a desire to change the behavior of Cuba and its policies, we will maintain our current policy toward Cuba. I trust this will put an end to the speculation that my government will ultimately improve relations with Cuba."[76]

As a prelude to considering improving relations with Cuba, Bush demanded that Castro hold U.S.-style elections, implement a multiparty system and democratic reforms, release counterrevolutionary prisoners, stop interfering in the internal affairs of other states, reduce the size of its armed forces, permit the free migration of Cuban citizens, give international human rights groups access to Cuba, and revert to a private market economy. Fidel realized that Nicaragua capitulated to similar demands from the United States and ultimately lost its revolution. If Cuba failed to meet these conditions, Bush stated, he would continue to oppose its readmission to the Organization of American States (OAS) and continue the broadcasts of the Voice of America–sponsored Radio Martí, designed to tell Cubans what they do not know about their country. Castro, ironically, sees Radio Martí, initiated in 1985, as a modern version of the imperialism Martí abhorred.[77] To Castro, calling it Radio Martí is analogous to naming a brothel after George Washington.[78] He notes that one cannot think that Reagan or Bush ever read Martí.[79] Yet Fidel does not oppose Radio Martí, favors free dialogue, and believes if the United States can broadcast to Cuba, Cuba should retaliate and broadcast to the United States.[80] When the United States inaugurated TV Martí for purposes identical to those of Radio Martí in the spring of 1990, Fidel said that it had gone too far and successfully jammed 90 percent of its broadcasts.

Castro found it incredible that Bush naïvely thought that Cuba would opt for the renewal of capitalism[81] because socialism declined elsewhere. He stated that Bush's attitudes heightened hostility in the United States toward Cuba, and he anticipated a more vigorous anti-Cuba campaign to remove the reminder that socialism lives. He says, "We are incorrigible, because we don't do what the imperialists say."[82] He accused Bush of traveling to Poland and Hungary in the summer of 1989 to encourage capitalist tendencies there but added that if those nations desired a peaceful transition to capitalism, Cuba would not challenge their independent decisions.[83]

Cuba subsequently approached the United States about mutual action against drugs, and the Washington government demurred. To demonstrate Cuba's good faith, Castro noted that between October 1970 and March

1986 the Cuban Coast Guard had captured 328 drug smugglers, confiscated 250 tons of marijuana, 1 ton of cocaine, and countless Quaalude tablets.[84] The United States dismissed Cuba's efforts to curtail drug running and the suggestion that the two nations cooperate in the venture. In fact, when Washington had knowledge that Cuban General Arnaldo Ochoa participated in drug dealings, it refrained from telling the Havana government, preferring to spread the lie that Fidel too was involved in the marketing of drugs. On the contrary, Castro claims that the U.S. Mafia has repeatedly tried, and failed, to gain his cooperation with its drug operations and has offered him enough money to solve Cuba's foreign exchange problem. He has responded by cracking down harder on drug traffickers.[85] In August 1989, when Castro again requested U.S. cooperation in controlling drug traffic, Washington accused him of creating the drug problem. He reminded the United States that as early as October 1958, before the triumph of the Revolution, he had issued the following law for enforcement in the territory under his control: "It is the responsibility and aim of the revolutionary movement and this administration to completely eliminate hard drugs and illicit gambling, which at present make the real physical, mental and economic development of the Cuban people impossible."[86]

Washington told Castro that before it would consider a mutual war on drugs, Cuba had to modify its behavior as outlined above and its relations with the Soviet Union.[87] Fidel asks those interested to compare the degree to which drugs are a problem in the United States and in Cuba and then to decide which nation has conducted a serious war on drugs. Those who have observed both societies firsthand, as I have, cannot help but conclude that the United States, if it so desired, could learn a great deal about curtailing the spread of drugs from the far more successful Cuban experience.

A year after rejecting Cuba's help in fighting drugs, George Bush announced his "Initiative for the Americas," a plan to promote neoliberal economics in the region. Fidel described it as an attempt to preserve Latin America as the privileged domain of the United States.[88] The Cuban leader was more convinced than ever that the United States would work with Latin American nations only on projects controlled by Washington.

Countries and their leaders tend to build diabolical and exaggerated images of their enemies, react to misperceptions, and sometimes act unrealistically. Fear exists whether the causes are real or imagined, and sorting out real from imagined fear is difficult. In light of the CIA's overthrow of the democratic government in Guatemala in 1954 and the U.S. invasions of Grenada (1983), Panama (1989), and Kuwait (1991) to remove governments it deemed undesirable, the foundation for Cuba's fear of U.S. aggression is legitimate. In contrast, it is doubtful, even after the Cuban Missile Crisis, that the United States fears an attack from Cuba.

Castro admits that with regard to the United States he would like to do some things over. But he doubts that the two nations would have ever ended up as close friends because Washington controlled Cuba too long and was determined to regain its domination over the island by ending the Revolution.[89] He would prefer a modus vivendi to the current antagonisms between the countries[90] and calls the lack of complete diplomatic accords poor politics, realizing that it is more intelligent to have full exchanges of ideas.[91]

Fidel feels that the United States would gain morally by having relations with Cuba, that diplomatic and economic intercourse between the neighbors would eliminate the stigma caused by a superpower persecuting a tiny Third World state, one that has been hurt at times by curtailed access to products available in the United States. For example, when an outbreak of dengue fever occurred in Cuba in 1981, the United States prohibited the export of medications to combat it. Cuba had to purchase the medicine in Japan, and while waiting a couple of days for the drug to arrive, some Cuban children died.

Castro insists that he would reestablish relations immediately if the United States did so on the basis of mutual respect and sovereign equality and if Washington terminated its economic blockade of the island.[92] Cubanologist Max Azicri said that for the reestablishment of diplomatic ties Cuba also requires U.S. subversion to stop, termination of U.S. violations of Cuban airspace and waters, and the return of the Guantánamo base. For its part, the United States wants compensation for property confiscated from U.S. owners, assurances that human rights will be respected, and Cuba's promise to cease participating in wars of national liberation in the Americas.[93]

The Reagan and Bush administrations insisted that Cuba dissolve close ties to the Soviet Union. After relations between the Soviets and the United States thawed in 1990, the Bush government again demanded that Cuba relinquish its socialist principles before Washington would discuss the resumption of relations. Castro defends his country's sovereign right to deal with whom it pleases[94] and contends that the United States is the terrorist in Central America and pursues harmful expansion in Latin America. He refuses to give people in the United States the impression that he would renounce any of his beliefs if relations with their government improved[95] or that a philosophical or ideological reconciliation is feasible. But he indicates that cooperation between the countries could be improved. For example, if the United States wanted a negotiated, instead of military, settlement of the conflicts in Central America, Castro would assist.[96]

Fidel says that he has, especially in the past fifteen years, extended numerous diplomatic olive branches to the United States, which has responded with a continuous flow of misinformation about Cuba to its people. He says that almost everything published in the United States about Cuba's government is negative but admits the same situation prevails in Cuba, where "we simply have a similar attitude."[97] He admits that a fairly free press exists in the United

States but finds that it ultimately supports policies delineated by the owners of the newspapers,[98] who hesitate to offend their advertisers. He acknowledges that in the United States it is possible to publish a book critical of the system because it poses no threat, but he reminds us that progressives in the United States have been persecuted in show business and the unions.[99] Fidel asks how U.S. citizens can judge the Cuban Revolution for themselves when their government prohibits them from traveling to the island. Did not the United States try to impede the televising of the 1991 Havana Pan American Games to prevent U.S. citizens from seeing Cuban reality, while simultaneously depriving Cuba of needed financial resources? Castro deplores repeated U.S. attempts to impose conditions regarding internal Cuban affairs in return for a normalization of relations, about which he holds little optimism.[100]

Although he would prefer better relations with the United States, Fidel knows that for over three decades the existence of the latter's hostility has united Cubans against a common enemy, a factor that has helped keep the island free. He expects long-term opposition from the United States, where free enterprise institutions wield enormous power. He saw the Republican administration of George Bush sign into law in October 1992 the Torricelli Bill, or "The Cuban Democracy Act," which extended the U.S. trade embargo against Cuba and banned all vessels stopping in Cuba from U.S. ports for six months. He noted that the government of Democrat Bill Clinton, inaugurated in 1993, supported the new legislation. He understands that U.S. recognition of Cuba would convey the impression to the other Latin American nations that the United States was willing to coexist with a Marxist-Leninist country. The United States in the foreseeable future will not appreciate socialism. If one day the people of the United States decide they want socialism, he asks, "Will the CIA agree? Will the Pentagon agree?"[101] He predicts that the United States will be the last place to adopt socialism and hopes that it ultimately can achieve social change in a parliamentary fashion.[102] He says that Englishmen never thought that their American colony would be independent. Slave owners never believed slavery would end, and "one day class societies will disappear."[103] He concludes that world peace will only come about on the terms desired by each nation's majority, not those imposed by another more powerful state, that effective force is not in arms, or laws, or state institutions, but in the masses, in revolutionary conviction, and in sincerity and consciousness.[104]

In conclusion, the Cuban Revolution has clearly affected the course of U.S. history. Tens of thousands of Cubans have sought exile in the United States, where a number of them have been implicated in the Bay of Pigs invasion, the Watergate scandal, illegal U.S. interventions in Latin America, and drug running. Also, U.S. intransigence has stiffened Cuba's resolve to fend off Yankee encroachments and has increased Castro's reluctance to compromise, which in turn provides additional reasons for U.S. opposition.[105]

Latin America

In recent years Fidel has been more interested in establishing closer diplomatic and economic ties to Latin America than in supporting revolution there. He still maintains solidarity, mostly in the form of moral support, for the area's national liberation movements. Cuba respects the area's capitalist regimes that reciprocate goodwill or provide trade benefits. Despite U.S. attempts to cast Fidel as the pariah of the hemisphere, his stature as a statesman has grown over the last two decades. He commands prestige because he has stood up to the United States. At recent presidential inaugurations in Brazil, Mexico, and Ecuador and at the 1992 Rio conference on the environment, Fidel received more attention and adulation than any other head of state. What has he done to attain such a position?

Initially a self-appointed spokesman for Latin America's downtrodden, he subsequently earned the right to function in that capacity through deeds and by example. He constantly reminds the people of Latin America that they liberated themselves from Spain, but not from exploitation. Local landlords assumed the authority of the Spanish governors. Indians continued in servitude, and minimal hope existed for the people under new oligarchs aided by foreign capital. He contends that today Latin America, Cuba excepted, languishes under imperialist control far more ferocious than Spanish colonialism.[106] He asserts that the region is ungovernable under capitalism, that conditions there approximate those that led to the French and Russian revolutions.

Fidel sees Cuba as an integral part of "Latin America historically, morally and culturally" and envisions an organization of revolutionary states there.[107] Many factors militate against such a prospect, among them the U.S.-controlled inter-American system, represented by the OAS, which extends the Monroe Doctrine, converts Latin America into a protectorate, and impedes revolution, and the U.S.-inspired cold war, which, despite recent events in Europe, rages on in the region and enables anti-Castro governments to receive economic and military assistance from Washington. He believes that the United States endeavors to prevent the unity of Latin American countries and tries to force them into bilateral talks with it.[108]

Fidel engages in a massive struggle with the United States for the hearts and minds of fellow Latins. For example, he strongly supports independence for Puerto Rico, which he claims became a U.S. colony as a result of the Cuban-Spanish-American War, and he maintains close ties to the Puerto Rican Socialist party.[109] He perceives that the United States has, in Latin America, for the most part, managed to capture the loyalties of only those who control the means of production. The majority of the masses of Latin America reject the United States and revere and/or respect Fidel. Castro's immediate objective, the restoration of solid diplomatic and economic relations with all Latin states, will take time and patience. He, in the best Marxian tradition, insists that time is on Cuba's side. He follows a simple rule of not subordinating the issue of relations to Cuba's interests, rather subordinating "that issue to the interests of each one of those countries."[110] He tells them to do what they consider most appropriate to their interests, reestablish relations with Cuba or wait.[111] By example, he negates the implied directive of the United States, "Do as I do or as I say."

Fidel understands the unique position of Latin American countries in comparison to some states in Asia and Africa. The Latin nations have achieved theoretical political sovereignty, do not require liberation in the conventional colonial sense, but remain economically dependent. He encourages them to study and comprehend dependency, a concept initially enunciated, but not defined, in the eighteenth and nineteenth centuries, forgotten for decades, and eventually revived by Lenin's theory of imperialism, which became popular in Latin America primarily thanks to studies about Cuba in the late 1960s and 1970s. He stresses that economic dependence diminishes political and social autonomy and that no state in the region is so weak that it must succumb to dependency. Strength exists in the form of the millions of people in nearby nations who share the "same miseries, harbor the same sentiments, have the same energy, and all dream about a better future."[112]

Fidel explains that Cuba took the revolutionary initiative in Latin America in the 1960s to create a kindred movement in the area and to alleviate its own feelings of isolation. Castro and his followers pushed for pluralistic Marxism in Latin America, not domination by Cuban ideology.[113] He expressed "the opinion that this hemisphere carries a child in its womb that is known as Revolution."[114] He believes that in Latin America the dynamics of nationalist and popular struggles will lead to the adoption of Marxist beliefs. Through class struggle the people will realize that what they fight for is also national liberation.[115] Naturally, he expects the successes of the Cuban Revolution to provide incentive to others.[116]

Castro accentuates the Bolivarian tradition of hemispheric confederation and solidarity, the belief that the people of the region can live, not balkanized, but united (in spirit and ideals) against imperialism. He promotes regional unity in Latin America. For instance, when Argentina invaded the British-held Malvinas (Falkland Islands) in 1982, Fidel immediately supported the claims of the right-wing Argentine military government, a selfless act that transcended ideology.[117] To Castro, Latin American unity against British imperialism superseded his distaste for Argentine fascism. In particular, he criticized the duplicity of the United States, which initially announced its neutrality in the conflict but, after Secretary of State Alexander Haig failed to mediate the dispute, joined the British against Argentina.

Castro and his cohorts have played a major role in unifying leftist political groups in Central and South America. There can be little doubt that the Cuban Revolution rehabilitated Marxism in the Americas from the 1960s through the 1980s. As a result of the Cuban Revolution many intellectuals in Latin America reexamined the feasibility of socialism in the area and dug deeper into the vast store of Marxist literature for ideas that could be applied creatively to twentieth-century conditions.[118] Neo-Marxist ideas as well as voluntarism and dependency thinking often replaced more rigid and ortho- dox European-oriented Marxist thought in Latin America. Latin American intellectuals increasingly accepted the theories of Castro, Guevara, Lenin, Trotsky, Mao, and Gramsci and combined them with aspects of Indian thought and culture, existentialism, feminism, nationalism, and Christian so- cial justice to work toward giving the masses some political and social power.[119]

Of course, many of Latin America's diverse Marxists evaluated the Revolu- tion differently, albeit positively. For example, Argentine thinker Alfredo Palacios admired Castro's successful defiance of the United States and de- fended the Revolution, especially its agrarian reform policy. He saw Cuba achieving, in a "creative" socialist fashion, some of his lifelong objectives.[120] Chilean *pensador* Raúl Ampuero Díaz, a Socialist party theoretician, praised Castro's flexibility and stated that if the Cuban leader had followed orthodox Marxist methods, the old regime would still be in power.[121] To Colombian Marxist thinker José Consuegra Higgins, Fidel is to Latin America what Le- nin was to the world.[122] Brazilian leftist intellectual Leôncio Busbaum noted that Cuba could attain socialism without a dictatorship of the proletariat be- cause Fidel acted as the conductor of the masses by interpreting their aspira- tions and helping them change their historical path.[123] Uruguayan Marxist writer Rodney Arismendi believed that Cuba's Revolution succeeded, in part, because Castro was willing to cooperate and collaborate, rather than form a class alliance, with Cuba's national bourgeoisie. He viewed Fidel as a revolu- tionary democrat, a social reformer inspired by socialist ideas, who eventually embraced Marxism-Leninism and allied with Cuba's established working classes.[124]

Castro also understands that after he revealed his Marxism, support for left- ists grew in Latin America, and in many countries the military assumed politi- cal control for "national security reasons." He also likes to mention that some of the area's military, exposed to Marxism as a part of anticommunism, have realized the need for change, questioned the social order, and moved to the left.[125] Despite the opposition created by the anticommunism engendered by the Cuban Revolution, he still believes that Latins owe a great deal to Cuba. He points out that the region has become more independent. Then again, since the Revolution, the United States has focused greater attention on Latin America, and that often translates into oppression. But some good has emerged. For instance, the United States has displayed greater respect for the area. It also has devised programs such as the Alliance for Progress. Between 1961 and 1971, the United States, through the alliance, intervened to deter socialism and to buttress capitalism,[126] and intervention aroused the revolutionary spirit.[127] Viewed from a capitalist perspective, according to Fidel, the alliance contained some altruism and benefited some poor people by providing a few viable reforms.[128]

Castro also maintains that the Latin American nations now know that if the United States crushes the Cuban Revolution, it will erode their sovereignty.[129] The Latins construe aggressive acts against Cuba as hostile to themselves. Thus they do not want to see the Revolution eradicated. He predicted in 1983 that possibly before the twenty-first century another socialist state, one not necessarily adhering to the Cuban model, would emerge in Latin America.[130] It appeared as if Nicaragua or El Salvador might fulfill his prediction, until the Sandinista party lost power in 1990 and the Salvadoran Marxist rebels in 1992 gave up armed struggle in favor of a negotiated political settlement, which included their integration into the nation's bourgeois electoral system.

Apropos of the Nicaraguan case, Castro concedes that U.S. imperialism works to destabilize Latin America, but in the long run, he thinks that the region's political and social upheavals, which have primarily internal, not external, origins,[131] will succeed. When they do, he would like Cuba to belong to an egalitarian regional organization, without headquarters in the United States, where he could serve as mediator between Latin America and the United States.

Mexico

The United States has always tried to create an unfavorable image of revolutionary Cuba in Latin America and has implored the nations of the region to join its economic blockade and to ostracize the island politically. Fidel indicates that Mexico has never complied with the wishes of the United States.[132] For instance, at the insistence of Washington the OAS expelled Cuba in 1962, and every Latin American nation except Mexico had dissolved diplomatic ties to Havana by 1964.[133] He feels a special warmth toward Mexico, where he prepared for his return to oppose Batista, for never breaking relations with Cuba and for upholding the precepts of nineteenth-century Mexican president Benito Juárez, who believed in peace through mutual respect. Fidel appreciates Mexico's adherence to the Mexican, or Estrada, Doctrine, a policy implemented by twentieth-century Mexican president Lázaro Cárdenas whereby Mexico recognizes all de facto governments and does not use diplomatic recognition as a tool of approval or disapproval.[134] Castro repeatedly applauds Mexico's noninterventionist foreign policy. Even when Mexico City disagreed with Havana, it has maintained open channels of communication to resolve differences. Since 1959, Mexico has regarded Cuba's leader as just another head of state, not as a threat to the world.

Mexico defends Cuba's right to self-determination[135] and shares its dedication to territorial integrity. Fidel knows that Mexico, which lost half of its land to U.S. expansionism, understands the consequences of imperialism. He refers frequently to Mexico's dedication to retaining control over its natural resources but fears for its sovereignty now that it has been proven oil rich. However, he also hopes that petroleum wealth increases Mexico's potential for independence.[136]

Castro praises Mexico for being a friend of underdeveloped nations and for its refusal to back genocidal governments even when prodded to do so by the United States. The Mexican people, from the outset of the Cuban Revolution, have respected Fidel's compassion for the underdog. I was in Mexico on January 1, 1959, and recall vividly seeing Mexicans dancing in the streets and proclaiming Castro's takeover "another Mexican Revolution." Mexico's feelings for Fidel have not abated over the years. President Miguel de la Madrid, in 1988, presented Castro with the Aztec Eagle Order, Mexico's highest award, and stated, "For Latin America, you represent the impassioned defense of our people's freedom and right to self-determination." Fidel expressed similar sentiments as he conferred upon the Mexican chief of state Cuba's top honor, the José Martí Order.[137] In the fall of 1991, Mexican president Carlos Salinas de Gortari, a close ally of the United States, stated publicly that Mexico intended to "contribute to détente and establish an open dialogue"[138] with Cuba, emphasizing potential trade and the reintegration of Cuba into the life of Latin America.

Although Castro has high regard for Mexico's independent foreign policy, he views the Mexican Revolution as a capitalist reform movement, one that did not break the bonds of economic dependence. The latter, he believes, can only be accomplished by genuine revolution that restructures a society's economic, political, and social institutions. He says that halfway reform measures simply do not work, and he supports his contention by referring to the failed reformist experiments in Guatemala in the 1940s and 1950s and in Bolivia during the 1950s and 1960s. He points out that in each of these cases democratic nationalists, together with unarmed people, could not withstand the onslaught of U.S. economic, political, and military pressures. The successful undermining of these democratic experiments convinced him that the only true road to political and social change is armed struggle,[139] and once you achieve victory you must remove all bourgeois types from positions of power. He acknowledges that where internal unity can be promoted in Latin America, reform might be possible, but in nations where it is impossible, such as Guatemala and Bolivia, revolution is the only answer.[140] With reference to Guatemala, Castro likes to point out that agrarian reforms and the implantation of democratic social justice there, not communism, led to U.S. military intervention in 1954 and subsequently the deaths of 100,000 people: "We have advanced on the basis of these experiences" and learned from Guatemala that nationalist reform movements will not be permitted to thrive.[141]

Chile

Because the United States intervened in Guatemala and Bolivia under the pretense of stopping Soviet subversion and protecting "national security," Fidel cautioned latter-day leftist movements in Chile, Grenada, and Nicaragua not to become as close to the USSR as did Cuba. By the time the democratically elected socialist Salvador Allende assumed the presidency in Chile in November 1970, Fidel thought that one cannot simply win election, but must hold power, before making a revolution. Castro believed that Allende could not build a revolution by adhering to Chile's constitutional institutions and that he did not have sufficient power or support to work outside of the established processes. He concluded that Allende could not move Chile toward socialism by passing legislation through a primarily bourgeois congress.

Fidel traveled in Chile for almost a month, beginning in November 1971, and remarked that Chile followed a unique process. Remembering that he had once stated, "Those who believe that they are going to win against the imperialists in elections are just plain naïve," he, for the sake of retaining a valuable ally, said, "If I am asked what is happening in Chile, I would sincerely say that a revolutionary process is occurring," but then he added, "a process is not yet a revolution."[142] In a speech to the Chilean people, he warned that some Latin American states are too small to think on a grand scale, that they should think in terms of the community of Latin American nations. He explained that you could not have a huge shipyard to build large vessels just for Chile, that it would have to construct them for other countries as well. It was not economically feasible for Cuba or Chile to run major specialized industries. Nations have to agree to distribute major industries among themselves or risk purchasing all large items abroad and running gigantic trade deficits.[143] Fidel made a plea for a community of cooperating socialist states in Latin America, with Cuba and Chile as charter members. Such an organization would function to collectively cancel members' debts and to stand up to the demands of capitalist nations.[144]

Although skeptical of Allende's ability to survive economically in the face of a U.S. trade boycott or to forge a revolution within the rules established by capitalists to maintain their control, he admitted that he hoped that he would be proven wrong, that perhaps a peaceful road to socialism existed. Also, while in Chile, Castro saw for the first time the revolutionary ability of the Christian Left and developed respect for it and its efforts to avert bloodshed. He returned to Havana with both hope and fear for the survival of the Allende administration. When, in September 1973, the Allende government fell victim to its internal opponents, including the CIA-financed military led by General Augusto Pinochet, Fidel expressed sadness and outrage, but not surprise. He realized that the CIA exaggerated the Cuba-Chile connection, which it moved to eliminate. He later indicated that the capitalist press clamored for the ouster of Allende throughout his administration, that under the Chilean pluralistic political system all of the socialist president's opponents had the right to conspire against him, and the powerful minority, representing the owning class, established a fascist regime. Castro pointed out that Cuba would never run similar risks.[145] He concluded, "The Chilean example teaches us the lesson that it is impossible to make the revolution with the people alone: arms are also necessary."[146] Fidel implored Allende to arm the workers to stave off the 1973 coup. But the Chilean president refused to do so on the grounds that such action would pit Chilean against Chilean and spill a considerable amount of blood.

A revolution must be able to defend itself and needs the support of peasants, workers, and the progressive bourgeoisie, which it did not have in Chile. The Chilean episode deepened Castro's conviction that progressives cannot attain power via the ballot box and remain in office. Once and for all, it invalidated the Soviet and orthodox Latin American Communist party idea of winning and retaining power through parliamentary procedures. He saw the tragedy of the overthrow of Allende and the damage it did to the Chilean people. He illustrated his point by noting that under Allende the government tried to feed everyone and had to import meat. After the socialist-oriented regime fell, repression followed. Pinochet fired civil servants, laid off tens of thousands of workers, cut wages, and restored the market economy. Chile could then export meat, Castro stated, because many people could not afford to buy it.[147]

From 1973 until 1989, when Pinochet stepped down as chief executive, Castro campaigned against him in international circles, claiming that he feared that Chile would become another Nicaragua, where the Somoza dynasty had ruled for over four decades. Fidel remarked that he would rather have middle-class civilians in political power than the brutal military under Pinochet.[148]

Grenada

In 1979, a few years after the collapse of the Allende experiment in Chile, the New Jewel Movement, led by socialist-oriented Maurice Bishop, took over the tiny eastern Caribbean island of Grenada, and the leftist Sandinista-led revolution triumphed over the Somozas in Nicaragua. These events left Castro feeling less isolated. He began to believe that his community of kindred-spirit states would emerge in the Americas. He called the Grenada uprising "a big revolution in a small country,"[149] one that he fully supported despite the fact that he did not consider Bishop to be building socialism. Fidel allowed that the Grenadian leader used some socialist theory to help develop the nation.[150] However, the United States, fearful that Bishop would be attracted to the Cuban style of revolution, warned him not to develop ties to Havana. Then, by denying the aid requested by the Bishop government, the United States drove Grenada to seek help from Cuba.

Cuba's people of African origin had a particularly warm spot for Grenada, a primarily black country. Fidel capitalized on his belief in Cuba as a Latin-African nation and developed close personal ties to Bishop and a solid working relationship with Grenada. Cuba sent teachers, physicians, and construction workers to help the embryonic revolution.

When an internal coup led to the murder of Bishop in 1983, Fidel was furious and believed that the Grenadian revolution had damaged itself. Internal divisions ruined Grenada's revolution and increased Castro's deep-seated fear of similar occurrences destroying the Cuban Revolution. Bernard Coard, who assumed some of Bishop's power and wanted to institute orthodox socialist measures, fancied himself a Marxist, a claim that Fidel said was diminished by his repugnant ambitions and desire for power.[151] Meanwhile, the Soviet Union viewed Coard's coup as necessary to attain better party discipline and condemned Cuba for not supporting Coard and, ultimately, for the loss of a socialist nation.

Before Castro could reduce Cuba's presence in Grenada, the United States, in violation of the UN and OAS charters, sent more than 8,000 troops to do battle with Grenada's 300-person military. The United States occupied the island and reinstituted its form of capitalism. While U.S. forces were en route to Grenada, Castro cabled the U.S. State Department and asked permission to remove 784 Cubans, including 40 military personnel, from the island before fighting erupted. Washington, claiming that 4,341 Cuban troops were in Grenada and needing the excuse that Soviet-backed Cuban forces had prepared the island as a launching site for attacks on the mainland of Latin America, ignored Castro's pleas. Ultimately, the Cubans in Grenada fought for their host nation, and the United States proclaimed that Castro's forces impeded its "war for peace." After the conflict, Cuba offered irrefutable evidence to disprove the U.S. allegations that Cuban workers were building a military airfield in Grenada. Months later, U.S. workers completed the St. George's airfield according to its original design for tourist use. The Cubans asked why they would be suspected of planning an attack from Grenada, when they had never launched one from Cuba in twenty-five years of revolution.

Fidel saw the invasion as pretentious, a preview of events to come elsewhere in the world. He asserted that the Pentagon had staged the war for television consumption in the United States. Not until seventy-two hours after its troops landed did the United States let "selected" journalists set foot on the island. Fidel notes that the press eventually let itself be carried away by "a wave of chauvinism."[152] Grenada became the first post-Vietnam war, one with selected aspects televised in the United States and the press serving as an nonobjective cheerleader for the invader. Grenada was a precursor to U.S. action in Panama in 1989 and in Iraq and Kuwait in 1991.

Whereas the Reagan government hailed the Grenada adventure as a blow to Cuba and communism, Fidel believed it damaged U.S. prestige by letting the world see a bully commit a cowardly and ridiculous act. Grenada, Castro insisted, strengthened Cuba's ties to Latin America, as Latins saw only a Pyrrhic victory by the U.S. intervenors, recalled Yankee complicity in the Malvinas the year before, and reenforced their dedication to anti-intervention.[153] In Fidel's mind, the Reagan administration had staged a "great victory" to save face for the U.S. defeat in Vietnam and for the 230 U.S. Marines killed in Lebanon a week before the invasion of Grenada. Fidel labeled the intervention "dangerous."[154]

With the fall of Grenada, Fidel and the Cuban people experienced a deep sense of loss. But ever the optimist, he concluded that the Grenada disaster intensified the fighting spirit among the progressive forces then combating the U.S.-financed military in El Salvador.[155]

El Salvador

On many occasions Castro has stated that Latin America, aside from Cuba, has received better treatment from the United States as a result of the Cuban Revolution. Immediately after Fidel assumed power, the United States undertook projects such as the aforementioned Alliance for Progress. These programs helped the Latin American republics to a very limited extent.

The economic, social, and political reforms of the 1960s and the move toward industrialization in countries such as El Salvador led to urbanization, increased trade union activity, and greater political awareness on the part of the urban proletariat. Demands for, and the implementation of, reforms increased foreign debts, leading more Salvadorans to claim that capitalism ruined their country. The example of Cuba, which proved that Revolution can bring dramatic social and economic changes rapidly, spawned new revolutionary movements such as El Salvador's Farabundo Martí National Liberation Movement (FMLN) and the Democratic Revolutionary Front (FDR). The United States, seeing its support for capitalist reforms backfire to a degree, reacted in two ways. First, it decided that the funds it formerly appropriated for such programs as the Alliance for Progress were being wasted and stolen by corrupt Latin American bureaucracies and also, inadvertently, that they stimulated nationalist and trade union activity by progressive Latinos. Thus, the Nixon administration, convinced that its foreign aid programs were too costly financially and ideologically, dropped any pretense at altruism vis-à-vis Latin America and reverted to the avaricious "dollar diplomacy" policies that had prevailed prior to World War II. Second, the United States, determined not to permit "another Cuba," embarked upon a national security course of using military force to combat whatever it declared "communism." Castro's contention, at least with respect to El Salvador, that the rest of Latin America benefited by the Cuban Revolution was true to the extent that heightened political consciousness had provoked political and guerrilla action. But it also led to government repression in El Salvador. Fidel denies that El Salvador's guerrillas followed the Cuban model. To him, the Central American state was far more backward than Cuba had been in 1959. First it had to be liberated, then developed economically, before it could proceed to build socialism.[156]

Castro goes on to say that El Salvador serves as a perfect example of the U.S. policy of encouraging peace among the powerful nations, such as the USSR (when it existed), and simultaneously waging war against small states with progressive movements like the FMLN-FDR. Washington fosters low-intensity conflicts in Central America to support the status quo and wear down the leftist opposition.[157] The United States during the Carter administration claimed that the FMLN was dedicated to establishing a Marxist, totalitarian government, and thus Washington armed, trained, and advised the Salvadoran army, hoping to solve militarily what were essentially social, political, and economic problems. Fidel declares that these problems cannot be rectified while the United States seeks military answers[158] and develops techniques to destroy revolutionary movements that use irregular warfare.

Fidel acknowledges that the Cuban Revolution stimulated the popular movement in El Salvador to combat dictatorship, the oligarchy, and U.S. influence. The Salvadorans learned from Cuba how to introduce revolutionary consciousness to the masses, how to integrate the petite bourgeoisie into the class struggle, and how to solidify the peasant-worker alliance.

Castro admits that Cuba sent military aid to the Salvadoran guerrillas during the early 1980s, but contrary to public opinion in the United States, since the mid-1980s Fidel has worked to promote dialogue between the FMLN-FDR and the government of El Salvador. He states that Cuba has placed no troops in El Salvador[159] and that it has moved to apply to the Central American nation the solutions of the Contadora Pact (1983) countries (Colombia, Mexico, Panama, and Venezuela): the demilitarization of Central America, including the withdrawal of all foreign forces, and guarantees of elections and democratic pluralism in each nation of the region.[160] He concurs with the FMLN-FDR, which repeatedly offered to terminate hostilities if it could participate fully in the constitutional process under terms agreed to by both sides. Fidel frequently offered to assist in mutually agreed-upon negotiations, with mutual concessions, not surrender (a word that does not exist in the revolutionary's lexicon),[161] to end the civil war in El Salvador. His offers were all rebuffed by the United States, which, he said, wanted to settle the conflict by exterminating all revolutionaries.[162]

Castro believed that the Salvadoran guerrillas possessed the capability to resist indefinitely without obtaining weapons from abroad.[163] Although Cuba continued to support the FMLN-FDR morally and with "opinions only when they ask us,"[164] Fidel found that, practically, it was very difficult to provide material assistance.[165] He envisioned a protracted struggle in El Salvador, one neither side could win.[166] By 1991, the stalemate he predicted continued, although thanks to UN diplomacy, a negotiated settlement, which the Cuban leader supported, appeared feasible. In the back of Castro's mind remained the possibility that an impatient United States might someday invade El Salvador and defeat its revolution. When the aforementioned negotiated settlement came to fruition in early 1992, Fidel remained skeptical that the Salvadoran government would abide by its agreement to reduce the size and curtail the power of its military and incorporate the FMLN-FDR into the constitutional process. He also doubted that the United States would refrain from intervening in the internal affairs of El Salvador.

Nicaragua

Revolutionary upheaval succeeded in Central America when Sandinista-led forces took over Nicaragua in July 1979. This temporarily confirmed Fidel's belief that ultimately all of Latin America could be turned into another Sierra Maestra. But when the FMLN offensive in El Salvador failed in January 1981, he decided, after careful evaluation, that Cuba should not once again advocate armed struggle in the Americas. The joyous Cuban leader asserted that from the Cuban Revolution the Nicaraguans had learned that their dreams could be realized, that radical changes could be wrought in what the United States thinks of as its sphere of influence. Castro cautioned the Nicaraguans to learn from the Cuban experience but to organize their revolution in keeping with national historical conditions. He said that what occurred in Nicaragua evolved from years of tyranny by the Somozas and over 150 years of foreign domination, decades of sacking the country, appropriating its wealth, repression, and continuous economic crisis for the masses.[167] Fidel neglected one vital aspect when he stated that Nicaragua had not imported its conditions.[168] The United States, in collusion with Nicaragua's oligarchy, bore responsibility for maintaining the Somozas in power for forty-two years.

When Washington responded to the Sandinista victory by warning of an impending Communist takeover, Fidel asked how the United States could explain its first occupation of Nicaragua in 1902 in terms of communism or blame Cuba for the exploits of Augusto Sandino, who had fought to expel the U.S. invaders in the 1920s and 1930s.[169] Nevertheless, Castro advised the Sandinista leaders not to offend Washington, as he had done twenty years earlier. He suggested that Nicaragua maintain good relations with the nation with which it historically conducted 84 percent of its trade. He also told the

Nicaraguans that the Cuban Revolution had erred by taking an abrupt leftward turn, which jarred and alienated liberals and social democrats.

Fidel appreciated the fact that the Sandinistas relied on his thinking and that of Lenin, Mao, Ho Chi Minh, and Che, along with the ideology of Sandino, which the Cuban leader knew well. To the Sandinista founders, Castro represented the resurrection of Sandino. The Sandinistas found that an updated version of Sandino's military strategy and political organization better suited Nicaraguan conditions than did Che's ideas on those topics. The Sandinistas, as did Fidel, saw class struggle as the motor force of their revolution. Also, Sandinista founder Carlos Fonseca Amador learned from the Cubans about the feasibility of revolutionary thinking emanating from revolutionary action. He also knew that concrete action is insufficient without revolutionary ideology and programs.

Although the Sandinista National Liberation Front (FSLN) was patterned after Cuba's nonsocialist 26th of July Movement, Castro pointed out that like the Cubans, the Nicaraguans had defeated the dictator without the help of the Soviet Union. He felt that it was absurd to view the situation in Central America as a result of Cuban or Soviet support and arms. He also mentioned that Costa Rica, Mexico, Panama, and Venezuela backed the Sandinistas.

Early in the Sandinista revolution, Castro stated that the Nicaraguans would never experience the same fate as the Chileans had under Allende because the Nicaraguan people had power and weapons.[170] Of course, he did not foresee the extent of the counterrevolutionary force (the Contras) mounted by the United States.

As he did with the Salvadorans, Fidel proclaimed, "We will never seek to tell the Sandinistas what they should do, or give or offer them free advice."[171] He noted that in many ways the Cuban and Nicaraguan revolutions were dissimilar. After visiting Nicaragua, he stated that the situation regarding the church was different in Cuba in 1959 and Nicaragua in 1979. Religious feeling had developed deeper roots in Nicaragua and elsewhere in Latin America by 1979 when the church stopped talking about rewards in the other world and focused on happiness in this life.[172] The Cuban Revolution ignored the church, whereas the Sandinistas incorporated the Popular Church and liberation theology into their movement. Christianity originally evolved as the religion of the poor, and Castro noted that the socialist movement could benefit from honest church leaders with the spirit of early Christianity.[173]

Fidel initially emphasized that he considered Nicaragua not socialist or reformist but revolutionary.[174] He later stated that President Daniel Ortega (1984–1990) spoke about the socialist essence, or character, of the Nicaraguan revolution but never said that it explicitly followed Marxist ideology.[175] Castro subsequently claimed that he could envision the Sandinistas pursuing long-term socialist goals.[176] Although Nicaragua copied Cuba's successful literacy campaign and instituted Sandinista Defense Committees, patterned after Cuba's Committees for the Defense of the Revolution, Fidel asserted that Nicaragua must pursue a different, less radical, path than did Cuba. He said that the Nicaraguans could not afford extremism, that they had to take time and plan each stage of their revolution carefully.[177] Proceed pragmatically, he suggested. For the moment, he believed Nicaragua needed a mixed economy and political pluralism.[178]

Castro put the services of Cuba at Nicaragua's disposal. To all who asked, he responded that Nicaragua had requested and received a few Cuban military advisers, many teachers and doctors, and some construction workers.[179] Also, he said, "We have trained [Nicaraguan] civilians and military cadre in Cuba."[180] Cuban solidarity extended to the financial realm as well. For example, in January 1985, Cuba canceled $70 million owed to it by Nicaragua for helping to build the Victoria de Julio sugar mill. Fidel explains dealings such as cancellation of debts as practices never followed by capitalists.[181]

Castro warned that as long as the United States believed that it could destroy the Nicaraguan revolution from within, it would attempt to do so and not seriously seek a political solution to its differences with the Sandinistas.[182] He refuted the U.S. contention that Nicaragua wanted to export its revolution to El Salvador. Fidel demonstrated that the conditions that precipitated the upheaval in El Salvador were manifest in the 1930s and that revolutionaries had existed there long before the Sandinistas took over Nicaragua.[183] He urged a negotiated settlement of U.S.-Nicaraguan problems and supported the aforementioned Contadora Pact,[184] which he interpreted as a move toward regional unity that could prevent war in Central America. He believes that the United States disregarded the Contadora initiative because Washington wanted a war to teach the lesson that nobody can conduct a progressive fight for independence and social justice in the area.[185]

Between 1979 and 1990, when the Sandinistas lost power in a freely contested election, Cuba, with years of experience combating various CIA schemes, advised the Nicaraguan government, primarily in terms of strategy, tactics, and international diplomacy, how to fight the U.S.-financed Contra war. After the 1990 election, Fidel applauded the Sandinistas for relinquishing power gracefully[186] and hoped that their revolution had not disappeared but had entered a new phase, one where they would prepare to once again win the backing of Nicaragua's majority. The Cuban leader reiterated that he does not believe that Cuba's political system per se would, or should, work elsewhere in Latin America. Nevertheless, he was hurt by the blow delivered to socialism in Nicaragua and felt increasingly isolated ideologically. His doubts about building socialism elsewhere in Latin America had to increase, but he renewed his determination not to let Cuba become another Nicaragua or Chile.[187]

Panama

Long before the United States intervened in Nicaragua, it had established its own enclave in the middle of Latin America. The Panama Canal and the surrounding zone, carved out with the assistance of President Theodore Roosevelt in 1903 and controlled by the United States ever since, has been the most prominent symbol of Yankee imperialism in the Americas and a convenient target for Castro's verbal attacks. The canal, a technological marvel, has been a source of U.S. pride and a rallying point for U.S. citizens who like to think of their nation in terms of military power. Since his student days, Fidel, like many other educated Latin Americans, has regarded the U.S. acquisition of the canal area as an act of piracy against Colombia, from which the territory was taken.[188] The Canal Zone has been the launching pad for many U.S. incursions in Latin America.

Castro considers the existence of U.S. bases on Latin American soil in the Canal Zone virtual colonization. To add insult to injury, at the bases special courses teach Latin American military personnel how to combat guerrilla warfare and how to conduct armed actions against insurgent peasants who oppose feudal exploitation. Fidel claims that in the Canal Zone the CIA converts Latin American armies into instruments for U.S. political and economic interests and equips and organizes "bands of fascists" to spread terror among workers' organizations, students, and intellectuals. He notes, for example, that the United States used the Canal Zone as a staging area for the troops that invaded the Dominican Republic in 1965 to assist the oligarchy and its military allies in a civil war against the supporters of legally elected democratic president Juan Bosch.[189] Similarly, Fidel avers that the United States has frequently used its bases in the Canal Zone to conduct exercises designed to prevent social revolutions that could lead to the nationalization of U.S.-owned property.

When Colonel Omar Torrijos took over Panama in 1968 and set as his primary goal the return of the canal and zone to native control, Castro supported his efforts to disengage the United States from the area. Fidel categorized the Torrijos regime, which in 1978 extracted some concessions from the United States, including a promise to turn the canal and environs over to Panama by the year 2000, as representative of a progressive military.[190] In contrast, the U.S.-trained Torrijos, at best a capitalist reformer, was condemned as a Marxist by some cold war warriors in the United States who resented the Panamanian strongman's willingness to cooperate with Castro and to stand up to Washington. The new Canal Treaties touched off a conservative reaction in the United States. Right-wing politicians and pressure groups united to prevent another "sell out" to Latin America. Their actions had two major consequences. First, their talk about "the next thing you know the United

States will recognize Cuba" undermined Jimmy Carter's efforts to restore diplomatic relations with Havana. Second, they rallied support for a new president who would safeguard sacred U.S. interests like the canal and subsequently helped place Ronald Reagan, a leader of the "keep the canal movement," in the White House.

In December 1989, the United States invaded Panama, ostensibly to remove from power corrupt and avaricious General Manuel Noriega, who had been on the CIA payroll since the 1960s, and whom Washington had used as a go-between with Castro. Thousands of Panamanians died and 18,000 of them were left homeless in the onslaught, which Washington also used to crush the trade union movement on the isthmus. After the invasion, the United States swore in as president Guillermo Endara, who had been elected to the office the previous May after a campaign openly financed by $9 million from the Bush government. Noriega previously had prevented Endara from taking office on the grounds that the United States had "bought" the election.

The majority of the OAS members refused to back the U.S. invasion or recognize Endara as the legitimate president. Castro noted, as a sign of progress, that even the OAS would no longer sanction the U.S. role of policeman of the hemisphere. Soon after Fidel remarked that the United States wanted to police the entire world[191] and refused to recognize the Endara government, Panama expelled Cuba's ambassador from Panama City.

Fidel construed the Panama episode as the result of U.S. reluctance to relinquish control on the isthmus. The United States corroborated Castro's beliefs. After U.S. troops removed, some say kidnapped, Noriega and took him to the United States for an unprecedented trial, a movement began in the U.S. Congress to renege on the 1977–1978 treaties with Panama and to retain ten U.S. bases on the isthmus beyond the year 2000.

The Panama takeover by the United States deepened Fidel's fears. Would Cuba be next? General Mark Cisneros, the U.S. deputy commander of the Panama invasion, lamented that it was a shame that Castro had not intervened on Noriega's behalf, so the United States could have finished off the Cuban dictator as well. After the European socialist states crumbled in 1990, U.S. Senator Robert Dole spoke about ousting Fidel, whom he called the last Communist domino. George Bush then fulfilled Castro's prediction, as he once again anointed the United States as the supreme arbiter of peace and started a war with Iraq ostensibly to liberate Kuwait, which the former had invaded. Castro's apprehension increased. He wondered whether the United States would someday employ in Cuba the same military tactics it used in Panama in Operation Just Cause and in Iraq in Operation Desert Storm, tactics designed to minimize Yankee casualties by needlessly destroying everything and everybody in their path.

Over a quarter of a century ago, Fidel Castro renounced his intention to incite a Cuban-style revolution in Panama. Since then *Fidelismo* has had much greater appeal in Panama than has orthodox communism. Panamanians see many connections between traditional Latin American personalism, coupled with nationalism, and the successes of the Cuban Revolution, with its anti-Yankee overtones. The Panamanians have not depicted Fidel as a representative of Soviet Marxism but as the idealistic eliminator of dictator Fulgencio Batista's pro-U.S., oppressive regime.

Castro and the Panamanians see valid parallels between their countries. Both attained independence as a result, to some degree, of U.S. intervention. Both were repeatedly subjected to Yankee involvement in their internal affairs and were economically dependent upon the United States. Geographically, both nations have played a strategic military role and have been of value to the United States in wartime. Above all, down through the decades, the masses in both countries have developed an intense dislike for the elitist-oriented policies of the United States that affected them adversely. Under Castro's direction, Cuba rid itself of U.S. influence; the Panamanian people view each Cuban gain as a step closer to the fulfillment of their own needs and aspirations.[192]

Debt Problems

Horrendous debts exacerbate the political and social problems of Mexico and the nations of Central and South America and the Caribbean. Referring to economic and living conditions in the area, Fidel says, "We are worse off now than we were in the period prior to the struggles of Bolívar, San Martín, O'Higgins, Juárez, Morelos and Sucre," in the nineteenth century.[193] He avers that you solve debt problems, not by technological formulas, but by people taking action. In uncanny fashion, he spews off the top of his head accurate debt statistics for all of Latin America, along with figures on the flight of capital from the area. He notes that in terms of interest payments alone, the United States extracts from Latin America $45 billion a year.[194] He predicts that if adequate solutions to the debt problems are not found soon, South America will explode as has Central America,[195] and such an explosion could lead to fascist coups.[196]

One can reduce debts by defending the region's natural resources, by extracting fair value in terms of trade, and by not permitting individuals and corporations to repatriate excessive profits. To attain these objectives Castro sees Latin America engaged in World War III, a basically economic struggle.[197] He finds:

> The crisis of the international economic system is not a phenomenon of a cyclical nature, but is rather a symptom of the underlying structural maladjustments and of a disequilibrium that are part of its very nature, and that imbalance has been

aggravated by the refusal of the developed market-economy countries to control their external imbalances and their high rates of inflation and unemployment.[198]

Early in the Revolution, Fidel had great faith in Cuba's economic relations with Eastern Europe and the Soviet Union, which he saw as a form of integration that fostered enormous gains in health care, education, and industrialization. Now that the European socialist economic community has disintegrated, Fidel feels stronger than ever about the necessity for Latin American economic integration to prevent the region from becoming totally economically dependent on the United States, Western Europe, and Japan, which would cause further drops in living standards.[199] Economic integration would become part of the "new economic order," a concept Fidel enunciated in the UN in the 1970s to promote international cooperation and protect the economies and development projects of the weaker nations. Economic integration, coupled with socialism, would enable Latin America to prosper, as has economically integrated Western Europe. He sees no need for Cuba to abandon its Marxism to be part of an integrated Latin American economy. Although Western Europe has advanced via capitalism, Fidel points out, under that system millions remain unemployed,[200] whereas socialism provides full employment.

Building new international economic relations in Latin America, which involves closer diplomatic ties, now takes precedence in Fidel's mind over armed struggle, and he concedes that the social revolution might have to be postponed to first cure the area's economic ills.[201] Cuba initially, in 1974, proposed the creation of the Latin American Economic System (SELA) as a step toward Castro's economic integration goals.[202] In 1975 Cuba and twenty-four other nations joined SELA, as they sought to collectively curtail Latin American economic dependence on the United States. Castro hoped that SELA would help reduce "unequal exchange," or higher prices for products of the industrialized states and lower ones for goods produced by the underdeveloped countries.[203]

Until 1985, Fidel believed that Latin American nations, which could not meet their debt obligations, needed a grace period of ten to twenty years without payment. He changed his approach when he found that even if a moratorium were granted, at the end of the term the debt would exceed $1 billion. He saw that over the past thirty years "unequal exchange" has increased.[204] Castro realized that Latin America hands over about $70 billion to wealthy industrialized nations annually, whereas its investment credit income is approximately $10 billion, a net loss of $60 billion a year.[205] He claims that the debt is economically, politically, and morally impossible to pay or collect. He understands that those who have tried to force sacrifices on people to pay debts have suffered politically. Because projected economic growth has never occurred, debts are literally unpayable.[206] Morally, he asserts, it is wrong to make people pay for loans they had nothing to do with or from which they received no benefits.[207] He proposes that Latin American states collectively cancel their debts, both principal and interest. Arguing that creditor nations should assume responsibility for the debts to their own private banks and allocate 12 percent of their military spending, or $1 billion a year, for this purpose, he says that would still leave them with $700 billion, enough for weapons to eradicate humanity.[208] With the debt situation under control, a new international economic order could foster development,[209] as could rechanneling the funds for the arms race.

Fidel uses the international debt crisis to establish Cuba's position as a leader among developing nations. He reminds them, "This problem of the debt, the IMF, and the horrifying, selfish measures that these countries adopt teach the masses more about the essence of imperialism and exploitation than ten of the biggest classics, because they can see it in actual practice."[210]

After the debt slate is wiped clean,[211] Fidel advocates the creation of a Latin American monetary fund to provide credit to stimulate business and an areawide common market to balance terms of trade.[212] He tells the 400 million people of Latin America that they should band together, that no one can blockade a continent.[213] He hopes that once the debt problems are resolved, the nations of the area will realize the need for changes in the social relations of production.

Lighter debt burdens mean that Latin American states could fulfill social obligations to their people.[214] Banana republics and unequal trade terms dating from the colonial era could be eliminated.[215] Fidel recalls that Latin America, with its precious metals and the sweat and blood of its indigenous people and the slaves imported from Africa, financed the development of Europe and later the United States. For five centuries, he states, Latin America has been financing the development of the industrialized countries: "This is why they are so wealthy and we are so poor. I believe that it is they who are the debtors and we are the creditors."[216]

He reasons that the debts should not be repaid, that you cannot hold children responsible for their parents' misdeeds. Under international law, contracts are valid only for a reasonable period. Fidel concludes that Latin America has no scientific model that will allow liquidation of the debt. Besides, a protracted period of repayment of debts would preclude the opportunity for economic growth and development, intensify exploitation, and drive the masses to greater poverty and misery. Since structural inequities in the global system of economic relations cause the debt crisis and since the wealthy nations refuse to amend the system, the Latin American states must take steps to break the cycle of Third World underdevelopment.

Castro acknowledges that the problem belongs to the Third World but proposes that Latin America, which is more developed than most parts of Asia and Africa, initiate the process of eliminating neocolonialism.[217] He holds the naïve, and definitely utopian, belief that many industrialized states, after considerable political negotiation, will support debt cancellation. He thinks that you can convince reasonable people in developed nations that if Latin American countries were not forced into horrible economic binds, conditions would improve and the underdeveloped states would become better customers for the industrialized nations.[218]

Cuba, Fidel says, feels qualified to lead the charge for economic change in the region because it has successfully defied the United States in the past and by so doing has created the highest standard of living in Latin America. He claims that no proof exists that capitalism can solve the growing social crises in Latin America, and he does not view the recent huge wave of neoliberalism there as the answer to the development needed in the hemisphere.[219] Also, Cuba feels no financial obligation to the nations that exploited it for centuries and has no qualms about canceling the debt. However, over the years, Fidel has felt committed to repay Cuba's debts to the socialist states, which did not charge exorbitant interest rates, extended Cuba long-term credits, and, at times, dismissed its debts entirely. Unlike the greedy capitalist nations that go to war for markets, the socialist states, which contributed significantly to Cuba's independence, in his opinion, understood the inseparable relationship between peace and development.

7

Democracy, Human Rights, and Freedom of Expression

Revolutionaries must express their ideas valiantly, define their principles and state their intentions so that no one is deceived, neither friend nor enemy.

—Fidel Castro

Socialism generally refers to a social system predicated on common ownership of the means of production and distribution, with emphasis on democracy. This chapter examines Fidel Castro's concept of democracy. It includes his definition of human rights and his response to the accusation that his regime violates them. It explains, according to Fidel, why censorship exists in Cuba and notes what forms it takes. The chapter explores the intricacies of Cuba's brand of socialist education and the role of intellectuals in the nation's educational processes. It examines Castro's views on the freedom of intellectual and artistic expression and the way he encourages writers and artists to strengthen the Revolution by creating thought-provoking forms of popular culture. Finally, it analyzes sports, which Fidel considers the physical side of popular culture, and shows how Cuba uses athletics to solidify the Revolution.

Democracy

The term *democracy* originated in the classical Greek city-states, where it meant the rule of the people, or the citizens (who were a minority), and their right to determine directly what matters concerned society. In modern nation-states democracy has generally become indirect, as elected representatives make determinations for the people.

Castro uses the term *democracy* often, but in a context most people in the capitalist world do not, or refuse to, comprehend. He believes in "unitary democracy," as distinguished from "adversary democracy." To some extent, "unitary democracy" is derived from Aristotle's idea of the body politic as an association for the expression of civic friendship, rather than the modern bourgeois concept of the state as an instrument to serve private ends. "Unitary democracy" implies the participation of all citizens in political, economic, and social debates leading to decisions that require a consensus. Fidel distrusts the "adversary democracy" advocated by liberalism because he has misgivings about the efficiency of representative institutions, which tend to support the needs and desires of the most powerful sectors of society.[1] He contends that democracy will be attained when people have a direct voice, without delegating their prerogatives and power to individuals who, once in office, can do as they please, which does not necessarily mean to work for the general welfare of society.[2]

Fidel understands that democracy requires participants to think, to discuss, and to act on rational ideas.[3] He concurs with Marx that the dictatorship of the proletariat, meaning democratic decisions made by and for the working-class majority, is the highest form of democracy.[4] He sees an analogy between Athenian democracy and the U.S. variety. In both societies class conflict existed: In Athens the aristocrats opposed the slaves, and in the United States the owners of the means of production combat the workers. To him, Roman democracy also approximated that of the United States. In Rome, senators and powerful men decided public issues and occasionally even assassinated caesars. Roman democracy, like that of the United States, had a military base, and its regiments intervened all over the world.[5]

Democracy, to Castro, connotes "just and timely criticism ... it involves calling attention to those that are mistaken, to change their ways and to prevent those who aren't from making mistakes."[6] It also includes freedom, which differs in capitalist and in socialist societies. Capitalist freedom, says Fidel, exists in a class-stratified system and correlates to your place in it, whereas socialist freedom means all are equal: There are no millionaires and no economic pyramid. Without equality there is no freedom and no democracy. He asks if democracy exists when you have beggars, prostitutes, the exploited people, and illiterates. Does democracy exist when you have the "freedom to write and speak for a man who cannot write, who cannot read"?[7]

Castro acknowledges the standing debate between advocates of the parliamentary system and those who believe in democratic centralism. Theoretically, democratic centralism, a basic tenet of Leninism, combines free political discussion and free election of leaders within a vanguard, or leadership, party, which functions hierarchically and wherein members follow discipline precisely as they execute decisions. Castro claims that when society is composed of different classes with varied, often antagonistic, interests, it is difficult to make laws of general benefit. But under democratic centralism and socialism, the party represents the majority, or working masses, and implements decisions beneficial to them based upon laws discussed by all workers.[8] In Cuba, domestic policies reflect a combination of ideas initiated and discussed at the top and the bottom, and foreign policies come from the top down.

As the leader of the party and elected government, Castro, in Rousseauean fashion, believes that he interprets the will of the people, which he views as reasonable and practical during the socialist stage of development, when society is guided by the dictatorship of the proletariat. Cuba has not reached the communist stage of democracy, in which those who produce control fully their own lives and futures. One might call Cuba's form of government benevolent socialist *caudillismo*, bearing in mind that in Latin America, traditionally the *caudillo* rules via patronage, loyalty, and real or implied force. The *caudillo* has the support of the people. When asked if this form of government is democratic, Castro responds that Cuba's brand of democracy allows more participation by the masses than does the U.S. variety, that Cuba is more egalitarian, and thus more democracy exists than under the U.S. electoral system.

When comparing liberal democracy and democratic centralism, one must bear in mind that the objectives of the respective systems differ. The former accentuates individual freedom and liberty; the latter stresses group goals. Both advocate civil and human rights. Castro charges that the United States uses capitalist ideas to analyze Cuba[9] and says that one cannot examine democratic centralism from a liberal democratic perspective and arrive at an honest evaluation. For example, if one judges Cuban democratic centralism by liberal democratic standards, one must be struck by the limits placed on certain kinds of dissent. Bourgeois political dissent does not exist in democratic centralism.[10] Fidel maintains that dissent is permitted within the Revolution and in the party.[11] Opposition from without is deemed counterrevolutionary, and those who engage in this type of dissent can lose their jobs or be subject to ridicule. Counterrevolution aimed at reinstituting a society run for the benefit of economic elites strikes a discordant note in Cuba, where fear of subversion directed from the United States is perceived as a genuine possibility.

Fidel believes there exists little or no potential for political dissent leading to socialism in the United States. There, Republicans and Democrats operate within the bounds of the accepted institutional framework. In the United States, Marxists, the equivalent of Cuba's counterrevolutionaries, can express their opinions through very few establishment channels. If and when their opinions are considered a viable threat to the established order, they are denied access to the media as well as to mainstream publications.

In existing socialist or capitalist societies, dissent aimed at destroying the established system is not permitted. In 1982, I heard an attorney from the United States ask the head of the Lawyer's Union in Cuba, who also served as a Supreme Court justice, if dissent was tolerated in his country. The jurist replied: "If tomorrow morning your dear little Ronnie Reagan appeared before his Congress and stated 'I am now, and will forever be, a Marxist-Leninist,' he would be regarded as either a lunatic or a traitor. If someone tells Fidel that his programs need revision, fine, but if that person supports a reversion to capitalist practices, he or she is a counterrevolutionary." There is some truth to the contention that the concept of dissent from without, construed as counterrevolutionary and treasonous, curtails dissent within the Revolution, as even those engaged in the latter fear that their actions might be interpreted as traitorous.

Human Rights

Bourgeois critics of Cuba condemn the right to dissent only within the Revolution, claiming that the Castro government fails to uphold human rights, and they act as if a gulag exists in the Caribbean. They tend to forget that under socialism, human rights, which people have by virtue of their humanity, not through law, supersede law-made property rights, which are paramount under capitalism. Fidel tells his critics: "Human rights are very often spoken of, but we must also speak of humanity's rights. Why should some people go barefoot, so that others may ride in expensive cars? Why should some be miserably poor, so that others may be exaggeratedly rich?"[12] He explains that human rights mean equal opportunity for people of all colors. He asks whether that exists in the United States, where whites earn three times more than blacks and many times more than Hispanics.[13]

When Castro responds to questions about human rights by widening the scope of discussion beyond the areas of political prisoners and torture, he is often accused by his detractors of obfuscating or circumventing the issue. He replies to specific points with broad answers, not to be evasive, but to exhibit disdain for simplistic answers to complex questions. Sometimes, however, one can pin down Fidel. For instance, he told Italian journalist Gianni Miná: "Not only after the triumph of the Revolution, but not even in our war of liberation was one single prisoner ever tortured, not even when someone could have justified it as necessary to save our soldiers or win a battle."[14]

He points out that never has a demonstration in Cuba been broken up by police or have trained dogs or tear gas been used against the people;[15] prisoners do not disappear, and rubber bullets are not used. Even the Bay of Pigs traitors, he notes, were not beaten or executed.[16] Castro is essentially correct. I have traveled from one end of Cuba to the other but of course have not been in all places at all times, and I have found no evidence of such abuses. Prison conditions in Cuba, as ascertained by international investigatory bodies, approximate those in the United States. Cuba has no labor camps.

Lay people in the United States hear repeatedly that Cuban jails overflow with political prisoners. Fidel claims that so-called political prisoners have committed counterrevolutionary crimes. They are guilty of treasonous acts, such as working with the CIA, and are not incarcerated for their beliefs.[17] Castro admitted that about eight hundred such people were serving sentences in March 1988.[18] By 1991 the number had diminished to less than a hundred. Fidel asserts that only those who take action against the state are in jeopardy, but no prisoners of conscience exist in Cuba.[19] He contends, with some justification, that most counterrevolutionary behavior results from U.S. encouragement and that one reason the United States focuses on political prisoners is that it worries that the Cubans it subverts will get caught and fears that subsequently other agents will be harder to recruit.

Powerful right-wing Cuban-exile lobbies in the United States have disseminated a great deal of propaganda about specific political prisoners in Cuba. One prisoner who attracted considerable attention is Huber Matos. About eight months before the triumph of the Revolution, Matos, a skilled organizer, joined the struggle on Fidel's side. Castro says that he was an ambitious and conceited man who released a lot of hype about himself when he led a rebel column. He also put forth a great deal of anticommunist propaganda. After Castro took over, Major Matos organized a revolt in Camaguey Province against the 26th of July Movement, which he saw as moving to the left. He was tried and convicted, according to Fidel, for instigating an insurrection. Despite international protests for his release, he served his full twenty-year sentence for counterrevolutionary crimes, as the Revolution refused to capitulate to external pressure.[20]

Another political prisoner who became a focal point for exile protest is Armando Valladares (see Chapter 6), arrested for terrorist activities against the Revolution. The French government, philosopher Régis Debray, and PEN, the international writers' group, begged for the release of Valladares, at best a mediocre poet, on the grounds that he was an invalid. A secret camera placed in his cell revealed that he could walk. Once confronted with the films, Valladares discarded his wheelchair and began a program of daily calisthenics. But segments of the exile community in the United States and their misinformed literary friends continued to campaign on behalf of the Cuban terrorist and blew his situation out of proportion in the press. Fidel contends that by distorting the truth about a few political prisoners, such as Matos and Valladares, Cuba bashers make headlines in capitalist countries like the United States, whose governments do not want the truth about Cuba known. Castro acknowledges that Cuban laws are strict, but all prison sentences are carried out after fair trials.[21] He urges people to think about what would have happened to counterrevolutionary traitors such as Matos and Valladares in most societies.

In addition to complaints about the prohibition on dissent and an overabundance of political prisoners, opponents of Castro's brand of socialism always point out that he took power in 1959 and the government did not promulgate a constitution until 1976. He retaliates by stating that even the United States, with its obsession for electoral democracy, did not issue a constitution and hold elections until thirteen years after its Declaration of Independence. Besides, he stipulates that genuine democracy is not enunciated by democratic constitutions, which are all too easily, and often, violated in Latin America, but by democratic institutions such as hospitals that serve equally without cost differentials, schools available for all, relatively equal living conditions for everyone, and a government committed to making progress for all citizens at an equal rate.[22]

Castro says that under Western constitutions, "democratic" leaders get elected by a majority of those who bother to vote and that these leaders do not necessarily heed the human rights guarantees in their constitutions. Thus a Ronald Reagan can win the presidency with less than 30 percent of the eligible electorate, and a few months after the election he is backed by even a smaller minority.[23] Reagan can then support the abuse of human rights in El Salvador, Guatemala, and elsewhere in Latin America, and most U.S. citizens are uninterested or uninformed. In contrast, in Cuba 97 percent of the electorate vote in elections that are not compulsory. Fidel wonders how people like Reagan have the audacity to express "the most absolute, arrogant, limitless scorn for the popular democratic form that our people have adopted in their own right."[24] For Castro:

> A revolution expressing the will of the people is an election every day, not every four years, it is a constant meeting with the people. ... The Revolution has exchanged the conception of pseudo-democracy for direct government by the people. ... Here, there is just one class, the humble, that class is in power, and so is not interested in the ambition of an exploiting minority to get back in power. Those people would have no chance at all in an election.[25]

In other words, those middle-class Miami-based Cuban exiles who supported Reagan's human rights abuses and who have been unrealistically clamoring to return to power in Cuba for over thirty years would hardly be welcomed by today's socialist masses.

In Castro's estimation, elections constitute only a segment of democracy. Democracy means respect for human rights, the right of everyone to employment, freedom from exploitation, the right of peasants to land, no high rents, no threats of eviction, no extortion by landowners. It means blacks' and women's right to be politically, civilly, and socially equal.

Censorship

Castro states: "We do not prohibit anyone from writing on any subject he likes. And let each choose the form that suits him, let each express freely the idea he wants to. We, for our part, will always judge his work through the prism of the Revolution."[26] *Mein Kampf* can be read in Cuba because Fidel believes that students of history should be acquainted with the theories of Nazism. The religious can read Bibles, and books for serious theoretical analysis of capitalism or socialism are welcome, but publications attacking or condemning socialism or the Revolution from a capitalist perspective are prohibited.[27] Lenin believed that you furthered political education and forged working-class consciousness by discussing issues rather than banning publications. Fidel disagrees. Castro, not the press, reveals genuine news to the people of Cuba. It appears in print only after he says that it can. When the press publishes stories, according to Fidel, they might be one-sided, especially when pertaining to the United States, but they do not contain lies, as found so often in the U.S. media.[28]

No discussion of democracy in socialist Cuba arises without reference to censorship. Almost all foreign Cubanologists, including strong supporters of the Revolution, agree that a freer press is desirable in Cuba. The government and Fidel require that all views in the nation's major newspaper *Granma* agree with those of the Communist party. They declare that this is necessary because of the persistent threat of counterrevolution.

Castro defends this system by calling attention to the fact that under socialism newspapers belong to the workers and operate in the name of the majority. He says that the government does not allow the press to oppose the majority or revolutionary class. He calls the Cuban system a "dictatorship of the exploited against the exploiters." Opposition can exist, but not class-based opposition, and criticism within the revolution is encouraged. According to Fidel, "What matters is that the democratic mechanisms function within the revolutionary institutions."[29]

"Direction," he says, is necessary to "channel the function of the press towards the service of society."[30] The Communist party decides what serves society. Fidel is often asked, if the overwhelming majority supports the party and the Revolution, what risk there is in permitting an opposition press. He replies, "It is not a question of risk, it is a matter of principle. We will not permit it."[31]

He asserts that some things must always remain in the family and should not be publicized in the media to prevent giving information to the enemy.[32] Most outside observers believe that this attitude reveals an exaggerated sense of insecurity, one no longer necessary after three decades of Revolution. Castro uses recent events in Eastern Europe, Nicaragua, Panama, and Grenada to validate his policy.

He claims that a similar form of censorship exists in capitalist society. He views "freedom of the press" as a euphemistic expression, one that implies the freedom to own the mass media in capitalist society. He indicates that a true dissenter from the system, a Marxist-Leninist, could not write for the *Washington Post* or the *New York Times*, nor would a communist advocating the restructuring of U.S. society likely appear on national radio or television in the United States.[33] Media analysts in the United States have shown conclusively that Marxist-Leninist views very rarely make the op-ed pages or television talk or news shows.

Those who run the United States do not generally fear for its ideological survival, and yet they encourage a form of censorship to preserve their institutions. Simultaneously, they criticize censorship in Cuba, which Castro attributes to his society's subordination to the desire to survive.[34] He insists that his government must protect its people from those in Cuba who concur with imperialism.[35]

Fidel explains that freedom of the press in capitalist nations means freedom of those who control the media to write what they want, that transnational corporations control the world's information flow, and that this constitutes censorship.[36] He believes that all nations defend their institutions by practicing censorship of one kind or another and that in the United States the people are deluded into thinking that a free press exists. Cuba's press has generally defended and lauded the Revolution. It has presented the illusion of popular unity and has not reflected the diversity of public opinion. But under the rectification process that began in the mid-1980s, the quality of the press, excluding *Granma,* has improved somewhat in terms of providing better investigative and analytical journalism and less uniformity of opinion. Cuban radio, in particular, and hundreds of periodicals, less well known than *Granma,* now present a broader spectrum of facts and interpretations than they did prior to rectification.

Today, most informed Cubans feel that the press can have a revolutionary aura without being "officialist." Cubans believe that the press can reflect more varied opinions, that the country is ready for more in-depth discussions, that official points of view are superfluous, and that alternative views within the Revolution should be discussed openly. To foster such openness the Communist party's Fourth Congress, in October 1991, stressed the responsibility of the press to raise the level of public information and to enrich political culture and ideological development.

Education

Anti-Castro propaganda organizations in the United States, such as the Cuban American National Foundation, funded by the U.S. government's National Endowment for Democracy, claim that because censorship exists in Cuba, education there is totally subjective. All nations, Cuba included, fill their children full of patriotic ideas and teach them about the verities of their ideological systems. Cuba inculcates socialism in its citizens by educating them about how capitalism has affected the Western world. In addition, Cubans are urged to think critically, to question, and to compare histories and cultures.

Many of the foundation blocks of Cuban education came from the thought of Argentine socialist Aníbal Ponce (1898–1938), as reflected in his 1936 volume, *Educación y lucha de clases* (Education and the class struggle). Ponce discerned in primitive education a social responsibility to build a sense of community. His book, republished in revolutionary Cuba, demonstrates that from classical time on, education became an agent of the ruling class that the state used to maintain slavery and feudalism. The state, in collusion with the church, taught irrationality, passivity, fatalism, and faith in the supernatural. According to Ponce, by the eleventh century and the origin of the university, the bourgeoisie, which viewed education as the road to benefits formerly reserved for the clergy and nobility, began to dominate intellectual life. He showed how the ruling class controlled the social organization of the state through education, which conveyed information but did not teach people how to think for fear that they question the system that education was designed to support. Ponce also rejected the concept of the "neutral scholar" and demonstrated the shallowness of those who believe that their judgments are objective and value free.[37]

Fidel understood that he had been a product of the bourgeois educational system described by Ponce, one subjected to Yankee propaganda,[38] where people were not encouraged to think critically. In 1953, when Castro wrote *History Will Absolve Me,* he believed education to be the key to developing Cuba socially and to the creation of human dignity. While fighting in the Sierra, he initiated a literacy campaign among the peasants as a step in making mass education a part of the Revolution. He disagreed with the unwritten philosophy that prevailed in Batista's Cuba that only those who needed to be literate in order to perform economically remunerative tasks would be taught to read and write well. He contended that the economic benefits available to the literate should be accessible to everyone; thus all should be taught to read and write.[39]

From the inception of the Revolution he stressed that the level of education in Cuba has to be raised.[40] To Castro, the way "to prevent cultural colonization from surviving economic colonization" is to teach people to think dialectically. This is done through education in socialist-oriented schools.[41] That does not make Cuban education primarily political propaganda. Fidel says that all education is political: All scholars view society through an ideological prism. He believes that Marxism enables people to understand the science of politics by interpreting the development of human history.[42] He agrees with the basic concepts of Marxist education, including compulsory and uniform public education, a need to combine education with work in order to narrow the gap between mental and manual labor, emphasis on cooperation rather than competition, and the development of the well-rounded person whose potential in all areas is reached.[43] He believes that every child has the right and the duty to study.

From the outset of the Revolution, Fidel has thought that people could learn while struggling, that the masses could further revolution through a profound process of understanding.[44] Through frequent public dialogues with the people, he has made Cubans want to learn, to improve themselves and society, and to please him. He has taught the masses that one cannot learn correct revolutionary behavior by merely studying Marxist-Leninist theory. He contends that "an enormous gap exists between general concepts and practice, between philosophy and reality."[45] He has convinced his people that education in diverse fields, both practical and theoretical, bridges that gap. The Cuban people now concur with his belief that oppression exists when people are denied education.

Fidel maintains that the nations most exploited economically, with populations that are the most politically oppressed, have the greatest percentage of illiterates. Only revolution can alter that situation by restructuring political, social, and economic relations.[46] In the course of the revolutionary process, Castro hopes to construct a collective genius in order to create a society where people pool their talents and successfully complete the most difficult scientific, technological, and practical projects.

Fidel cringes when he sees that in today's world only 20 percent of all schoolchildren can identify their national leader, but 90 percent know who Superman is.[47] He wants a Cuban society where every worker is a student and every student a worker.[48] Like Marx and Martí, he advocates linking study and work to prepare people to face life in every respect.[49] Ideally, schools should be adjacent to workplaces, and where that is not possible, the latter should function as centers of higher learning. For example, in hospitals doctors take postgraduate courses.[50] At work and while studying, citizens should gain respect for the scientific outlook, including dialectical materialism, and reject supernatural and pietistic values.[51]

According to Fidel, industrial technology and science in general have developed incredibly, but the social sciences are underdeveloped. Thus, intelligent people with advanced degrees in physics can explain intricate formulas but have no idea how societies work, do not understand politics, and accept blindly what their government and religious leaders tell them. Castro finds that nothing teaches better than the Revolution, where you learn to assess and evaluate the experience of other people and how to contribute to the underdeveloped science of politics and society.[52] He insists that Cuba must train social scientists and humanists, that without an opportunity to study history or sociology it is doubtful that one will devise a revolutionary theory. He indicates that the exploited have not generally had access to humanistic education[53] and not many revolutionaries have come from their ranks.

Castro understands that Cuba cannot compete, or even survive, without scientific advances. "Independence is not a flag, a hymn or a coat of arms. Independence is not a question of symbols. Independence depends on development, independence depends on technology. Independence depends on science in today's world."[54]

According to Fidel, people do not learn by indoctrination, by having their heads filled with bits and pieces of theory. They learn by thinking, analyzing, and searching history for lessons and answers. In Castro's ideal revolutionary society, people go to school to learn, to dissect, to understand.[55] In reality, Cuba's educational system, like that of most mass programs, suffers from passivity on the part of the students, who too often accept information and fail to probe its depths.

In 1961 Cuba undertook a massive literacy campaign, which eventually enabled over 90 percent of its citizens to read and paved the way for the comprehensive educational program desired by Castro, which now ranks first in the Third World. Fidel told the thousands who spread out over Cuba to teach everyone who could not read, "You are going to teach, but as you teach you will also learn much more than you can possibly teach, and in the end you will feel as grateful to the *campesinos* as the *campesinos* will feel to you for teaching them to read and write." From the students, he envisioned, the teachers would learn why the Revolution was fought, the value of the hard honest life, and to understand moral rectitude.[56]

Dedicated teaching became the key to Cuba's innovative educational system. Castro likes to remind people that Cuba has 15,000 more teachers than it needs. He points out that this permits them to take time off to study.[57] He insists that teachers constantly renew the spirit of the Revolution by bringing up-to-date theories and information into the classroom. He implores them to pursue their studies and to impart new ideas in an aura of optimism, whether they teach in elementary school or in the universities.[58]

To be admitted to a university to become a teacher or to pursue another occupation, one can have an inquiring attitude but must not be a professed counterrevolutionary. Cuban students do not hesitate to question. One of the first things I have been asked by Cuban university students is to explain life in the United States and its government's policies because they want to ascertain whether their teachers have been accurate and truthful. Cuban university students tend to think more critically than their counterparts in the United States, who rarely question what they are told by their professors unless it contradicts what they are told by their government or their religious leaders.

All universities in Cuba now have courses that deal with Marxist theory. Despite Cuba's rich tradition of radical thought, few of these courses existed in the 1950s. In late 1960, Castro established Schools of Revolutionary Instruction to build a foundation for the socialism he wanted to construct.[59] These schools existed considerably before the 26th of July Movement and the Revolutionary Directorate joined forces to form the Integrated Revolutionary Organization (ORI) and before Castro announced his Marxism-Leninism. In 1963, he founded the Institute of Higher Studies of Marxism to pursue theoretical Marxian analyses of Cuban society.[60]

Fidel reiterates that in all revolutionary processes, those who elaborated the ideology came from educated backgrounds. After all, he says, Marx and Engels were hardly proletarians. But, he boasts, in Cuba the universities are open to everyone, not just the exceptional student. That way Cuba can forge the aforementioned collective genius and still develop the talents of exceptional individuals and future leaders.[61] Castro takes a deep interest in university students, whom he considers academic apprentices, part of the intelligentsia dedicated to demystifying power by engaging in and promoting socialist self-criticism. He encourages students of all ages to comprehend the causes of social unrest, exploitation, poverty, illiteracy, disease, unemployment, and economic and political instability.[62]

Intellectuals

Marx and Lenin spoke about workers' representatives as working people, not merely as negotiators for those who labor for wages. Castro believes that as long as intellectuals do the thinking, negotiating, and planning for the workers, the latter will remain exploited. He expresses skepticism about pure intellectuals: "The embryo of chauvinism and of the petit-bourgeois spirit affecting those of us who reached the road of revolution by a merely intellectual way develops, sometimes unconsciously, certain attitudes that may be regarded as self-sufficiency and excessive self-esteem."[63] He dreams of molding worker-intellectuals.

People with an intellectual orientation, said Marx, are attracted to the Left because of their interest in critical evaluation, and in the restructuring, of society. Lenin felt that political class consciousness could be developed only by well-informed, educated intellectuals who stood back from the productive processes and analyzed the class relations of bourgeois society. The class consciousness developed by these intellectuals, he said, is adopted by the working class after being transmitted to it by the professional revolutionaries in the political party. If we accept Lenin's thinking rather than Fidel's dreams, we conclude that, generally, the Left will be led by worker-oriented intellectuals, not worker-intellectuals.

Marxist intellectuals from all backgrounds and occupations, according to Fidel, must engage in a never-ceasing process of renewing ideology. They must not be content to follow outdated or unrealistic theories, nor must they think that they can win anybody over by uttering tired clichés.[64] They must adapt to current conditions. Fidel, perhaps reflecting on his own position, emphasizes that "philosophical and artistic geniuses have considerably greater scope in time and history than political geniuses who are locked into the world of reality and action, the only setting in which they live."[65] He denies being an intellectual and repeatedly refers to himself as a man of revolutionary action, but he takes pride in frequent association with intellectuals and in his ability to understand them. While daily duties have prevented him from spending a great deal of time theorizing, he has become somewhat of a pragmatic, often impatient, philosopher and interpreter of Cuba's Revolution for its people. He appreciates intellectuals and their ideas but realizes that ideas alone are insufficient to make a revolution. He maintains, "Many times practice comes first and then theory,"[66] meaning that most people arrive at Marxism-Leninism via revolutionary struggle, not intellectual effort. In Cuba, the Revolution began with a basically nationalist orientation; the struggle then led to the development of class consciousness, which in turn led to socialism.[67]

Once the revolutionaries took power in Cuba, Fidel, a man with an insatiable appetite for knowledge about all revolutionary movements and their intellectual leaders and theoreticians, sought to produce and nurture a new generation of intellectuals to analyze Cuba's past and help guide its future. By the time he took over, Fidel had developed a bit of the moral and intellectual arrogance that causes disdain for others who do not have the benefit of the answers that Marxist analysis provides. He wanted to surround himself with advisers who shared his privileged insights, those whom he called "creators."[68]

Castro endeavored to create an intellectual cadre to become the conscience and the critic of society. He understood that although intellectuals did not play a major role in the early phases of the Revolution, he needed them as a support group to sustain it. He wanted the new intellectuals either to be, or appreciate, activists. He wanted them to devise solutions to societal problems and to actively engage in solving them.[69] Critics complain that since 1959 intellectuals in Cuba have generally conformed to governmental policies. These critics often fail to realize that in a socialist society intellectual work is deemed a part of the socialization process. Intellectuals are guided by those directing the course of society and, in turn, influence them to change direction when necessary. All nations choreograph intellectual currents and are choreographed by them to some degree.

Fidel's fear of counterrevolutionary activity extends to intellectuals as well as to political activists. He generally invites to visit Cuba only writers and *pensadores* who tend to understand the Revolution and analyze it in relatively sympathetic terms. Fidel places little faith in liberal intellectuals, whom he fears will never comprehend Cuban society because they examine it from an alien perspective. For that reason, he has seen fit to expel from Cuba liberal writers, such as anthropologist Oscar Lewis.[70] Nevertheless, although Castro does not invite conservative intellectuals to assess the Revolution, he is more receptive to their requests for interviews than to those of liberals. The latter, he thinks, can do more harm by negatively influencing potentially sympathetic progressive readers, whereas potential supporters of the Revolution know what the conservatives stand for and take their views with a grain of salt. Fidel has courted the support of writers whose revolutionary themes have inspired him, such as Colombian novelist Gabriel García Márquez and the late Julio Cortázar of Argentina. Upon seeing Cuba firsthand in 1961, Cortázar commented that it made him a political person. He said, "I know that when I go to Cuba its leaders will turn to me—not to manipulate or use me, but to talk and engage in a dialogue. I would consider it manipulation if they told me what to say or not to say in a speech, but this has never happened."[71] García Márquez writes regularly for _Granma_, and his books are bestsellers in literature-hungry Cuba. Fidel encourages Cubans to develop their own literary genre and refers to the works of Cortázar and García Márquez as revolutionary models. The latter has so much influence with Fidel that the Cuban leader listens to his criticism, and on occasion García Márquez has convinced him to negotiate the release of political prisoners.[72]

During the first decade and a half of the Revolution, Castro did not forgive Latin American intellectuals who criticized his attempts to silence counterrevolutionary writers and thinkers. For example, prize-winning poet Herbert Padilla was imprisoned in March 1971 for being vain and egotistical and placing himself above the Revolution. He was released from jail a month later, after a strong campaign by Latin American and European intellectuals, including García Márquez. Padilla lived in Cuba for another decade, translating foreign literature, before García Márquez was instrumental in gaining permission for him to emigrate. Fidel resented the interference in the Padilla affair by foreign writers.

In the 1960s and 1970s, Cuba's intellectuals, taking a cue from their leader and prompted by fear of criticism, displayed disdain of some well-known Latin American intellectuals. For example, during the early Castro years, Mexican novelist and anti-imperialist commentator Carlos Fuentes was insulted by leading intellectuals in Cuba and vowed never to return to the island. Fuentes, who later signed a letter critical of the Padilla incident, still feels estranged from Cuba's intellectual elite.[73] For its part, the Cuban government hesitates to invite Fuentes to visit for fear that he will impugn the Revolution with a liberal critique.

Over the decades Castro's policies have antagonized intellectuals in the Americas, especially those who insist on judging Cuba by bourgeois standards. As recently as December 1988, a hundred intellectuals from Latin America signed and published a petition calling on Fidel to permit a plebiscite or hold a liberal democratic election. Cuba's Foreign Ministry rejoined that the Cuban people selected their destiny thirty years ago and "renew that commitment daily with their resolute activity to construct socialism." To this, Mexican liberal poet Octavio Paz replied: "A people does not marry its government for an eternity as in a church wedding. They are tied together in a modern way that allows a change of relationship when things do not work."[74] Some intellectuals outside of Cuba think it does not work; to most who live in Cuba, it does.

In addition to political and human rights questions, writers and artists in the Americas concern themselves with how the Cuban Revolution treats intellectual property, or abstract property that emanates from human intelligence. Traditionally, those who have created such products have lived in poverty and have not benefited fully from their labor. Those who wrote books in prerevolutionary Cuba found that their publishers held the copyrights to their works and often took advantage of them financially. At the beginning of the Revolution, Cuba had to spend tens of millions of pesos to purchase copyrighted materials in order to educate its citizens. The government then decided to disallow copyrights. Fidel explained that the work of those who create is the patrimony of all humanity, that you cannot deny the poor the benefits of technology because someone owns the property rights. In socialist fashion, Cuba placed the creations of its citizens at the disposal of everyone.[75]

Castro believes that artists, novelists, and writers of technical books deserve compensation but that what they produce should be printed everywhere without a fee being paid to copyright holders.[76] Early in the Revolution, he recognized that certain items, such as books on Latin American (not Cuban) history, were rarely published in Cuba and determined that they should be made available to his compatriots at low cost.[77] To do so, Cuba could not pay copyright fees.

Fidel also feels strongly about freedom of intellectual and artistic expression. Since 1975, by which time Castro had more confidence in the stability of the Revolution, writers and artists have had greater latitude in expressing themselves. He contends that each writer should produce what he or she wants, and if it is not good, that is his or her problem. In other words, the Revolution will not tell people what to write.[78] Moreover, the Revolution has not seen fit to make the writer or intellectual the "critical conscience of society"; that right was reserved to the people. Castro has opposed building an intellectual class that could, alone, criticize society.[79]

Fidel has always supported a sound dialogue between the Revolution's leaders and Cuban writers.[80] At a famous meeting held in June 1961 in Havana's National Library, he delivered "Words to the Intellectuals." In this talk the Cuban *jefe* divided the intelligentsia into three categories: those who were committed in thought and action to the Revolution, counterrevolutionaries, and the uncommitted, who understand the need for change but could not bring themselves to participate actively—a common characteristic among middle-class and even self-proclaimed socialist intellectuals.[81] Castro told Cuban intellectuals that the Revolution valued and utilized Cuba's intellectual heritage, that it demanded cooperation from the nation's honest old (prerevolutionary) intellectuals, and that it would train new thinkers.[82]

"Words to the Intellectuals" set the tone for the actions of writers and artists in Cuba, and outlined Fidel's conception of their function.

> The Revolution should try to win over the greater part of the people to its ideas, the Revolution should never give up counting not only on the revolutionaries but on all honest citizens who, although they may not be revolutionaries, that is, although they may not have a revolutionary attitude toward life, are with it. The Revolution should only renounce those who are incorrigibly counterrevolutionary. And the Revolution must have a political plan for these people, the Revolution has to have an attitude toward those intellectuals and writers. The Revolution must comprehend that reality and meanwhile act in such a way that that sector of artists and intellectuals who are not genuinely revolutionary may find within the Revolution a place where they can work and create and where their creative spirit, even when they are not revolutionary writers and artists, will have the opportunity and freedom to express itself within the Revolution. This means that within the Revolution, everything, against the Revolution, nothing.[83]

Castro encouraged creativity by writers and artists and, following Gramsci's dictum, explained to them their vital role in developing a revolutionary popular culture. He especially wanted the people of Cuba to learn from their writers and thinkers how to analyze and criticize from a revolutionary perspective.[84] These ideas have endured since 1961. The phrase "within the Revolution, everything, against the Revolution, nothing" resurfaced in 1988 at the Fourth Congress of the Writers Union when Vice-President Carlos Rafael Rodríguez asserted that the Revolution was "not a narrow path only with enough room for apologists and acolytes."[85] That year Fidel again urged intellectuals to explore all aspects of form and content within the Revolution.

Popular Culture

Cuba incorporated Gramsci's idea of using revolutionary struggle to strengthen the cultural superstructure. The Italian thinker believed that you unified society by building a revolutionary popular culture that appeals to everyone.[86] Cuba has succeeded very well in this realm. Proportionally more Cubans participate in cultural activities than do the citizens of any other Latin American nation. One way that Cuba has accomplished this is by adding sports to Gramsci's list of cultural activities, which included art, crafts, literature, music, theater, and dance.

Marxists who utilize popular culture as a vehicle for spreading the revolution cannot trace this idea to the German master. Marx never propounded any general theory of aesthetics, nor did he study art or literature or their role in society's development. He focused on overcoming the unequal division of labor, as does Fidel. To Marx and Castro painters per se do not exist; at most there are people who among other things paint. Castro agrees with Marx that in a communist society no one has an exclusive sphere of activity and anyone can become proficient in any area where she or he has specific abilities. All are free to develop individual skills or talents to the fullest. Artists, whether they be painters or writers, do not exist in Cuba only for art's sake, but also to promote political and social goals, to support revolutionary Third World anti-elitist and anti-imperialist endeavors.[87]

Fidel views writing and art as weapons of the Revolution. Art, as defined by the Revolution in the broadest sense, as part of culture, exists as a historical and social phenomenon conditioned by the needs of social classes and thus always has a political dimension. Castro asserts that at the beginning of class society the ruling classes did primarily political and cultural work, characteristics that endured during the eras of slavery and feudalism. Under capitalism, according to Fidel, bureaucracies, generally devoid of creativity, were conceived to support their masters and further their social influence by handling many of the political affairs of state.[88] Under capitalism, culture still received its direction from the ruling hierarchy. Fidel contends that if revolutionary culture were turned over to bureaucracies, which eliminated individualism, Marxism would be acting like a pseudorevolutionary church, not a revolutionary force.

At the same time, Fidel opposes placing cultural or artistic control in the hands of a small, elite group. To him, the greatness of a culture emanates from its creation by the people. He understands that the masses cannot all be political and social theorists or artists but contends that theory and art can be predicated on the thoughts and needs of the masses and articulated by their representatives, who have special abilities.[89] He agrees with Lenin that artists, writers, and thinkers should put their talents at the service of the people and the party. They assimilate the national and world cultural heritage, add to it the fruits of their own labor, and express it in proletarian terms. It is the job of Cuba's artists and intellectuals to convey this cultural heritage, which includes the great classics of art and literature, to the people, and it is the duty of the state to subsidize their efforts by providing them with jobs and disseminating what they produce to the general public free or at a cost it can afford.

Castro reveres tradition and the high culture of Western civilization as well as Cuba's folk culture. He maintains that culture must buoy up people's spirits. It enriches life and must be considered part of the standard of living.[90] He claims: "We ... value cultural and artistic creations in proportion to their contribution to the revindication of man, the liberation of man, the happiness of man. ... There can be no esthetic value in opposition to man ... to justice."[91]

In Fidel's ideal comradely society all people have cultural ties. These ties exist in their most fulfilling form only when abundance replaces want. One of the ways that society achieves abundance is by creating and developing shared values and motivation, or the ethic of service to society.[92] The artist and writer furthers the revolution by contributing to society's values by regenerating the spirit through culture. Castro states that as Cuba's socioeconomic revolution develops, it will lead to a cultural revolution,[93] one in which the masses can re-

ceive the greatest cultural values developed by humanity from time immemo-
rial to the present.[94]

Castro does not see Cuba as a pluralistic society, where diverse ethnic
groups develop their own cultures. He attempts to unify society by having all
people relate to the same cultural composite.[95] Raising the cultural level of a
society takes years, perhaps generations. Fidel knows that artists do not create
for future generations or for posterity.[96] They direct their work toward their
contemporaries, although their creations can be cherished for posterity. How
can culture contribute to revolutionary continuity when so much of it is present oriented? Castro believes that by linking the past to the present, the artist
or writer becomes a link to the future. Also, he understands that artistic and
literary excellence transcends the ages and contributes to the happiness and
liberation of generations to come.

As the Revolution progresses and becomes more secure, freedom and alienation decrease and the nonalienated artists become more creative. Recently,
Cuban artists have been encouraged to do what they please, the content of
their work bears less governmental scrutiny, and they pursue fewer social realism and revolutionary themes than they did some thirty years ago.

Since 1959, when Fidel established the Casa de las Américas (House of the
Americas), a cultural organization dedicated to publishing fine literature and
to promoting cultural exchanges in Latin America, Cuba's artistic, literary,
and intellectual communities have grown in size and quality. The Casa, together with the Union of Journalists of Cuba, the National Union of Writers
and Artists of Cuba, and professional organizations and institutions such as
the National Library, the National Institute of Motion Pictures, the National
Council of Culture, and various publishers cited in the notes to this book,
have overseen three decades of incredible literary and cultural output. Cuba's
emphasis on literary production and book publication has turned reading into
the national pastime. At this writing, Cuba's new generation of revolutionary
intellectuals is coming into its own, and some solid original work in the areas
of literary criticism, political and social thought, and Marxist theory has begun to take its place alongside the literature, poetry, and histories produced
since the inception of the Revolution.

Sports

"Sports have been like a school to me, they taught me willpower, tenacity,
steadfastness, perseverance and made me healthy. I'm always competing, even
with myself. I do two things, eat little, and exercise."[97] Some Cubans who
identify with Fidel's love of athletics and competition might take issue with
my contention that reading has become Cuba's national pastime. Those who
know the Cuban leader's affinity for gourmet cooking and have seen photo-
graphs of his waistline might question his remark about eating little. Never-

theless, Fidel tries to link his love of activities of the mind with his infatuation with athletics and physical exercise. He talks about the intellectual aspects of sport. For example, he theorizes that basketball, at which he excelled in high school, requires tactical and strategic planning, speed, and agility, all good preparation for guerrilla warfare.[98] Castro's attraction to sports is overshadowed only by his love for politics and, perhaps, good food.

With the knowledge that athletics requires discipline, abnegation, modesty, and valor, all solid revolutionary traits, Fidel, upon taking power, promoted sports and turned Cuba's aristocratic athletic clubs over to the masses.[99] In 1959 Cuba had 200 sports facilities; by 1989 it had over 7,000.[100] Sports, which exist as a right of the people, have become an integral part of the populace's health, the nation's educational system, and its popular culture. According to Castro, health, education, and culture do not contribute directly to the gross national product, but they increase the standard of living.[101] They promote a team, or collective, spirit and a sense of physical well-being and provide the society international heroes like sprinters Ana Fidelia Quirot and Alberto Juantorena, boxer Teófilo Stevenson, and high jumper Javier Sotomayor, who serve to unify Cuba.[102]

Fidel claims that before the Revolution Cuba did poorly in international sports competition, and the nation had an inferiority complex. Since he took power, he has accentuated athletics, raised the nation's level of international competition, and thereby raised morale.[103] He insists that Cuba needs athletic champions as symbols to the young, and as a yardstick of the development of the Revolution. He is convinced that sports develop good habits and serve as an antidote to vice and other counterrevolutionary behavior.

Athletics and exercise always played a fundamental role in Fidel's life-style. He finds it difficult not to seek excellence in sports. In a 1977 Cuban film, *The New School*, we see Castro berating a student for sloppy volleyball playing. "Come, you can do better than that," he exclaimed. "How could you live with yourself if you let the girls beat you?" The film censors let the maximum leader be cast as a far too severe critic, and as a sexist one at that.[104] Does Fidel demand that everyone perform up to the standards he sets for himself? Despite occasional impatience with what he deems inadequacy, as depicted in the example above, he generally asks only that people do their best. He is aware of the negative aspects of competition, the fact that it causes wars, disastrous rivalries, and greed.

No other athletic event carries the international stature of the Olympic Games, which according to Castro were created to show off the exploits of the wealthy industrialized nations during a time when colonialism ran rampant. Every four years, he says, the Olympic Games measure the inferiority of the Indian, black, yellow, and mestizo countries, as the white-ruled nations win the preponderance of medals. Although blacks win the majority of medals for the United States, he notes that the white establishment controls that country.[105] Needless to say, he was ecstatic when he attended the 1992 Olympics in Barcelona, Spain, where Cuba ranked fifth out of 172 nations in terms of total medals won.

To reduce inequality in athletics, Fidel favors placing the Olympics under the jurisdiction of a UN agency run along the lines of the United Nations Children's Fund (UNICEF) and designed to advance and promote sports in the Third World. According to his plan, proceeds from the Olympics, like the $200 million taken in at Los Angeles in 1984, would be used in the underdeveloped world rather than remain in the host country, since the funds were derived from the efforts of athletes from all nations.[106] He believes strongly that we do not need counts and dukes and millionaires running the field of athletics, and he construes the noblesse oblige of such people as condescending.[107] He criticizes the inclusion of professional athletes in some Olympic sports, preferring to retain the games as a purely amateur competition.

Western capitalist powers have manipulated the Olympic Games from their inception, says Fidel, and, contrary to their claims, have always politicized them. Castro does likewise. For example, he stated that the 1988 games, held in Seoul, hid the South Korean dictatorship behind the trappings of international sport.[108] To Castro, lending prestige to South Korea, occupied by U.S. forces and controlled by Yankee corporations, did not enhance international unity.[109] In addition, he felt that Cuba's friendship with the People's Republic of Korea (North Korea), which was denied the right to co-host the games, was worth more than winning some awards.[110] He believes that socialist states are obligated to boycott, and thereby call attention to, Olympics sponsored by dictatorships such as South Korea and inhumane imperialist powers like the United States. Cuba thus spurned the 1984 Olympics in "the empire" (Los Angeles) and sent no team to Seoul in 1988.[111] "We do not exchange our ideals for a few medals," Castro exclaimed.[112] In Fidel's view, politics always comes first.

8

Social Progress

When the exploitation of man by man disappears, when capitalist ownership over the means of production disappears, humanity will have entered history. And we have entered history. ... If others want to return to prehistory, it's up to them.

—Fidel Castro

Social and intellectual history has shown Fidel that for decades bourgeois thinkers and writers have talked about the role of social classes but have denied that it affects history.[1] He disagrees and concludes that class struggle has been a primary element in effecting the social change and progress for which he has been fighting most of his adult life. Even before he read Marx, he worked for the rights of the underclass and for social change—major thrusts of the Cuban Revolution. This chapter looks at Castro's views on social revolution and indicates how he has helped to implement it in Cuba. It demonstrates how assorted "rectification" plans have fostered economic and social change. It shows how the Revolution has wrought considerable progress in race relations and how it has endeavored to eliminate sexism. It notes to what degree Cuban society has changed as a result of the Revolution's effect upon organized religion.

Social Change

Cuba's Revolution proved the possibility of destroying the old capitalist order without enunciating a guiding theory. But Castro quickly realized the impossibility of sustaining the revolutionary process without theoretical guideposts. Moreover, the fact that nowhere in Latin America was the Cuban experience repeated successfully led him to see the need for revolutionary theory to support action.

Fidel has read extensively about class struggle and revolutionary political theory. He is convinced that at the beginning of civilization humans fought

149

the common enemy, nature, and a primitive communism existed. People struggled for the necessities of life, and poverty and misery existed, but not exploitation. Class relationships began to evolve, he says, with the advent of the classical societies and slavery. By the Middle Ages, and the development of feudalism, the situation was not drastically different from the present. For example, he cites contemporary Peru, where latifundios exist and are worked by exploited Indians. With the advent of the commercial and industrial revolutions, economic systems began to shape social structures. The proletariat emerged, and class struggle reached another plateau. He credits Marx with interpreting these historical developments, then devising the historical laws of determination and the theory of the working class and scientific socialism.[2]

In the writings of Marx, Castro found a suitable explanation for historical development and a workable plan for social change, subjects that preoccupy him. He insists that "the people must be given something more than liberty and democracy in the abstract, decent living must be given to every Cuban."[3] Everyone should be guaranteed a job; unemployment is unnecessary.[4] These objectives cannot be met unless society is controlled by the working class, which he views as the most effective agent of social and economic development.

Under his guidance, for over three decades, Cuba has created a value-oriented social movement, one dedicated to changing society radically. Cuba views progressive development as inextricably linked to social justice and the quality of life.[5] Fidel has worked tirelessly to change class relations and build socialism and has directed the reorganization of Cuban society. As a result of his powers of persuasion, Cubans have gotten involved in revolutionary institutions, have mobilized for numerous tasks, and have repeatedly sacrificed for the Revolution.[6]

He has supervised the administrators who have reorganized society and has insisted that they be fully grounded in the technology and ideology of production as well as in its human dimensions.[7] He has worked to prevent new classes, especially a "leadership class," from evolving and has eliminated all traditional elements that tend to divide national communities.[8] In contrast to what existed in the Soviet Union, Cuba has no new ruling class with extraordinary privileges. Fidel feels strongly that only the masses can effect change. He commented to critics who incorrectly depicted Cuba as a Caribbean version of the drab, barely changing Eastern European socialist societies that life evolves and so does the Revolution.[9]

The Revolution has altered social relations radically. Cubans now have entitlements or claims on the government for employment, health care, education, and facilities for self-development.[10] For example, no longer is a university education a privilege: Every qualified person has the right to pursue a degree at the government's expense. To effect these, often expensive, entitlements, Cuba has needed economic development. Fidel points out that the

economy grew at the rate of 4 percent annually for thirty years, and this enhanced progress in many areas. During the course of his July 26, 1988, ad-
dress, he demonstrated societal change by referring to comparative statistics
(see Table 8.1).

Castro likes to show that elsewhere in Latin America 60 percent of the population lives in slums, whereas in Cuba the figure is less than 3 percent and
hunger and homelessness have been abolished.[11] Visitors to Havana will find
that sections of the city have deteriorated, but Fidel stresses that is because resources are allocated to the countryside for better overall distribution.[12]

In 1959 Castro felt that the greatest need for social change existed in rural,
basically agricultural, areas. He moved to expropriate and collectivize land to
enhance economic development and consolidate the Revolution.[13] He realized that in a modern society people could not survive by hunting, fishing,
and gathering. They must, with the aid of modern technology, pursue inten-
sive farming, fish breeding, and deep-sea fishing.[14]

Through agrarian reform, Cuba ended rural unemployment, increased production, and protected water supplies.[15] Unlike other socialist states that divided the land, Cuba retained many large land units and developed them as
production enterprises. However, he knew that breaking up the larger sugar
plantations would mean that the new owners might cut the production of
marketable items and raise crops for their own use. He was willing to let this
occur in some instances, believing that ultimately, after sufficient political education, the farmers would want to raise production for the market.[16] Fidel
told small farmers that they could retain their plots but that he preferred state
farms, which were superior economically and socially and could best, if used
optimally, benefit the nation. "We must be patient," he exclaimed, "if we
have endured the ranches, the corrals, the latifundia and the minifundia all
these centuries, what does it matter if we wait ten, fifteen, twenty or thirty or
fifty years for isolated cases?"[17] Sharecroppers and tenant farmers received
land but were never forced into cooperatives. Many elected to join cooperatives because of the advantages provided to them by the state, such as schools,
housing, and guaranteed income.[18]

By the late 1980s, over two-thirds of Cuba's farmers belonged to cooperatives.[19] Agricultural efficiency increased at a rapid pace. For example, in 1970
Cuba needed 350,000 sugarcane cutters. By 1990, thanks to improved technology, only 77,000 cane cutters were required.[20] Despite such advances and
the ones noted previously, Fidel claims that Cuba has not developed as quickly
as desired or made all of the requisite social changes because its terms of trade
are subject to the dictates of major capitalist powers. If we carry this thinking
to its logical conclusion, Cuba will prosper only when capitalism collapses and
Cuban products, in an international socialist system, will be priced according
to the labor required to produce them. At the time of this writing, such a sce-
nario appears highly unlikely, thus leading to the conclusion that sufficient de-

TABLE 8.1   Province of Santiago de Cuba

	1959	1959
Population	570,000	968,000
Workers	85,000	349,000
Working women	8,000	120,000
Cement (tons)	250,000	400,000
Oil refined (tons)	1,000,000	3,700,000
Citrus fruit (tons)	3,900	82,000
Health facilities	33	127
Doctors	180	1,470
Dentists	15	551
Nurses	76	4,529
Infant mortality	60%	11.8%
Primary school enrollees	(less than) 27%	100%
Illiteracy	35%	5%

SOURCE: *Granma Weekly Review*, August 7, 1988, p. 2.

velopment to provide the climate for full social change without extreme sacrifices is not in the near future.

Castro asserts that the desired social change could be instituted easily in the world at large by using a fraction of the funds spent on the military. The United Nations, he says, has demonstrated that disarmament could bring about a 3.7 percent increase in the world's gross national product and that billions of dollars a year in military expenditures could be used for nobler purposes.[21] Fidel avers that you cannot solve the complex problems of the world through the indiscriminate use, or threat of, force that endangers human survival. Resources that can kill humanity many times over can best be used for social change. He notes that the cost of one Trident nuclear submarine equals that of sending 16 million children to school or housing for 2 million people.[22] He prefers to see a halt to building nuclear weapons but advocates the use of nuclear energy as a power source alternative to expensive liquid fuels imported by nations such as Cuba.[23] He believes deeply that significant social change can occur in his ideal new society, where profits do not exist, the contradiction between people and power disappears, and the nation can finish the phrase attributed to Louis XIV, "I am the state," by adding, "I am the power, I am the owner."[24]

Rectification

For three decades critics of Cuba labeled it a satellite of the Soviet Union. Now, when Cuba rejects the bourgeois reformism of the former Soviet Union, it is called intransigent. According to Castro, Cuba has no need to follow the lead of that nation; it has its own program of rectification. To him *rectificación*, the most recent phase of Cuba's endeavors to build socialism, does not represent something new; it reasserts the concepts of vigilance and sacrifice that prevailed in the earlier years of the Revolution. It forms part of the ongoing revolutionary process and could be obsolete by the time these words appear in print. To some of Fidel's critics, it merely represents reinventing the wheel. They can point out that very early in the Revolution, when longtime Communist party leader Carlos Rafael Rodríguez advocated material incentives, Che Guevara claimed that such attitudes needed rectifying, and he predicted correctly that they would breed competition among enterprises and lead to the breakdown of collective central management.[25]

Rectification is not a model, but rather the absence of a model. Contrary to the common view outside of Cuba, it does not eliminate material incentives; it reduces their excesses. Rectification calls for a better balance between moral and material incentives. It emerges from Fidel's belief that each socialist state must pursue its own path to development, although Cuba shares some of the goals of Soviet *perestroika*, such as eliminating corruption and increasing economic efficiency. But rather than look to the market economy for reform, rectification abolishes the market concept.[26] Cubanologist Max Azicri wisely speculated that by launching a rectification process now, Cuba saves itself from being forced into *perestroika* or the resurrection of capitalism in the future.[27] In contrast, Castro's critics claim that he fears *perestroika* would weaken his power, as did the reforms of the early 1960s, which enabled market mechanisms to get out of control, and those of the 1970s and 1980s, which led to the weakening of central authority.

Cubans point out that rectification permits economic change but does not radically alter the system as *perestroika* did in the Soviet Union. They generally agree that the outdated Soviet system became dysfunctional but believe that moves toward socialism, not capitalism, would have solved the USSR's problems. Rectification, initially designed to improve economic productivity, according to Vice-President Carlos Rafael Rodríguez, restores "the true value of a worker's labor to his productive output."[28] No longer are salaries geared to output or norms lowered to make productivity appear higher, factors that encourage materialistic mentalities. According to Fidel, rectification corrects two types of errors made by the Revolution: using idealism to correct the mistakes of idealism and government involvement in "market mania" or bourgeois commercialism.[29]

Historically, Castro has supported necessary political and economic change. In the early 1960s, he tried to rectify sectarianism within revolutionary thought, as exemplified by the Escalante case (see Chapter 2). In 1970, he moved to rectify the error of monocultural agriculture after Cuba proved unable to produce its goal of 10 million tons of sugar a year. Cuba underwent a relative economic boom in the late 1970s, which lasted through the middle of the 1980s. By 1984, the economic system had begun to deteriorate, and Fidel, in 1986, announced publicly the need for *rectificación* or change. We see that the Revolution has undergone a continuous process of rectification, with periods of greater or lesser emphasis.[30]

Cuba's Third Party Congress outlined the rectification process in 1986 to combat the economic liberalization that had permitted the existence since the late 1970s of free peasant markets. Those markets had enabled some to acquire wealth by selling surplus products for what the market would bear after filling their production quotas at set state prices.[31] The government moved in 1986 to eliminate food distribution through private, or parallel, unregulated markets, which engendered corruption but also enabled people to believe that someday conditions in the county would not be so austere. It began to evaluate state enterprises by their output of socially necessary goods and services rather than by their profitability; to decrease market competition; and to reduce the use of bonuses and individual material incentives.[32] By making these changes, Fidel hoped to eliminate demoralization and political demobilization. He sensed that the gap between the people and the party was widening, and he sought to bridge it and to improve *poder popular* (people's power).

Specifically, he noted that technocrats related to others in bureaucratic fashion, that middle-level administrators meddled in lower-level affairs, that workers did not participate in decision-making, as bureaucrats coordinated from above. In other words, bureaucratic centralism, at times epitomized by Fidel himself, supplanted democratic centralism and functioned as a form of class stratification. He believed that rectification would limit bureaucracy. Simultaneously, it would give him more control.

He also hoped to reduce the false sense of security created by the socialist state and to impress upon his fellow citizens the need to confront future concerns.[33] He feared that the Communist party was "starting to go to pot,"[34] that it must reunite and instill in the people the need for moral incentives. He charged that a layer of administrators had emerged in state enterprises, ones who "dressed up like capitalists, but without capitalists' efficiency."[35] Before rectification, a manager might say to a worker, "Sleep on the floor and I'll pay you extra for abnormal conditions."[36] Fidel sought to eliminate this type of corruption that sprang from the philosophy that everything had to be done for money. He wanted virtue to "become a mass phenomenon."[37]

Castro considers rectification a long-term struggle, not a five-year plan. It is not a cultural revolution or a propaganda campaign. It is an offensive, taking up arms from the Palace of the Revolution, not the Sierra Maestra, an economic reform program that can solve social problems, an attempt to "find the hidden seed in every man" that will enable him to put forth his best for the Revolution.[38] In reality it presents no coherent plan partially because Fidel distrusts the bureaucracy and will not permit it to formulate comprehensive programs. By 1988, Castro believed, rectification had rid the country of some paternalism and a legacy of old, substandard ideas.[39] He wants to make rectification responsive to the needs of the people in order to win the broadest possible approval and build political cohesion. Fidel maintains that rectification defends the gains of the Cuban workers and peasants, which are inseparable from the progress of humanity.[40]

To Castro, rectification renews the socialist spirit. He realizes that in planning for the future, Cuba cannot become a consumer society like the United States if it wants to retain equality. Public consciousness predicated on Marxist-Leninist values must be preserved if Cuban's basic needs are to be met. Moral incentives must take precedence over material ones if equality is to prevail, since Cuba does not have a large material base.[41] He asserts that in a socialist society you cannot have individuals who live parasitically from the wealth that others create. For instance, he refers to candy vendors who make more money than those who work the fields. The vendors get paid by those who create wealth, and the vendor does not work nearly as hard.[42]

Castro contends that rectification is not idealism, but it is realistic use of economic planning and management, which he says had become "like a lame nag with two-bit capitalist hucksters."[43] He seeks to eliminate the same type of shoddiness that dragged the Soviet system down. He calls rectification "a revolution within the Revolution," a move to negate the mediocrity that negates "Che's ideas, revolutionary thought, style, spirit and example." In particular, he strives to eliminate high prices charged by plants, chaos in wages, work competition, the desire to use money as a regulatory agent, and markets with prices determined by supply and demand.[44] He states, "We're rectifying all those things—and there are many that strayed from the revolutionary spirit, from revolutionary work, revolutionary virtue, revolutionary effort, revolutionary responsibility; all those things that strayed from the spirit of solidarity among people."[45]

Fidel admits that Cuba suffers from low productivity, poor quality of goods, wastefulness, lack of worker participation in economic and governmental planning, overstaffing, cynicism, bureaucratic intransigence, poor distribution of goods, agricultural and industrial inefficiency, and high rates of managerial turnover. To solve these problems he has initiated more centralized planning and has eliminated areas where some individuals, driven by the profit motive, operated independently of state controls.[46] Castro also opposed rewarding inefficiencies such as a bus driver—paid by the hour—extending the length of trips. No longer would the concept of "to each according to his work" enable workers to receive overpayments for little or no work.

In addition, rectification has to a small degree altered the previously noncontroversial press in Cuba. More open criticism of the government, within the Revolution, has been permitted since 1986. Young artists have increasingly criticized political stagnation and bureaucratic inefficiency. At times they have gone too far and have been censored; nevertheless they have become a more powerful tool for constructive criticism. In addition, rectification has eliminated some sexual discrimination against women, raised minimum wages, and upgraded living conditions for the lowest paid sector of society.[47] It has led to voluntary Sunday labor by approximately 2 million workers, the resurrection of the minibrigade concept, whereby in Havana alone 30,000 people, working in groups of forty, volunteer their labor. Prior to the minibrigades, plans existed in Havana to build five new day care centers over a five-year period. The brigades built over fifty in one year.[48] The brigades, which make use of professionals and industrial workers who are released from regular jobs and paid their normal salaries but who work sixty to seventy hours per week instead of the regular forty-four, also built housing, hospitals, and athletic facilities. Simultaneously, regular construction contingents, composed of full-time skilled workers, continue to function. Together the minibrigades and the regular workers hope to build 20,000 new dwellings annually in Havana, a city with over 2 million inhabitants.[49]

Fidel considers Cuba's successful family doctor program, designed to put a physician into each neighborhood, factory, school, and day care center, a victory for the rectification program. Under this plan, each physician cares for about 120 families. As of 1990, the program operated in parts of Havana and in some countryside areas. Castro projects that it will eventually serve the entire nation. He believes that when you take care of people's health and they do not need money to be well, materialism will diminish.

Fidel claims that rectification prevents the use of a privileged, elitist bureaucracy, like that which existed in the Soviet Union. He believes that in the initial years of socialism, the bureaucracy should develop and strengthen the Revolution. But unlike in capitalism, where public employees serve the dominant class and work for the benefit of private entrepreneurs, in Cuba the bureaucracy serves the people as a guiding force.[50] Under capitalism, bureaucracies divide intellectual from manual labor, something that socialism must resist. He realizes that bureaucracies, even with good intentions, tend to run things in accord with their own interests but emphasizes that Cuba's socialist bureaucracy must subordinate itself to the interests of society.[51] Castro asserts that bureaucracies can be kept in check by greater worker control, which permits the laboring sector to confront society's administrators.

According to Fidel, the 1989 Ochoa incident exemplified the need for rectification. During the summer of 1989, General Arnaldo Ochoa, hero of the Africa campaigns, and other administrators were charged, tried, and convicted of drug trafficking, and General Ochoa was executed. Ochoa had admitted dealing in drugs, claiming that he used the profits to purchase food and medicine for his troops and the Cuban people. Critics of Castro implied that Ochoa's "philanthropy" provided him with a popular base of support sufficient to enable Fidel to perceive him as a rival for political power and to eliminate him. No hard evidence exists to support this theory. Ochoa's behavior, predicated on greed and lax political consciousness, was surrounded by an aura of corruption, which Fidel moved quickly to stamp out. Emphasizing the fact that flouting the law is antisocialist, Castro ruled against Ochoa and his cohorts: "Treason is to sell your country, and they sold the country. Treason is to put the nation in jeopardy, and they placed the nation in serious jeopardy. Treason is to undermine the nation's morals and the Revolution's prestige. They have been doing things that undermine the Revolution's morale and prestige. They weaken it in every sense."[52]

To Fidel, those involved in the Ochoa case mocked the principles of rectification. He stated that the Ochoa affair signified growing political demobilization and demoralization and gave rise to a dangerous portent in terms of bureaucratic mismanagement, indifference, and fraud. It exacerbated his frustration in dealing with these problems in piecemeal fashion. The Communist party reacted by establishing a new, younger leadership on all levels in all organizations and institutions.

Castro commented that if Ochoa and his cohorts were not punished, you could not speak of rectification. At a time when socialism was being questioned in all quarters, he stressed that Cuba had to remain honest, serious, and truthful.[53] Despite the fact that Miami-based critics alleged that Fidel rapidly silenced Ochoa to cover up his own involvement in drug dealings and to prevent a loss of his own internal power, all evidence points to the contrary. Castro has assiduously endeavored to maintain a drug-free Cuba and has never been implicated in drug dealings.

The Ochoa case damaged the Revolution psychologically and morally, weakened its cohesion, and cast aspersions on its leadership. It proved that Fidel was not aware of all that transpired within the government, including detrimental initiatives by supposedly trusted officials.

Immediately after the execution of General Ochoa, the rectification process was intensified. Public dialogue between opposing groups and generations increased as Cubans sought to find out what went wrong and how to change it. Fidel noted that the Ochoa case did not cause party disunity and that the questioning within the Revolution was part of the dialectical process. As a result of the Ochoa episode, Castro dug in his heels, took a harder line toward bourgeois reform and corruption, and emphasized that he could not let the unfortunate events lead to exile politics becoming enmeshed with Cuban politics, thereby causing a backlash. He used the Ochoa affair to strengthen the revolutionary mass movement, an integral part of rectification, and to demonstrate to the world that Cubans would not permit actions detrimental to their socialist objectives. The Ochoa case also served to diminish some bureaucrats' desire for privilege and induced them not to exceed the bounds of their offices.

Seven years after the most recent rectification program began, it cannot yet be assessed precisely. One cannot tell what degree of ideological cohesion it has fostered. The process has caused a resurgence in the popularity of Che's ideas about the new socialist person. It has also reinvigorated Castro's populist style of the 1960s and has buttressed political consciousness, a major weapon employed against Yankee and capitalist aggression. Initially, as a result of rectification, corruption receded a bit and morale improved, but after the collapse of European socialism, the former increased and the latter declined. Economic hardships forced Cuba's government, in summer 1993, to legalize the use of U.S. dollars by Cubans and to permit some small businesses to operate free of governmental regulation, situations that undermine the ideals of the 1986 rectification project.

Race Relations

The various rectifications of the Revolution have changed the structure of Cuban society. Nowhere is that more evident than in the area of race relations. According to Fidel, during the colonial era, Cuba's relations of production were based on slavery and racism, as native-born whites controlled the island's wealth.[54] Racial discrimination had an economic base, a fact that perturbs Castro, who likes to quote from Martí: "To be Cuban is more than being White, more than being Black. A Cuban is simply someone who belongs to no race in particular."[55]

While a student at the University of Havana, Fidel often spoke about racial equality and pursued integration through membership in the Biracial University Committee Against Racial Discrimination. Paradoxically, in the 1950s, when he fought to overthrow a "colored" president, Batista, a man of African, Asian, and Caucasian ancestry, some blacks initially refused to back his efforts. After taking power in January 1959, Castro won over those who opposed on racial grounds his ouster of Batista.

Upon assuming control of the nation, Fidel identified two types of racial discrimination: The first took place in cultural and recreational centers, the second in the workplace.[56] To him, racial integration appeared to be the simple answer to the problems of discrimination. During the early years of the Revolution, he did not concern himself much with the "ethno-political and psycho-cultural aspects of discrimination."[57] He knew that discrimination ran rampant on the island, that blacks held subordinate jobs and constituted the greatest proportion of the unemployed.[58]

By the 1970s many of Cuba's upper- and middle-class whites, the perpetrators of racial discrimination, had departed the country, and its demographic profile began to change. Fidel noted that the vast majority who went to Miami were bourgeois and white, and that by and large the blacks, those formerly discriminated against, supported the Revolution.[59] By 1990 Cuba's government estimated that approximately 58 percent of its citizens were black. As the Revolution progressed, Fidel cited racism as something that the world revolutionary movement had to eliminate. He saw South Africa as the quintessence of racism bred by imperialism, and he began to speak of Cuba as an ethnic ally of the black Africans.[60] In keeping with his antidiscrimination stance, Cuba moved to defend black African states under siege, such as Angola.[61]

Fidel realized that blacks sought power, not just access to resorts, universities, and country clubs. To facilitate this, he established the National Movement of Orientation and Integration, composed of prominent black and white professionals. He also lashed out frequently at racial discrimination directed at blacks and Indians in the United States and used the example of his Yankee neighbor to link economic exploitation to racism.

Since assuming power, Castro has maintained: "The Revolution will not force anyone to dance with anybody. But everybody will have to dance with the Revolution."[62] Under his aegis, blacks have advanced steadily and have become more secure and assertive. Most scholars who have examined racial relations in Cuba feel that discrimination has faded. Feelings of white superiority still exist in some quarters; some still consider blacks as best in music and sports; and mulattoes occasionally prefer to identify with whites, but Cuba is not a racist society. Racial harmony is especially strong among Cubans born after the Revolution. Two generations from now, if the Revolution continues on its present course, the question of race will be moot.

Fidel likes to point out that neither Marx nor Martí understood racial problems as they existed in Cuba in the 1960s.[63] He claims that Cuba has combated those problems by pursuing proletarian internationalism and universal culture that transcends ethnic, racial, cultural, and national frontiers. To him, all people should be treated equally, and no person or group should be singled out for special attention. He eschews the Pan-African point of view, as we shall see. This policy, to some degree, negates some of the African culture and religion that had existed in Cuba. Although some citizens complain that black cultural distinctiveness has been played down by the Revolution, it is more precise to say that revolutionary objectives have taken precedence over the preservation of ethnic ties.

Castro-bashers will tell you that he exhibits traces of white superiority, but his friends say that his aura of superiority derives from personal confidence, perhaps arrogance, but not racism, and would exist even if Fidel were black. They emphasize that he is an ardent integrationist because he does not believe in racial differences. His attitudes are far more progressive than those of Karl Marx, who spoke about "race peculiarities" and "inborn race characteristics," or Friedrich Engels, who referred disparagingly to certain people, like the Poles, and who thought that Germans had superior physical and intellectual abilities.[64] Marx attributed the chasm between the laborer and the philosopher primarily to the capitalist divisions of labor and class conflict. Fidel also sees racism as a product of class conflict and part of the superstructure of the capitalist system. He believes that it will wither away under socialism.

Although the Revolution has abolished all aspects of legal racial discrimination, Fidel understands that the establishment of equality takes time and education. He has assigned the Communist party the task of elevating the lot of people of African and mixed blood. "We have to straighten out what history has twisted," he asserts.[65] Carlos Moore, a critic of Castro who was born in Cuba but who now resides in the United States, complained that a "*gracias Fidel*" syndrome exists whereby blacks in Cuba who have been oppressed are overly grateful to Castro for whatever gestures his regime has made to them.[66] Moore accused Fidel of racial demagoguery when the Cuban leader recognized outstanding achievements by blacks in Cuba. But Moore incorrectly assessed this as racist paternalism. Fidel's paternalism is pervasive and knows no racial bounds.

Some view Castro's early negative response to African cults as discrimination, but most see it as part of his egalitarian nature. Fidel supports the activism of black nationalists as an integral part of the class struggle but does not regard cultural separatist tendencies as a healthy course for a socialist society. His stance on this matter has mellowed over the years. In 1981 the Cuban government began to see some validity in the African religions. About the same time, it began to soften its approach to religion in general. The fact that Fidel does not support all aspects of black nationalism or Pan-Africanism does not make him a racist. He has struggled long and hard to keep Cuba unified, and he has a latent fear of black nationalism spreading to the extent of a largely black province such as Oriente demanding to be a separate black state. However, black nationalists complain that the whites who dominate Cuba's Communist party fear that black consciousness would lead to greater demands for a more equitable racial distribution of power in Cuba.[67] Fidel responds angrily to this allegation by noting that the Revolution has never been racist. He acknowledges that initially the majority of its leaders were white and male because most individuals who had the requisite leadership skills and education came from those groups. But he insists that as the Revolution has matured, more and more blacks and women have assumed leadership roles.

I should also point out that in a society with a great deal of miscegenation it is often difficult to make racial distinctions. For example, for years I thought of Communist leader Carlos Rafael Rodríguez, whom I have seen frequently, as white. In the course of reading his collected works, I found that he has African blood and could be categorized as black.

Under the 1986 rectification program, according to Carlos Moore, Cuba has embraced a type of affirmative action program whereby it has endeavored to place more blacks as well as women into positions of leadership.[68] Fidel has said that racial prejudice has been eliminated in Cuba, and he has constantly maintained that it had exacerbated the economic exploitation of blacks. Those who do not want to integrate, but who seek power, not equality, for their own group, are in his view dividing society or building a class whose very existence contradicts basic socialist tenets. Since the inception of the Revolution Castro has encouraged scholars to explore in depth the history and sociology of African culture in Cuba and to make the population as a whole conscious of the contributions of blacks. He implores sociologists and cultural anthropologists to get to the roots of racial discrimination and to seek scientific ways to overcome it.

Sexism

Spanish-speaking visitors to Cuba generally agree that the Revolution has done a better job in eliminating racism than it has in reducing sexism. It has been more difficult to overcome the Hispanic traditions of *caudillismo* and militarism, which extol male supremacy. Cuba currently suffers from some latent prejudice against homosexual men and women. Nevertheless, great strides have been made in altering how women are perceived by men and by other females. Fidel, aware of the fact that he was brought up as a traditional Cuban male supremacist and that he embodies the cult of virility, an integral part of machismo, has sought to eliminate discrimination against women and homosexuals.[69] He claims that he has not been prejudiced against homosexuals, acknowledges that strong sentiment existed against them in the 1960s, but feels that it has lessened in the 1990s.[70]

Historically, Cuba's women—even those who had demonstrated great self-sacrifice for their country—lived in positions of legal and social inferiority.[71] Capitalists in Cuba relied upon sexual inequality to generate surplus value by underpaying female workers and by placing them in jobs not likely to lead to trade unionism. Nevertheless, Cuban women have always been involved in the struggle for liberation. Castro notes that Martí stated that the work of women, made with the heart, was invincible.[72] But Castro neglects to mention that Martí, although he thought of women as the intellectual equals of men, believed that they should be trained well to function as companions rather than playthings and that they belonged in the home.[73]

In 1959, 9.8 percent of Cuban women held jobs, 70 percent of them as domestic servants. The working-class female suffered from double exploitation, according to Fidel. She was looked down upon because she was poor, and her own class relegated her to a lower status as a female. The competitive capitalist class system encourages everybody to strive to be better than someone else. Castro believed that the Revolution had to liberate women from their class and their roles within that class. He maintained that without the necessary material base, someone will always be subjugated. But an adequate material base frees women from some exploitation and alleviates some of their double burdens.[74] He stresses his desire to save women from working full-time jobs and then doing housework and child raising at home. He insists that men do their share of the latter.[75] Despite considerable progress in these areas, women still do a disproportionate share of housework and child raising.

Fidel claims that prior to the Revolution, young females were prepared for matrimony, preferably to someone of a higher class. Their lives depended on marriage. Many who did not marry ended up in brothels. Those lucky enough to find minor jobs in stores, offices, bars, and hotels were generally chosen for their looks. The Revolution technically freed women, but prejudices about them persisted. As equals, they had to prove that they could shoot and fight as well as men.[76]

Castro points out that of the almost 7 million people in Cuba in 1959, 100,000 worked in some form of prostitution. Those exploited in marriage were victimized by backward attitudes toward divorce, which forced them into virtual slavery or prostitution at home.[77] Black women, he declares, suffered from greater discrimination than whites. The former, for example, were excluded from some professions, such as nursing.[78]

Fidel did not regard himself as prejudiced against women before the Revolution but now admits that he was.[79] In light of his own prejudice and that of most Cuban males of his generation, he realized that the Revolution must wage a massive social and educational battle to integrate women into society. After the military phase of the Revolution, Castro organized the Mariana Grajales Platoon (named after a black woman who fought in Cuba's initial war of independence), designed to involve females in the process of building a new society. Many women participated in Cuba's Committees for the Defense of the Revolution[80] in order to pursue what Fidel calls "another revolution in the Revolution,"[81] or the battle for equality. In August 1960, with his support, the Federation of Cuban Women (FMC) formed to help promote Marxist-Leninist and feminist ideas. Incidentally, from Castro's conversations it becomes clear that he believes that feminism can be achieved only through socialism.

Fidel's endeavors to integrate women into society have not always followed the teachings of the Marxist masters. Lenin said that the people could not win a complete victory until women were totally liberated,[82] and Marx, who wrote little on feminism, viewed the female-male relationship as a most natural tie, which, when studied, could determine a great deal about human development. In *The Origin of the Family: Private Property and the State*, Engels visualized the family as an artificial element that buttressed the class system. He referred to monogamy as a tool of the bourgeois state that would be eliminated under socialism. Castro rejects Engels's ideas and those found in the *Communist Manifesto*, which calls for the abolition of the family. He views the heterosexual nuclear family as the basic component of society. He regards women as equal parts of couples.[83] He concurs with Marx, Engels, and Lenin that you must terminate women's economic dependence on their husbands, put women into the workplace, and eliminate economic bonds that force incompatible spouses to stay together so that relationships can be based on love, not economic need. In addition, he feels that you must socialize household tasks traditionally performed by women by building public cafeterias, laundries, and child care centers.[84] Women, Castro believes, must live as equals, as comrades, not at men's feet as toys.[85] He agrees with Lenin that "petty housework crushes, strangles, stultifies and degrades" women and chains them to the kitchen and the nursery[86] and that the church's prohibition on the dissolution of marriage and its inclination to view the man as the head of the household have proved detrimental to women. Some fifty years after Lenin issued decrees providing for "The Dissolution of Marriage and Civil Marriage," the Cuban government passed similar laws.[87]

Castro feels that access to equal employment will emancipate women from the drudgery of unpaid slave labor. Once women are freed from the class system, which is in itself discriminatory, they will have equality, dignity, and opportunity.[88] These three elements, he believes, must be promoted in mass organizations, youth organizations, and by the Communist party.[89]

Incorporating women into the mainstream of Cuba's social, economic, and political life, in Castro's estimation, strengthens the Revolution by adding to its supporters.[90] Integrating women into the work force also develops the economy. Economic development enhances industrialization, which provides more machinery (for example, washing machines) to perform the tasks formerly done by hand by women.[91]

Cuba's program to incorporate women into the labor force has succeeded. In 1959, with a population close to 7 million, fewer than 200,000 women worked; in 1990, with a population of 10 million, women constituted 38.7 percent of the work force and occupied 58.3 percent of the nation's technical positions. Also, 55 percent of the country's university students were female, as were the majority of its medical students.[92] By 1991 more than half of the members of the executive committee of the National Assembly were female and three women served on the Political Bureau, but less than 20 percent of the Communist party members were female, and 20–21 percent of the candidates nominated for office were women, figures that Fidel hoped would improve to 40–60 percent. Until the inequities between the sexes are rectified and more females have leadership roles, he feels that a need exists for the Federation of Cuban Women, which now enrolls over 80 percent of all Cuban females over fourteen years of age. He believes that as the sexual division of labor or employment changes, more women will assume leadership positions. However, he maintains that a Federation of Cuban Men would be superfluous.[93] Castro contends that the Revolution is more popular among women than men because of the great gains the former have made.

Under the Family Code, which views sexual relations as a manifestation of love and human warmth, not male dominance, the family is defended on the basis of public ownership of the means of production. The Family Code, whose precepts also pertain to unmarried people who cohabit, gives Cuban women the right to eighteen weeks of paid pregnancy leave of absence and another year off without pay. To eliminate oppression, the code provides for abortion on demand. This helps to obviate the need for a population control system, which Engels once claimed that Communist societies might have to implement to preclude overpopulation. Women have the same rights as men in the family. Television and newspaper ads cannot use the female body to sell products through sexuality. Fidel rails against beauty contests or similar sexist exhibitions. Equality decreed by the Revolution has not eliminated sexuality, but it has eradicated, for the most part, the idea of using sex as an inducement or for compensation. Sexual harassment has been banned, and very rarely are women on Cuba's streets subjected to unsolicited physical contact or verbal abuse.

Fidel's attitudes toward women have evolved as the Revolution has progressed. The general consensus in Cuba is that for a man steeped in the macho tradition, Castro has developed a remarkable feminist consciousness. He views women as mental and spiritual equals, acknowledges that they are physically less strong, declares that physical strength should not be a cause for discrimination, understands that females hold special responsibilities such as childbearing, and maintains that they warrant extra respect because they can do what no man can. He contends that women must contribute their labor, which according to Marx shapes them as human beings. Castro spends considerable time discussing feminism with writers, artists, and reporters. He continuously calls for strengthening the "Continental Women's Front" and sees Cuba at the forefront of the feminist movement in Latin America.

Religion

Just as feminist consciousness has changed in Cuba over the past three decades, so have ideas about religion.[94] At the outset of the Revolution, Fidel believed that Cubans lived in an epoch in which politics permeated organized religion. Regarding religion, Castro likes to refer to Hatuey, the first Indian chief in the Americas to confront Christianity. According to Fidel, Hatuey told his native Cubans that the invading Spaniards worshiped gold, and "if Christians go to heaven, I do not want to go to heaven. I want to go to hell, so as not to be with people so cruel and evil as Christians who kill and enslave the Indians." Castro followed that remark with the thought that if he had to accept aspects of capitalism in order to go to heaven, he would not do so.[95]

Fidel stresses that in Cuba before the Revolution, for most people religion consisted of baptism, no religious instruction, and little understanding of Catholicism. Few churches existed in the countryside, where 70 percent of the people lived. Not many rural Cubans had systematic religious beliefs and standards. In the cities people attended mass, but religious practice was still hard to find.[96] Institutionally, he claims, the Cuban church was linked to the economic, political, and social system that the Revolution sought to replace.[97] Castro wanted to break that link but not meddle in the internal affairs of the church.[98] He strove to eliminate approval of the idea that Columbus bore the sword and the cross and used the latter to sanctify the right to conquer.[99] Fidel's initial task was somewhat easier than it might have been elsewhere in Latin America, where priests often worked side by side with *campesinos* in the fields. Cuba, compared to the rest of Latin America, experienced far less evangelization. Virtually no religious education existed on the island outside of the private schools run by clerical orders.

According to Fidel, historically the church never condemned the enslavement of blacks or Indians, nor did it denounce the extermination of the indigenous people. It is no wonder, he claimed, that the Revolution had an inherently antireligious spirit, a spirit of liberation found in the French Revolution, the philosophy of Jean-Jacques Rousseau, the French encyclopedists, as well as in the Bolshevik Revolution.[100]

Castro saw Catholicism as the religion of the wealthy and African religions and Protestantism as having more ties to the poor.[101] He repudiated religion for the benefit of one class and rejected religion for its own sake, but he believed that religion that served the people was all right.[102] In his early leadership days he concluded that religion constituted a sacred part of some lives, and like the Peruvian Marxist thinker José Carlos Mariátegui, he believed that the struggle for social, economic, and political change would foster religious changes, that it was not necessary to wage an anti–holy war on organized religion.[103] He decided that the successful Revolution would take away the church's reason for being, to help the poor, and thus the government could leave the church to decay on its own. According to Vice-President Carlos Rafael Rodríguez, Fidel cast off the old, the soldiers, the priests, and religion, and with the new, the workers and peasants, fostered Latin America's first socialist Revolution.[104]

Castro likes to compare those persecuted for religious ideas in ancient Rome with the systematic brutal persecutions in modern times of those with communist beliefs. In earlier eras, he points out, reactionaries hated the name "Christian" as much as they now hate "Communist," but "to be a Christian in the age of the Roman emperors was worse than being a Communist in Pinochet's Chile."[105] He cites as analogies the persecutions in the United States during the McCarthy period and the executions of the Rosenbergs, not because they were guilty of treason, but because they were Communists.[106]

In 1960, Fidel declared that no reasons existed for problems with the Catholic church, that his government recognized the right of citizens to engage in any religious practice.[107] At that time the church opposed the Revolution, even though Castro had not yet declared its Marxist orientation. The next year he expelled a few priests, Spaniards and Cubans, accused them of associating with the wealthy and the privileged instead of the poor, where Christ would have expected them to work. He stated: "The doctrine of Christ found an echo among slaves and humble people. It was persecuted by the aristocracy and dominant classes."[108]

Fidel tried to sidestep religious issues until August 7, 1960, when a pastoral letter emphasized the dangers of communism. He replied angrily: "I would like to see a pastoral letter condemning the crimes of imperialism. ... And then we would see that those who condemn a Revolution which is with the poor and the humble, which preaches time for one's neighbor and fraternity among men, which preaches equality, which practices love, generosity and the common good, those who condemn a Revolution like this are betraying Christ and at the same time they'd be capable of crucifying him again."[109]

In 1961, the Marxist direction of the Cuban government frightened many Catholics, even though no antireligious laws were enacted. After Fidel professed his Marxism-Leninism, numerous church leaders departed the country. The secular tone of the regime implied antireligious sentiments to ardent Catholics, some of whom were discriminated against by citizens who believed that the church had retarded Cuban society over the years.

Church leaders began returning to Cuba in 1962 and 1963, intent upon staying out of domestic political affairs and concentrating on spiritual matters—precisely what Castro preferred them to do. His strategy had worked, and the church lost popular support. Whereas in 1954, 17 percent of Cubans attended services regularly, by 1976 2 percent of Cubans openly identified themselves as Christians, and by 1987 the number had dwindled to slightly more than 1 percent.[110] Fidel attributed the defections from the church to a revulsion of the impoverished for the affluent,[111] basically a class conflict.[112]

After avoiding the major issues of the Revolution between 1963 and 1967, in 1968 the church began to work toward a rapprochement with the government. Cuba's 1976 constitution stipulated that the state based its religious policy on the "scientific materialist conception of the universe" but stressed that it protected the freedom to practice any religion.[113] By the late 1970s the church had entered into friendly dialogues with Castro and his colleagues. By this time the church had taken a more progressive stance in Latin America, pursued more options for the poor, and was looked upon in a different light by Fidel. He realized that new, more progressive, church people believed that one cannot love universally and be anticommunist or anti-Marxist in one's social actions. He now felt safer supporting liberal and radical elements in the church.

Castro contends that he has always had an intellectual fascination for the church, and his speeches and writings contain many references to Western religious values. He admired Jesus, whom he views as a revolutionary who fought injustice and human depredation.[114] He prefers the early, persecuted church with its fairer, more moral values to the later church, which turned persecutor.[115] To him, Christ's teachings were perverted by Christians who used religion as an instrument to hide the vices and defects of the dominant classes and forgot "today's slaves"—the landless peasants and the workers. When the church separated itself from the exploited masses, according to Fidel, it "prostituted the essence of primitive Christianity."[116]

Castro repeats Christ's saying, "It is easier for a camel to go through the eye of a needle, than for a rich man to enter into the kingdom of God."[117] He feels that as communism emerges, it reiterates early Christianity in its most just, human, and moral aspects. Both Christ and communism pursue austerity, humility, the spirit of sacrifice, and love of neighbor.[118] He recognizes parallels in Christianity and communism, but his faith is political, not religious. Even though he learned from priests as a boy, he claims that religious faith was never inculcated in him[119] and that the Revolution is his religion. He attributes his interest in philosophical and ethical questions to his religious education.[120] He also equates revolutionary solidarity with Christian love. To him, both mean fraternity.[121] He sometimes draws analogies between his penchant for work, struggle, and dignity and the Protestant work ethic.

When Cardinal Silva Henríguez of Chile presented Fidel with a Bible as a gift, the cardinal asked if it annoyed him. Castro replied: "Why should it? This is a great book. I read it, studied it as a boy."[122] Then he commented: "How, for example, can any spiritual guide of a human collective ignore its material problems, its human problems, its vital problems? Can it be that those material human problems are independent of the historical process? Are they independent of social phenomena?"[123] Despite his criticism of the Bible, Fidel believes that it can enrich lives, and Cuba permits the church to import tens of thousands of copies annually. When Cesare Zacchi, papal nuncio to Cuba from 1962 to 1976, was asked if he considered Fidel a Catholic, he responded that ideologically a Marxist-Leninist cannot be a Christian, but ethically he was one.[124]

As a child, Castro rebelled at the idea that you have to believe in God. He concluded that if not to believe was a terrible sin and punishable, then belief was predicated on fear of punishment. He preferred to think that religious faith, like political belief, should be based on reason and on the development of thought and feelings.[125] To him, religion is not a question of imposition, but a matter of awareness, something that one decides for her or himself.[126] Fidel states that a person can be a revolutionary and still have religious faith: The latter need not be understood rationally. He says that faith without work equals selfishness, and that religion compounded by dedication to a particular form of justice is more honest.[127]

Fidel maintains that it is an error to emphasize philosophical differences with Christians, of whom most are victimized by the system. He would rather persuade them to unite in common struggle for justice, especially in today's Latin America, where faith is no longer just a tool for domination and oppression.[128] In his personal relations with Christians, he prefers to relate to earthly concerns and avoid conflict over matters of another world.[129]

Fidel views today's church as more closely tied to a Western hierarchy based in Europe, the United States, and Latin America, as opposed to former links with the Spanish church. He points out that even subversive priests, those with CIA affiliations, have never been mistreated in his nation.[130] He mentioned to students at Chile's University of Concepción that his government has been lenient with counterrevolutionary priests and has tried not to make an example of them in order not to portray to the imperialists that Cuba opposes religion.[131] He notes that in contemporary Cuba the church hierarchy is more receptive to dialogue with the government than has been any other Catholic hierarchy in a socialist nation. Paradoxically, he avers that Cuba's church leaders are less critical of Vatican policies than their counterparts elsewhere in Latin America.[132] He takes pride in Cuba's solid diplomatic relations with the Vatican.[133]

The Cuban Catholic church has not tried to carve a niche for itself in the socialist state, as has the Popular Church in Nicaragua, although Castro has recently provided opportunities for it to do so. Unlike in El Salvador and Nicaragua in the 1980s, no Church of the Poor has emerged from among the ranks of Cuba's Catholics. Fidel attributes this to the historical tendency of Cuba's church to work with society's political and economic leaders, not its grass-roots elements.[134] He maintained until 1991 that if Cuba had a Church of the Poor, Catholics would have been eligible for Communist party membership.[135] He says that the appearance of the book *Fidel y la Religión* (published in English as *Fidel and Religion*) in 1986 created a better climate for church and state, as he appealed to the millenary wisdom of the church to draw the positive elements from liberation theology.[136] His twenty-three-hour interview with Frei Betto in 1985, which led to the publication of the book, might be considered a watershed in Cuban relations with religion. Incidentally, the book sold over 200,000 copies in a few days in Cuba, and over a million in a few months, as one out of every ten Cubans purchased a copy.[137] In the interview Fidel reacted positively to the new social conscience of the church and the fact that some clergy were no longer afraid to take a stand against the cold war. Moreover, the fact that Christians had become aware of revolutionary functions confirmed his belief in Che's idea that an alliance with the church would be possible.

Soon after the appearance of the book, Castro met with Mother Teresa of Calcutta, who remarked, "The most beautiful gift that God has given me is my meeting with President Fidel Castro."[138] Members of her Missionaries of Charity Order, an organization that fights against birth control and abortion, subsequently arrived in Cuba, at Fidel's request, to care for the sick. He drew analogies between these missionaries and the internationalists, primarily teachers and physicians, he sent abroad. A few years later, in 1988, John Cardinal O'Connor of New York visited Havana and met with Castro for three hours. The Cuban leader told him that he welcomed more nuns in Cuba and appreciated the efforts of the U.S. church to reduce the dangers of nuclear war.[139] Fidel made no mention of wanting more priests in Cuba. Nevertheless, the cardinal commented that Castro is "definitely reaching toward the church" and that "I don't think that I've ever met anyone who believes more intensely in what he's doing and in himself than President Castro."[140]

Despite the apparent rapprochement with the Catholic church, Fidel still takes exception to a number of its teachings. He, like Marx, contends that human awareness of reality is earthly, not celestial.[141] Marx believed that religion would speak to people only as long as it helped them achieve secular freedom. By working toward this goal, Castro can foresee a meeting of the minds taking place between atheist-humanists and religious-humanists. For example, Fidel believes that Christians for Socialism see religion, not as the opiate of the people, but as a stimulus to liberation. They believe that the commitment of both God and Marx was fundamentally to humanity, that no classes existed in the eyes of God. To them, the worldview of Marxism and Christianity is historical. Theoretically, both are oriented to assist the struggle for justice and human freedom, and both advocate a mixture of theory and praxis. Christians for Socialism believe that social Christianity tried to liberate humanity from the evils of capitalism and that historical analysis reveals that capitalism ended up using social Christianity for its own ends. Thus it became necessary for those who believe in social Christianity to look elsewhere—to historical materialism—for solutions to human problems.[142]

Christians for Socialism believe that Marx felt that religion could be a force or catalyst for social protest, an idea not generally followed by most Marxists, who have usually viewed religion as conservative, even reactionary. Marx also contended that revolution radicalized people and altered their religious ideas. He depicted religion as part of an oppressive society but thought that under altered relations of social production, it would disappear. Fidel concurs, believing that by the time the true communist state evolves, religion in Cuba will at least be marginalized. Castro points out that when Marx established the International Workingmen's Association, Christians joined it, as they participated in the First International and the Paris Commune. Nowhere, says Fidel, did Marx or Lenin exclude Christians from the historic mission of advancing the social revolution.[143]

Castro credits Lenin, not Marx, with making atheism into a metaphysical rather than a political rule.[144] Lenin demanded the disestablishment of the church; Fidel never has. Castro, like most Marxists, regards religion as a social development that originates with people, not God, an institution predicated on conformity and hope for life in a future world. He would prefer to integrate the church into the world, rather than convert the latter into a church. Thus the church could solve problems rather than make them.[145] Pursuing this line of thought, Castro can turn around 180 degrees Marx's comment about religion being the opiate of the people. He also can assert that religion has been a truth only under specific historical conditions.[146] "From a political point of view," he says, "I think one can be a Marxist without ceasing to be a Christian and can work together with a Marxist Communist to transform the world. What is important in both cases is a question of sincere revolutionaries disposed to abolish the exploitation of man by man and to struggle for the just distribution of social riches."[147] This line of thought echoes what Italy's Communists have said for decades.

Fidel claims that socialism and the church both criticize avarice,[148] teach neighborly love, and have utopian elements, but that socialism generally maintains better touch with reality.[149] He sees "10,000 times more congruity between Christianity and Communism than between Christianity and capitalism."[150] He says that Marxists need not be dogmatic and abide by the standard Communist party myth that Christian-Communist understanding cannot exist. He states that it is not enough for Christians and Marxists to respect each other; they must cooperate to change the world, and a strategic alliance between religion and socialism can be built.[151] He views leftist Christians, such as Christians for Socialism, as strategic, not simply tactical, allies in the revolutionary process.[152]

Despite his rhetoric, Fidel has received considerable criticism because Cuba's Communist party excluded from membership those who worshipped God. The party since its inception has advocated liberty of conscience, the right to practice any religion, the idea that all religions have equal rights, that believers and nonbelievers have revolutionary obligations and the same rights and relationship to the state, that religion cannot be used as pretext to oppose socialism or the Revolution, that atheists have the right to their convictions, and that education shall not include a religious component.[153] The PCC regards religious supernatural power as explainable natural phenomena. It ensures that religion is a private matter for each citizen to decide and works to eliminate the odious social conditions that cause a need for religion.

The rationale of the party for excluding practicing Christians until 1991 and keeping them out of influential positions in the armed forces and government, thus out of leadership capacities, was that it reduced the potential for counterrevolutionary activity by a politically active church hierarchy. Undoubtedly, Christian Cubans feel about as home in their country as most nonbelievers do in the United States.

Castro indicates that all Catholics are not perceived as counterrevolutionaries. Over the past three decades, active Christians who, it was assumed, had renounced their beliefs and ties to the church have joined the party. In 1985 the party established a Religious Affairs Office in the Central Committee to facilitate better relations with the church, a move motivated by the rise of the Christians for Socialism movement in Latin America and by liberation theology. At its Fourth Congress in October 1991, the Communist party decided to broaden its base, especially at the grass roots, and it voted to permit believers to join its ranks. Catholics, Protestants, as well as followers of African religions, many of whom were staunch supporters of the Revolution, could become party members. Fidel concurred with the party's decision.

In Castro's view both Christians for Socialism and liberation theology represent a reversion to Christianity's social roots.[154] Simultaneously, he acknowledges that whereas Marxism recognizes the dialectical relationship of the exploiters to the exploited, liberation theologists often believe that Marxism forgets or disregards the dialectical tension revealed by history and confirmed by faith.[155] Although Fidel takes issue with their contention, he has a soft spot for the concept of Christian faith involving love translated into efficient service to all people, as enunciated in the 1960s by Colombian priest–freedom fighter Camilo Torres. Castro points to Torres's death in battle in Colombia's mountains as the consummate Christian intellect's commitment to the people's revolution.[156] To Fidel, Torres understood about the international imperialism of capital and died combating it.

Currently Cuba's Catholic church is the weakest institutionally in Latin America. In 1985 it had only 1 priest for every 52,948 Cubans,[157] and its hierarchy had not totally accepted the precepts of Father Torres, liberation theology, and Christians for Socialism. The church is still more concerned with survival than with adopting a humanist stance. At this time, one cannot tell if there will develop out of the recent relaxation of tension toward religion in Cuba critical Christian Base Communities, as exist elsewhere in Latin America, or if such organizations would be superfluous given the predominantly revolutionary character of the Cuban people.[158] Castro sees no need for Christians for Socialism or Christian Base Communities, since Cuba is socialist and people may be Christians.

Fidel contends that the Revolution has never been inspired by antireligious feelings.[159] He now strives to get state and church to accommodate to each other, and in 1991 the Cuban government gave the church permission to publish literature in the country. But he notes that reconciliation that allows a communist to be a Christian and a Christian to be a communist does not mean they are one in the same. Faith will forever be that, and political ideology can never be faith in the religious sense, although some critics see it as such in terms of the acceptance of dogma. As a result of these differences, Castro admits that domestically subtle discrimination exists against Christians, basically as a lack of confidence in them.[160]

In the international context, Fidel detests the invocation of God by a Ronald Reagan or an Augusto Pinochet, which he regards as idolatry and hypocrisy.[161] He says, "There are many people in the world who call themselves

Christians but do horrible things, Pinochet, Reagan and [South Africa's] Botha, for example, consider themselves Christians."[162] Castro particularly despises Sunday Mass broadcast from the United States on Radio Martí. He considers it a foreign incursion, but a futile one that has little influence on Cuba's few practicing Catholics.

9

Final Observations

Cuba is the country where many hoped to see socialism fall, and they placed time limits on its survival and they're still doing so, but time goes by and the suitcases they've packed have become moth-ridden.

—Fidel Castro

The cry "Fidel! Fidel! Fidel!" still reverberates throughout José Martí Revolution Square in the 1990s. Cubans continue to express their loyalty, or *Fidel*idad (fidelity), by cheering the only leader most of them have known, as he weaves his magic through a three-hour explanation of how their nation will survive, with difficulty, without the assistance of European socialist allies, during the current "special period" of hardship. Many changes have been wrought in the country since 1959 when a younger, slimmer, and more belligerent Castro spoke from the same historic site and conveyed to the people his dreams for their future. Today, to almost 11 million Cubans, and many others, Fidel represents one of the most intriguing and unique political figures of the twentieth century. In a country of chronic complainers, where most condemnation has traditionally been reserved for politicians, Castro is an institution, a living legend, the creator of one of the few socially beneficial societies where there exists a *consciencia comunista* (communist consciousness). When problems arise, Cubans still tend to absolve Fidel of blame and direct their criticism to a lazy and corrupt bureaucracy, whose size and rigidity retards progress.

After more than three decades of control, Fidel, despite his denials, acts paternalistically and uses his prestige as a source of power. Unlike Stalin, who used violence, Castro has through persuasion prevented rivals from usurping his position. His supporters and critics agree that in the 1990s Castro exhibits greater intellectual and ideological maturity and more refined statesmanship than he did in the 1960s. They also recognize that his revolutionary ardor has not waned, that his passion still sustains the movement and galvanizes the Cuban people for collective action.

Three decades later, critics call his public pleas for criticism insincere gestures to gain power. They forget that he has had that power all along. More precisely, Fidel's one-way dealings with the people are intended to retain power and approval. Some accuse him of exaggerating his importance, but his confidants will tell you that his efforts are designed to gain attention and respect for Cuba. Have these tactics succeeded? What other nation of Cuba's size has received as much acclaim and notoriety?

One secret to Fidel's success is his belief that you cannot subordinate reality to theory. He excels at the art of recognizing the possible. His ideas may not be original, but his applications of them to the Cuban reality are. By applying socialist ideas pragmatically, he has attained a modicum of his goals and held power. Fidel learned well from the lessons of his Cuban radical predecessors. He has had the courage to try their theories and the sense to jettison the ones that proved impractical.

One of Castro's biographers noted that his accomplishments are limited only by the degree of his vision.[1] The latter has changed over the years. One scholar found him to be an opportunist prior to 1965, an idealistic revolutionary between 1966 and 1970, and a pragmatist thereafter.[2] Experts in human behavior claim that those phases correspond to the normal maturation process. In the same vein, as he ages, his dealings with people are more direct. Moreover, he attempts to demonstrate his courage and creativity in public less often.

Contemporary Cuba represents a uniquely pragmatic Marxist state where, as Fidel articulated: "Today we are not fighting against men—unless those men be ourselves; we fight against the past; we fight in the presence of that past which is still with us; we fight against limitations of every kind. But this, sincerely, is the greatest challenge that we face in our lives and the greatest challenge that the Revolution has faced."[3] When he assumed power, he knew that Marx had outlined as a major challenge the possibility that it would take the workers fifteen to fifty years of civil war to alter existing conditions and to prepare themselves for political rule. Castro met and overcame that challenge in a few years and filled the vacuum of a society devoid of strong middle-class institutions with new, radical values.

Cubans like to think that if Marx and Lenin had never existed, Fidel would have invented communism. They imply that theirs is a unique communism, not a Soviet or orthodox version. They are proud of the fact that Castro used Marx as a guide, not as gospel, that unlike the German thinker, who set his ideas down in ponderous fashion, Fidel has insisted that Cuba's Marxists put Marx's thought into a native context, expressed in terms easily understood by laypeople. In a very straightforward way, as we have seen, he has applied dialectical logic to Cuba's historical process and has demonstrated the primacy of economic factors in the development of Cuban society.

Most Cubans call what they have *Fidelismo* or Castroism, an indigenous movement shaped by Cuba's history, culture, economy, and the effects on them of external influences. Castroism still perpetuates the myth of the purity of guerrilla struggle, a concept some think almost alien to Marx, which somehow enables Cubans to have higher moral self-perceptions. *Fidelismo* does not represent a closed model but provides a step in the revolutionary direction for other Latin American nations to examine and then construct their own radical movements based on their historical conditions and social contradictions. Castro tells his fellow Latins that revolutionary orthodoxy fosters anticommunism.

Over the years, as his knowledge of Marxist theory has deepened, his social and political analyses and revolutionary points of view have become more concrete and less abstract. Nevertheless, his thought does not display theoretical precision. He claims that he is neither dogmatic nor pragmatic (he is both), but dialectical: Thus nothing is permanent and all changes.[4] Latin American intellectuals do not view him as a theoretician or philosopher; he is seen as the implementer of a Marxist vision for Cuba. They see that as his understanding of Marxist thought has become more sophisticated, he has tended less and less to find in it answers for all questions. To him, such rigidity hinders development. He increasingly portrays Cuba's Revolution as humanist, indicating that love for humanity and the desire to eliminate injustice and misery gave rise to Marx's ideas.[5]

Despite recent attempts by anticommunists to foster the idea that Marxism is on its way to oblivion, Fidel feels that no one can say with certainty that Marxism has been surpassed or that it merely represents political aspirations or value judgments. He claims that this is partially attributable to the fact that during the 1970s and 1980s the Cuban economy outperformed those of the region's developing capitalist nations in terms of growth and equity for their citizens. Marxism, to Castro, still stands as a major school of thought that in its infinite varieties unifies the historical processes. But he admits that "to talk about a socialist camp today is a euphemism."[6] History will not judge Fidel on his merits as a Marxist thinker but on how successfully he implemented Marxist ideas and what the Cuban Revolution achieved under his aegis. Under Fidel's direction, in a few years the market economy was eliminated, civil society advanced, the land tenure system altered, the educational philosophy revamped, U.S. influence removed, a new national security system installed, and a politically conscious citizenry worked to create a classless society. After observing the changes in Cuba over the last three decades, even his opponents conclude that Castro has many accomplishments to his credit. If you ask him what he is most proud of, he says that Cuba gained sovereignty, altered its dependent relationship to the United States, took over ownership of its means of production, assumed control of the fruits of its labor, ended poverty, and is willing to share what it has with others less fortunate. Cuba, he declares, is no longer a slave to the past, and its government has greater popular support than does the United States and the nations of Western Europe.[7] He points with particular satisfaction to the inability of the United States to stop Cuba's joint business ventures with Western capitalist states, a situation that has lost U.S. businesses billions of dollars over the years.

The Cuban people still see their revolutionary reflection in Fidel, whom they regard as a man who has never been afraid to take action to move ahead. For a revolution to succeed, it must continue to move forward, and until the 1990s, even though it often deviated from its original plans and promises, Cuba moved ahead socially and economically and demonstrated how social-ism could work for the benefit of the nation's majority. Unfortunately, too of-ten the Cuban system and its accomplishments have been evaluated by outsid-ers guided by the bourgeois ideals, which Castro has endeavored to avoid. Fidel has supervised the construction of a socialist society, which must be judged by socialist values.[8] You cannot measure Cuba by what it was never in-tended to be or by Yankee standards. Fidel feels that because of his bourgeois background, he understands the Yankees' thinking. Most of them, however, have never seriously studied socialism and cannot comprehend Cuba's new way of life. Cuban accomplishments must be measured by what the Revolu-tion set out to achieve—the replacement of the old capitalist economy. Ac-cording to one scholar, Fidel, in his attempt to overcome capitalist relations of production that prevented Cuban development, took the only course open that could benefit Cuba—the socialist road. He never betrayed the Revolu-tion, as some of his early bourgeois followers insist, but he pursued the only option to success.[9]

Cuba's founding generation of socialists, including Fidel, take enormous pride in their achievements but do not hesitate to mention their mistakes. For example, they admit that their initial desire to build communism immediately and to skip the socialist stage was overly ambitious. They respect their fellow Cubans who succeeded, and they talk like new grandparents about the cur-rent generation of socialists that they helped produce.

Fidel's generation of revolutionaries feel good because the Revolution has saved over 300,000 children from premature death.[10] They point out that un-der the new economic system far fewer are engaged in cane cutting, whereas sugar production has increased, thus freeing hundreds of thousands of work-ers for diversified agricultural tasks.[11] Despite such gains, they agree with Marx, who said that the abolition of scarcity brings freedom and that until that time arrives, freedom is relative. They also know that before Fidel's vic-tory in Cuba and the progress of the Revolution, many Latin American intel-lectuals, tired of the unfulfilled promises of the Left, often referred to Marx-ism as a philosophy whose founders did not have the Americas in mind.

Cuba's Revolution forced some of them to reexamine the applicability of flexible scientific socialism to the region, to study Marxist theory more closely for ideas to apply to contemporary conditions in their countries.[12] Castro and the Revolution helped change Marxism from a European to a Latin American form. Revolutionary theorists and activists throughout the hemisphere, especially in El Salvador and Nicaragua, learned many lessons from Cuba.

In addition to the Cuban ideas introduced elsewhere in the Americas, the best testimony to the accomplishments of the Revolution guided by Fidel is found when one travels throughout the nation and witnesses communism in the making. Some observers find the relations between people and property the major change in the country, but the most significant differences are in the relations between people. Social life organized around collective, noncompetitive principles and the lack of materialistic greed and jealously are what most observers consider impressive. A few critics claim that Cuba now has two classes, the ideologically integrated and the ideologically alienated. Such an assertion distorts reality. All societies have some alienated people who do not fit in. The Seventh Day Adventists provide a good example for Cuba. But there are not a sufficient number of alienated people in Cuba to constitute a class. If you talk to a random sample of twenty-five Cuban dissidents, you will find infinite variations of disgruntlement, but basically they are disparate individuals and lack a substantial social base, group consciousness, or cohesion.

Cubans appreciate the fact that Castro has presided over a nation relatively free of drug addiction, gambling, prostitution, unemployment, extreme poverty, sexual exploitation, and social discrimination. Castro asks whether the United States can make comparable claims. He then adds that there exist in Cuba far fewer acts of violence and bloodshed perpetrated by individuals against individuals or the government against individuals than in the United States.[13]

No Cuban will tell you that the nation is a utopia. A great desire still exists for a better way of life, for better television sets and clothing, for more automobiles. Fidel does not criticize consumerism but contrasts it to conspicuous consumption. He realizes that consumer goods contribute to a better quality of life and a greater sense of well-being. He is quick to criticize the consumer excesses and conspicuous consumption of the United States, where advertising extols the need for Jaguars and BMWs, products he considers superfluous. All of the money spent on these overpriced cars does not increase their functionality, but he believes that the cumulative differences between the prices of Toyotas and cars in the BMW category would be sufficient to eliminate malnutrition and homelessness in the United States.

When commenting on the scarcities and desires of the Cuban people, Fidel says repeatedly, *"Hay problemas, hay contradiciones"* (there are problems, there are contradictions). He acknowledges that at times he has not perceived how difficult it is to create the material conditions necessary for communism and consumerism. He admits that his government has sometimes used coercion to handle special problems that arise from the lack of consumer goods, such as the black market, which now appears to be growing. His critics say that if he did not insist on trying to solve problems his way, more might be accomplished. In essence they assert that his omnipresence can and does retard progress, another difficult claim to substantiate or disprove.

Above all, Castro wants socialism to succeed in Cuba, a tall order in a capitalist world. He has remarked on how much easier it was to destroy the old order than to create and sustain the new one. He believes that he can, and that he has, accelerated the historical process. Whether he is primarily responsible for the changes and the Revolution is a question that is often asked and cannot be answered. Fidel insists that historically in the West the "great person theory" prevails and individuals are given too much credit for social change; publicly he dismisses the idea that a "Castro's Cuba" exists and that he is indispensable to the Revolution.[14] He rejects this notion, which he believes has primarily been created by the United States because it finds dislike of individual villains easier to justify than dislike of ideological systems. To illustrate the point, he asserts that the United States, preoccupied with the question of who will succeed him,[15] finds it difficult to comprehend the feasibility of a collectively run democratic socialist society without a tyrannical leader or of the existence of a popularly supported government headed by a strong leader who believes that bourgeois elections and legislatures are not essential to promoting social justice and development. Nelson Valdés, a perspicacious Cuban-born observer of Cuba's political scene, says that the "Fidel is the Revolution" theory remains to be proven. He notes that the fact that Castro announces all major policies makes him the great communicator but that other forces are at work in Cuba.[16]

Leftist analysts Michael Albert and Robin Hahnel saw one-person rule through a bureaucratic hierarchy controlled by the Communist party. They viewed Fidel as the hub, the party as the spokes, and the participatory democracy, in institutions like People's Power, subordinate to party control. They believed that the Leninist party monopolizes political power and ensures that only one political party exists, that Castro's ubiquity leaves little room for popular elements to decentralize power. Albert and Hahnel agreed that the United States, the perpetual antagonist, was responsible to a great degree for Fidel's reluctance to relinquish or delegate power. Contending that Cuba lacks workplace democracy, as technocrats make decisions carried out by workers, they maintained that a ruling coordinator class plans workers' projects and establishes their pay scales, thus contributing to their alienation. They found that the "coordinator economy" has made enormous gains in the areas of health care, housing, nutrition, literacy, and national security. These analysts insisted that Cuba's system is not socialism because a ruling hierarchy, not the workers, make the decisions.[17] Considerable truth exists in their assessments, but more worker and group participation exists than they realize, especially in predecision discussions and postdecision implementation. In other words, worker participation in decision-making exists; worker control does not.

Limited concrete evidence exists on decision-making in Cuba, and pro- and anti-Castro Cubanologists speculate on the subject. Most of his critics say that Fidel makes all decisions, whereas others claim that an authoritarian political apparatus sometimes controls him, a contention that he denies. His supporters believe that state administrators wield considerable power. They reject the idea that Cuba is totalitarian because its government acquired power by contravening previously existing laws and its institutions are dominated by the state, which is regulated by the Communist party, which is run by the Central Committee, which follows the will of the Political Bureau, which is controlled by Castro. In addition, they point out that at the 1991 Fourth Party Congress, because the leaders felt that Cuban democracy did not live up to expectations, they extended democratic debate and participation within the party. Supporters of the Revolution note that critics who try to reduce Cuba to the will of Castro find their theory impossible to prove.[18]

My suggestion is that a two-tiered policy-making process exists in Cuba. On one level, Fidel decides; on the other, the state apparatus formulates policies. In the final analysis, if Castro's decision does not concur, or cannot be reconciled, with that of the bureaucracy, his word prevails. By remaining independent of the bureaucracy, Fidel reduces its potential for becoming an elite body.[19] He reserves for himself the ultimate power primarily because he fears that as long as the state's organizations and policies are not totally communist, there exists a danger of the bureaucracy becoming a privileged stratum of society or a new ruling class.[20]

Undoubtedly, Fidel feels a deep responsibility to build socialism for his people and takes every opportunity to tell them so. He feels a great need to oversee the ideological solidarity and purity of the Revolution.[21]

Perceptive critic Janette Habel claimed that Castro has become sclerotic, that "the political project and collective aspirations no longer coincide."[22] According to her, he has run out of new ideas and thus continues to renew plans that have often worked in the past, and he finds it extremely difficult to deal with the possibility of radically modifying Cuban socialism or employing new methodologies. He sees liberalization and a market economy on one side and centralized planning on the other.[23] He does not believe that a viable alternative to centralized planning exists.

Cuba now has sufficiently strong institutions to permit it to run under a democratic form of socialist government without Castro. Currently, he fears letting go of the reins of power. He feels that if he steps down, the oppressor class will regain control of Cuba. He responds quickly to external pressures, and when he perceives that the Revolution is threatened from without, he tends to curtail internal dissent, as illustrated by recent arrests of a small number of vehement opponents of the government. He justifies his actions by portraying Cubans as "the unfailing frontier line defenders of the noble causes of the world's poor and exploited."[24]

Fidel's generation finds it difficult to transfer control or power to younger Cubans. Nevertheless, he talks about empowering a new generation. He says that he wants the nation to depend less on him and believes that if his work lasts only as long as he is in power and the Revolution is not institutionalized, he has failed. The government promises to help institutionalize the Revolution by involving more young people in the decision-making process and has done so since the beginning of the 1986 rectification. Currently, Fidel is surrounded by about thirty intelligent young administrators who act as his eyes and ears and, along with the old guard, coordinate the government's programs and function as a vanguard within the vanguard party. They represent Cuba's future leaders, who in the absence of Castro would probably distribute governing power in a more collective fashion and liberalize some of Fidel's policies.

Fidel constantly points out that half of the Cuban people are under thirty, thus born within the Revolution. These young people tend to be better educated and more politically conscious than their parents and have a better grasp of, and more confidence in, socialist theory. They are less hesitant to criticize it than was the preceding generation, which grew up in the insecure atmosphere of the Batista dictatorship. A 1991 survey by the Cuban Academy of Science demonstrated that half of Cuba's population born after 1959 has a high degree of loyalty to the system. The young are faithful to the party but not always overly enthusiastic about the direction of the Revolution.[25] Young Cubans have mounted a subtle generational challenge to the government and Fidel. They regard Castro as an old man who has performed well, but one whose limited ideas do not always work. They press for an opening up of society, not for a capitalist-style multiparty system, but for a Communist party or parties with more diversity of opinion. Fidel fears that if these socialist critics make progress, the Cuban exiles will be close behind. Thus he stifles some dissent. By now he should realize that socialist dissent might not play into the hands of the exiled critics but could strengthen pluralistic socialism, give people the feeling that Cuba is theirs, and help the Revolution. That is not to say that more democratic pluralistic socialism will guarantee the increased productivity and governmental efficiency that Cuba needs. Despite the aforementioned conundrums, Cuba's youth are at a loss to find a successor to Fidel[26] and fear that revolutionary gains will evaporate without him.

The question of transfer of political power from Fidel has been raised frequently in discussions by Cuba's younger intellectuals, but they have not articulated it in print.[27] Young members of the government leadership would like to replace the 26th of July Movement people who hold government and

Communist party positions with men and women of their own generation.[28] But Castro's presence impedes their initiative in this delicate area. Occasionally some venturesome journalists or foreign intellectuals ask Fidel when he intends to retire. He then quotes Plato, who said in *The Republic* that the ideal age to take charge of a government was fifty-five, when one had sufficient wisdom. He goes on to refer to wonderfully creative seventy-five-year-old intellectuals and great musicians who played at ninety-five.[29] He infers that his longevity in office provides valuable continuity to the Revolution. But most experts agree that when Fidel no longer heads Cuba, his style of leadership—keeping the bureaucracy in line while controlling the mobilization of the masses and ruling paternalistically—will not survive him.[30] A successor regime will find it difficult to keep society supportive of the Revolution by perpetuating a state of siege and advocating and working for equality while not relinquishing its grip on power.[31] Fidel is an institution, and we do not know precisely how the gaps left by his departure will be filled when he is gone. For example, will an individual or a group be able to balance the party against the state as he has done? In 1990, when an NBC correspondent asked Castro to reply to a Cuban exile's comment that Fidel would be gone within a year, he stated, "Well neither they nor I can know that, only God knows whether one year from now I'll still be here, dead or alive, healthy or not healthy." Then he added that he had been saying the same thing for thirty-one years.[32]

Castro estimates that 90–92 percent of the Cuban people support the Revolution, and 8–10 percent oppose it sufficiently to engage in counterrevolutionary activities, figures that a former high-ranking member of his government disputes.[33] The supporters reflect two different approaches to how the state should be run. Fidel's close allies favor "common will" among people, or unity. They identify Castro with the Revolution, the Communist party, and the people. In contrast, as noted above, some of his more distant supporters prefer a more pluralistic system, with greater diversity within the Revolution and more individual initiatives. They would like to place limitations on the party, which they would prefer to see as a guiding, not governing, institution.[34] Both groups of supporters concur with the 1990 slogan *socialismo o muerte* (socialism or death), which replaced the old one, *patria o muerte* (homeland or death). The new slogan has multiple meanings. It signifies that the proud Cuban people will not capitulate, that they are determined to struggle for their goals, that Yankee imperialism will not kill revolutionary aspirations. By 1991, Fidel had begun to use just the slogan *socialismo,* implying that the survival of socialism was paramount.

His supporters know that the socialist community of nations no longer exists but prefer socialist development to capitalist marginalization, which is what they think would occur if Cuba followed the current route of Eastern Europe's formerly socialist countries. Castro contends that capitalism has failed in more than one hundred Third World states, including some in Latin

America,[35] and that under a privatized market economy Cuba could become another Haiti, whose people face continuous economic and social crises, monumental class antagonisms, and poverty so severe that it defies description.

One cannot predict what the future holds for Cuban socialism or whether the nation will ever reach the communist plateau. In fact, the significance of the Cuban Revolution, beyond the factors discussed on preceding pages, will have to be assessed by a future generation of historians with the benefit of years of hindsight. However, it is safe to say that without Fidel Castro there would not have been a Revolution that radically transformed Cuban society.[36] Under Castro's direction Cuba endeavored to terminate the Latin American traditions of *caudillismo,* excessive military control, monoculture, and economic and political dependence and to reinstitute constitutionalism. Has Fidel succeeded? He definitely possesses the characteristics of the traditional *caudillo,* albeit a benevolent one who has not hesitated to impose his views on society in order to share with it the benefits of his revolutionary vision. Although the majority of *caudillos* perpetuate the cultural tradition of hierarchical decisions and use their authority for the benefit of a limited group, Castro does not. Moreover, he differs from most *caudillos,* who generally have not transformed their societies and then institutionalized the positive changes. Paradoxically, although Fidel opposes the cult of personality, his presence perpetuates it. The military, which includes 250,000 active-duty troops and 200,000 reservists, does not run Cuba but plays an integral role in government and is consulted on most major issues and on all national security concerns. During the early years of the Revolution, Cuba could be categorized as a monocultural nation, relying chiefly on sugar for foreign exchange. In recent years other products and industries such as citrus, fish, paper goods, and tourism have earned hard currency. Most dependency theorists state that when the nation aligned itself with the Soviet bloc, ownership of the nation's means of production and control over its political and social systems were reclaimed by Cubans. Finally, the Revolution turned away from bourgeois institutions and pursued another variety of constitution, one that places checks on Fidel's authority, a characteristic uncommon to most dictatorships.

One cannot attribute all the successes and failures of the Revolution directly to Fidel. What has been accomplished, he points out, is not a miracle but the result of much planning, hard work, and tenacity on the part of countless teams of people.[37] As you travel about Cuba you rarely hear, as you did in the 1960s, "Fidel will resolve the problems." Since the 1970s and the advent of the elected National Assembly, popular sophistication about the machinations of government has grown, and people realize that one man cannot govern alone.

Recently, optimism in the country has waned, as the Cuban people no longer assume that world peace and economic prosperity are just over the horizon, especially in light of the fact that by 1992 lack of fuel had caused Cuban factories to close, newspaper production was decreased, and all foods were rationed. Cubans foresee protracted hardships for themselves and increasing political and social turmoil for the world but still hope that the latter will lead to revolutionary solutions for others. Castro and his people realize that even if the cold war has ended between the United States and the Soviet Union, for Cuba and the United States it rages on. Despite his legitimate fear of the United States, Fidel still places too much blame for some socialist failures on the United States.

The Castro of the 1990s does not fear confrontation, but neither does he court it. At the same time that he insists that the Revolution will not collapse, he frequently pursues détente. He now prefers to pursue a mutual live-and-let-live policy vis-à-vis the United States and its most reactionary allies.[38] With regard to other nations, Fidel still verbally supports revolution where it appears feasible, but where it seems improbable, he has resolved to back de facto regimes. He admits that of late Cuba's international influence has decreased outside of Latin America, especially in the Third World. Cuba currently has virtually no direct involvement in Asia, Africa, or the Middle East.

Castro does not believe that anyone in the world possesses the ability to turn the clock back historically, yet paradoxically he feels that if Cuba meets a fate similar to that of Eastern Europe's socialists, the Miami-exile critics, with the assistance of the U.S. government, would be back in control, and Cuba would again become a neocolonial possession. He thinks that it is about time that his Miami-based Cuban opponents realize that new ideas have taken hold in Cuba, that the Revolution has made viable social gains, and that the exiles should relinquish their dreams of restoring some form of bourgeois democracy or dictatorship under their control.

Fidel does not maintain that there can exist identical historical events but claims that elsewhere in the world the workers can assume a greater role in society, as they do in Cuba.[39] He states that the Cuban Revolution has disproved the contention of Marx and many of his disciples that revolutionary leadership, in terms of eliminating capitalism, would emanate from major capitalist states. To him, the Cuban Revolution has demonstrated that henceforth revolutionary leadership will come from smaller nations, especially ones with a substantial radical tradition.

When confronted with the anti-intellectual position of the George Bush administration that ideological wars are over, that history is coming to an end, Fidel responded in true Marxist fashion that, on the contrary, history has hardly begun. He pointed out that Marxism, in terms of the history of the world, is a recently implemented method of analysis, not a historical interlude or a failed political system. He has faith in the inexorable historical process that Marx predicted would lead to socialism. He declared that, to date, most of the capitalist Third World knows only discrimination, misery, and exploitation and minority social, economic, and political control over majorities. The present might appear to belong to capitalism, but Castro does not accept the fact that the future does, as long as class struggle continues in capitalist societies. Today most of the people of Latin America suffer under neo-liberalism, the legacy of capitalist economics, which does not promise to alleviate the region's problems of underdevelopment. Fidel refuses to believe that tyranny, deprivation, and subjugation is all that the future holds. He understands from the Cuban experience that the Marxist promise of a perfect life cannot be attained, that the transformation to socialism does not resolve all of the contradictions in society, and that communism might never be reached. He realizes that nations such as Cuba might never go beyond socialism with its continuous struggles, but he thinks that hope exists for struggles to lead to the improvement of the human condition and to economic and social justice.

Notes

Preface

1. Nelson P. Valdés, "Revolution and Paradigms: A Critical Assessment of Cuban Studies," in *Cuban Political Economy: Controversies in Cubanology*, ed. Andrew Zimbalist (Boulder: Westview Press, 1988), p. 188.

Chapter 1

1. See Sheldon B. Liss, *Roots of Revolution: Radical Thought in Cuba* (Lincoln: University of Nebraska Press, 1987).

2. Gabriel García Márquez, "Plying the Word," *NACLA Report on the Americas* 24 (2) (August 1990):42.

3. Gabriel García Márquez, "Fidel, el oficio de la palabra," *Areíto* 2 (56) (July 1989): 19–20.

4. John Griffiths, *Castro* (London: Batsford Academic and Educational, 1981), p. 27.

5. Nelson P. Valdés, taperecorded talk on Castro and the Revolution, presented at conference: "Thirty Years of the Cuban Revolution: An Assessment," Halifax, Canada (November 1–4, 1989), tape no. P. 5.

6. García Márquez, "Fidel, el oficio," p. 16.

7. Fidel Castro, *Fidel Castro habla con Barbara Walters* (Colombia: Carlos Valencia Editores, 1977), p. 68.

8. García Márquez, "Plying the Word," p. 43.

9. Janette Habel, *Cuba: The Revolution in Peril* (London: Verso, 1991), p. 108.

10. Fidel Castro and Frei Betto, *Fidel and Religion: Castro Talks on Revolution and Religion with Frei Betto* (New York: Simon and Schuster, 1987), p. 90.

11. John Gerassi, *Fidel Castro: A Biography* (Garden City, N.Y.: Doubleday, 1973), p. 1.

12. Tad Szulc, *Fidel: A Critical Portrait* (New York: William Morrow, 1986), p. 20.

13. Castro and Betto, *Fidel and Religion*, p. 11.

14. Fidel Castro, *Fidel Castro Speaks on Marxism-Leninism* (New York: Fair Play for Cuba Committee, 1961), p. 31.

15. Fidel Castro, *Fidel Castro Denounces Sectarianism* (Havana: Ministry of Foreign Relations, 1962), p. 32. Speech of March 26, 1962.

16. Szulc, *Fidel,* p. 33.

17. Fidel Castro, *Political, Economic, and Social Thought of Fidel Castro* (Havana: Editorial Lex, 1959), p. 189.

18. Michael Taber, ed., *Fidel Castro Speeches 1984–85: War and Crisis in the Americas* (New York: Pathfinder Press, 1985), pp. 156–157.

19. Ibid.

20. Lee Lockwood, *Castro's Cuba, Cuba's Fidel* (New York: Random House, 1969), pp. 147–148.

21. Fidel Castro, *Nothing Can Stop the Course of History,* interview by Jeffrey M. Elliot and Mervyn M. Dymally (New York: Pathfinder Press, 1986), p. 194.

22. Castro and Betto, *Fidel and Religion,* p. 286.

23. K. S. Karol, *Guerrillas in Power* (New York: Hill and Wang, 1970), p. 241.

24. Marta Harnecker, *Fidel Castro's Political Strategy: From Moncada to Victory* (New York: Pathfinder Press, 1987), pp. 10–11.

25. *Granma Weekly Review,* March 27, 1988.

26. Castro, *Nothing Can Stop,* p. 224.

27. David Deutschmann and Deborah Shnookal, eds., *The Right to Dignity: Fidel Castro and the Nonaligned Movement* (Melbourne: Ocean Press, 1989), p. 22.

28. Max Azicri, "Twenty-six Years of Cuban Revolutionary Politics: An Appraisal," in *Democracy in Latin America: Visions and Realities,* ed. Susanne Jonas and Nancy Stein (New York: Bergin and Garvey, 1990), p. 147.

29. Carlos Alberto Montaner, *Fidel Castro and the Cuban Revolution: Age, Position, Character, Destiny, Personality, and Ambition* (New Brunswick: Transaction Books, 1989), p. 18.

30. Samuel Farber, *Revolution and Reaction in Cuba, 1933–1960: A Political Sociology from Machado to Castro* (Middletown, Conn.: Wesleyan University Press, 1976), pp. 18–25.

31. Lockwood, *Castro's Cuba,* p. 329.

32. Szulc, *Fidel,* p. 34.

33. Karol, *Guerrillas,* p. 480.

34. *Granma Weekly Review,* August 28, 1988, p. 3.

35. Castro, *Nothing Can Stop,* pp. 284–285.

36. Theodore MacDonald, *Making a New People: Education in Revolutionary Cuba* (Vancouver: New Star Books, 1985), p. 195.

37. Fidel Castro, *Socialismo y comunismo: un proceso único* (Mexico City: Editorial Diógenes, 1978), pp. 100–107.

38. Castro, *Nothing Can Stop,* p. 213.

39. Montaner, *Fidel Castro,* p. 23.

40. García Márquez, "Fidel, el oficio," p. 18.

41. Castro, *Nothing Can Stop,* p. 237.

42. Fidel Castro, *De los recuerdos de Fidel Castro, el Bogotazo y Hemingway, entrevistas* (Havana: Editora Política, 1984), pp. 81–87.

43. Peter G. Bourne, *Fidel: A Biography of Fidel Castro* (New York: Dodd, Mead, 1986), p. 200.

44. Castro, *Socialismo y comunismo,* pp. 52, 55.

45. See García Márquez, "Fidel, el oficio."

46. Castro, *Nothing Can Stop*, p. 23.

47. Boris Goldenberg, "Radicalization of a Latin American State: The Establishment of Communism in Cuba," in *The Anatomy of Communist Takeovers*, ed. Thomas T. Hammond (New Haven: Yale University Press, 1975), p. 591.

48. Karol, *Guerrillas*, p. 489.

49. Lockwood, *Castro's Cuba*, p. 172.

50. Jean Stubbs, *Cuba: The Test of Time* (London: Latin American Bureau, 1989), pp. 47–48.

51. John Krich, *A Totally Free Man: An Unauthorized Autobiography of Fidel Castro* (Berkeley: Creative Arts Book Co., 1981). This quotation is located on an unnumbered page preceding page 1.

Chapter 2

1. Fidel Castro and Frei Betto, *Fidel and Religion: Castro Talks on Revolution and Religion with Frei Betto* (New York: Simon and Schuster, 1987), pp. 241–242.

2. Communist Party of Cuba, *First Congress of the Communist Party of Cuba* (Moscow: Progress Publishers, 1976), pp. 18–19; and Michael Taber, ed., *Fidel Castro Speeches*, vol. 2, *Building Socialism in Cuba* (New York: Pathfinder Press, 1983), p. 307.

3. Fidel Castro, Osvaldo Dorticós, and Raúl Roa, *Así se derrotó al imperialismo*, vol. 1, *Preparando la defensa* (Mexico City: Siglo XXI, 1981), p. 81.

4. Sheldon B. Liss, *Roots of Revolution: Radical Thought in Cuba* (Lincoln: University of Nebraska Press, 1987), p. 152.

5. Fidel Castro, "Words to the Intellectuals," in *Radical Perspectives in the Arts*, ed. Lee Baxandall (Baltimore: Penguin Books, 1972), p. 296.

6. Max Azicri, *Cuba: Politics, Economics and Society* (London: Pinter Publishers, 1988), p. 251.

7. Castro and Betto, *Fidel and Religion*, p. 94.

8. Peter G. Bourne, *Fidel: A Biography of Fidel Castro* (New York: Dodd, Mead, 1986), pp. 14–18.

9. Ibid.

10. Castro and Betto, *Fidel and Religion*, pp. 12–13.

11. Ibid., sect. 2, pt. 1.

12. Bourne, *Fidel*, p. 20.

13. Ibid., p. 30.

14. Fidel Castro, "Interview with Barbara Walters," *Foreign Policy* 29 (Autumn 1977):32.

15. Castro, "Words to the Intellectuals," p. 292.

16. Liss, *Roots of Revolution*, pp. 83–103, 119–151.

17. Castro and Betto, *Fidel and Religion*, p. 145.

18. Ibid., p. 148.

19. Jorge I. Domínguez, *Cuba: Order and Revolution* (Cambridge: Harvard University Press, 1978), p. 111.

20. Lionel Martin, *The Early Fidel: Roots of Castro's Communism* (Secaucus, N.J.: Lyle Stuart, 1978), pp. 50–81.

21. Ibid., p. 81.

22. Castro and Betto, *Fidel and Religion*, p. 149.

23. Martin, *Early Fidel*, p. 30.

24. Bourne, *Fidel*, p. 41.

25. Fidel Castro, *De los recuerdos de Fidel Castro, el Bogotazo y Hemingway, entrevistas* (Havana: Editora Política, 1984), pp. 70–77.

26. Ibid., pp. 66–68.

27. Ibid., p. 26.

28. Ibid., p. 15.

29. Martin, *Early Fidel*, p. 28.

30. Castro, "Interview with Barbara Walters," p. 32.

31. Martin, *Early Fidel*, p. 64.

32. Marta Harnecker, *Fidel Castro's Political Strategy: From Moncada to Victory* (New York: Pathfinder Press, 1987), p. 67.

33. Martin, *Early Fidel*, p. 65.

34. Ibid., p. 107.

35. Lee Lockwood, *Castro's Cuba, Cuba's Fidel* (New York: Random House, 1969), p. 155.

36. Fidel Castro, *Political, Economic, and Social Thought of Fidel Castro* (Havana: Editorial Lex, 1959), pp. 108–109.

37. Tad Szulc, *Fidel: A Critical Portrait* (New York: William Morrow, 1986), p. 228.

38. Castro and Betto, *Fidel and Religion*, pp. 152–153.

39. Liss, *Roots of Revolution*, p. 173.

40. Martin, *Early Fidel*, p. 121.

41. Ibid., p. 95.

42. Bourne, *Fidel*, p. 73.

43. Ramón Bonachea and Marta San Martín, *The Cuban Insurrection 1952–1959* (New Brunswick: Transaction Books, 1974), p. 63.

44. Ibid., p. 62.

45. Fidel Castro, "Renewal or Death," *New International* 6 (1987):247. Speech to Communist Party of Cuba, Third Congress, February 7, 1986.

46. Martin, *Early Fidel*, p. 93.

47. Ibid., p. 101.

48. Harnecker, *Fidel Castro's*, p. 41.

49. Mirta Aguirre, Denia García Ronda, and Isabel Monal, "El leninismo en la historia me absolverá," *Casa de Las Americas*, November 16, 1975, pp. 67–70.

50. Liss, *Roots of Revolution*, p. 11.

51. Maurice Zeitlin and Robert Scheer, *Cuba: Tragedy in Our Hemisphere* (New York: Grove Press, 1963), pp. 52–53.

52. Harnecker, *Fidel Castro's*, p. 7.

53. Martin, *Early Fidel*, p. 155.

54. Harnecker, *Fidel Castro's*, pp. 11–12.

55. Fidel Castro, *Fidel Castro habla con Barbara Walters* (Colombia: Carlos Valencia Editores, 1977), p. 30.

56. Castro, *De los recuerdos*, p. 66.

57. Martin, *Early Fidel*, p. 155.

58. Harnecker, *Fidel Castro's*, p. 43.

59. Liss, *Roots of Revolution*, pp. 113–119.

60. Castro, *Political, Economic, and Social*, pp. 57–58.

61. Rolando E. Bonachea and Nelson P. Valdés, eds., *Cuba in Revolution* (Garden City, N.Y.: Anchor Doubleday, 1972), pp. 218–219.

62. Fidel Castro, *Fidel Castro Denounces Sectarianism* (Havana: Ministry of Foreign Relations, 1962), p. 41. Speech of March 26, 1962.

63. Joel C. Edelstein, "The Evolution of Goals and Priorities in the Thought of Fidel Castro Ruz," Doctoral Dissertation, University of California, Riverside, 1975, p. 21.

64. Arthur MacEwan, *Revolution and Economic Development in Cuba* (New York: St. Martin's Press, 1981), p. 213.

65. Bonachea and Valdés, *Cuba in Revolution*, p. 183.

66. Castro and Betto, *Fidel and Religion*, p. 208.

67. Liss, *Roots of Revolution*, p. 113.

68. Carlos Franqui, *Diary of the Cuban Revolution* (New York: Viking Press, 1980), p. 66.

69. Ibid., p. 70.

70. Liss, *Roots of Revolution*, p. 173; and Martin, *Early Fidel*, p. 154.

71. Liss, *Roots of Revolution*, p. 173; and Franqui, *Diary*, p. 71.

72. Szulc, *Fidel*, p. 307.

73. Bourne, *Fidel*, p. 95.

74. Fidel Castro, *Nothing Can Stop the Course of History*, interview by Jeffrey M. Elliot and Mervyn M. Dymally (New York: Pathfinder Press, 1986), pp. 230–231.

75. Szulc, *Fidel*, p. 305.

76. Harnecker, *Fidel Castro's*, p. 27.

77. Martin, *Early Fidel*, pp. 169–172.

78. Castro, *Political, Economic, and Social*, pp. 129–130, 143.

79. Wayne S. Smith, *The Closest of Enemies: A Personal and Diplomatic Account of U.S.-Cuban Relations Since 1957* (New York: Norton, 1987), p. 15.

80. Nelson Valdés, "Ideological Roots of the Cuban Revolutionary Movement," in *Contemporary Caribbean: A Sociological Reader*, vol. 2, ed. Susan Craig (Maracas, Trinidad and Tobago: Susan Craig, 1982), p. 216.

81. Liss, *Roots of Revolution*, p. 113.

82. Harnecker, *Fidel Castro's*, pp. 24–25.

83. Fidel Castro, "Interview with ABC Television," *I. F. Stone's Bi-Weekly*, May 27, 1963, p. 6.

84. Régis Debray, *Revolution in the Revolution?* (New York: Grove Press, 1967), p. 20.

85. Castro, "Interview with Barbara Walters," p. 44.

86. Fidel Castro, Speech, *Granma Weekly Review*, August 7, 1988. Speech of July 26, 1988.

87. Liss, *Roots of Revolution*, p. 197.

88. Communist Party, *First Congress*, p. 49.

89. Fidel Castro, *El partido marxista-leninista* (Buenos Aires: Ediciones La Rosa Blindada, 1965), p. 75.

90. MacEwan, *Revolution and Economic,* p. 32.

91. Castro, *Political, Economic, and Social,* p. 173.

92. Herbert L. Matthews, *Revolution in Cuba* (New York: Scribner's, 1975), p. 135.

93. Fidel Castro, *El pensamiento de Fidel Castro: selección temática, enero 1959–abril 1961,* vol. 1 (Havana: Editora Política, 1983), pp. 18–19.

94. John Griffiths, *Castro* (London: Batsford Academic and Educational, 1981), p. 25.

95. Castro, *Political, Economic and Social,* pp. 213–219.

96. Peter Shearman, *The Soviet Union and Cuba* (London: Routledge and Kegan Paul, 1987), p. 7.

97. Liss, *Roots of Revolution,* p. 192.

98. Theodore Draper, *Castroism: Theory and Practice* (New York: Praeger, 1965), p. 58.

99. Max Azicri, "Twenty-six Years of Cuban Revolutionary Politics: An Appraisal," in *Democracy in Latin America: Visions and Realities,* ed. Susanne Jonas and Nancy Stein (New York: Bergin and Garvey, 1990), p. 155.

100. Fidel Castro, Speech of July 26, 1967, in *The Quest for Change in Latin America,* ed. W. Raymond Duncan and James Nelson Goodsell (New York: Oxford University Press, 1970), p. 305.

101. Castro, *El partido marxista-leninista,* p. 88.

102. Louis A. Pérez, Jr., *Cuba: Between Reform and Revolution* (New York: Oxford University Press, 1988), p. 324.

103. Miguel Jorrín and John D. Martz, *Latin-American Political Thought and Ideology* (Chapel Hill: University of North Carolina Press, 1970), p. 293.

104. Edelstein, "The Evolution of Goals," p. 3.

105. Donald C. Hodges, *The Latin American Revolution: Politics and Strategy from Apro-Marxism to Guevarism* (New York: William Morrow, 1974), p. 228.

106. Jorrín and Martz, *Latin-American Political Thought,* p. 293.

107. Castro and Betto, *Fidel and Religion,* pp. 209–210.

108. MacEwan, *Revolution and Economic,* p. 70.

109. Michael Taber, ed., *Fidel Castro Speeches 1984–85: War and Crisis in the Americas* (New York: Pathfinder Press, 1985), pp. 164–165.

110. James O'Connor, *The Origins of Socialism in Cuba* (Ithaca: Cornell University Press, 1970), p. 312.

111. Castro, *Fidel Castro Denounces,* p. 13.

112. Ibid.

113. David Childs, *Marx and the Marxists* (London: Ernest Benn, 1973), pp. 313–314.

114. Castro, *Fidel Castro Denounces,* pp. 35–36.

115. Terence Cannon, *Revolutionary Cuba* (New York: Crowell, 1981), pp. 253–254.

116. Edelstein, "The Evolution of Goals," p. 238.

117. Azicri, "Twenty-six Years," p. 146.

118. Liss, *Roots of Revolution,* p. 209; and Carla Anne Robbins, *The Cuban Threat* (New York: McGraw-Hill, 1983), p. 149.

119. Liss, *Roots of Revolution,* p. 194.

120. Sebastian Balfour, *Castro* (New York: Longman, 1990), pp. 98–99.

121. Ibid., pp. 116–118.

122. Ibid.

123. Pérez, *Between Reform*, p. 349.

124. Theodore MacDonald, *Making a New People: Education in Revolutionary Cuba* (Vancouver: New Star Books, 1985), p. 4; and *Granma*, July 25, 1971, p. 2.

125. Fidel Castro, *Discursos*, vol. 2 (Havana: Editorial de Ciencias Sociales, 1975), pp. 11–12.

126. Ibid.

127. Shearman, *The Soviet Union*, p. 78.

128. Robin Blackburn, ed., *Strategy for Revolution: Essays on Latin America by Régis Debray* (New York: Monthly Review Press, 1969), p. 152.

129. *New York Times*, July 28, 1989.

Chapter 3

1. Peter G. Bourne, *Fidel: A Biography of Fidel Castro* (New York: Dodd, Mead, 1986), p. 95.

2. Sheldon B. Liss, *Roots of Revolution: Radical Thought in Cuba* (Lincoln: University of Nebraska Press, 1987), p. 46.

3. Frank Mankiewicz and Kirby Jones, *With Fidel: A Portrait of Castro* (Chicago: Playboy Press, 1975), p. 56.

4. Fidel Castro, *Nothing Can Stop the Course of History*, interview by Jeffrey M. Elliot and Mervyn M. Dymally (New York: Pathfinder Press, 1986), pp. 31–34. Heading Fidel's "most despised" list is Adolf Hitler, who he believes appealed to people's most base instincts and had no leadership ability.

5. *Granma Weekly Review*, October 13, 1968, pp. 2–5.

6. Fidel Castro, *Socialismo y comunismo: un proceso único* (Mexico City: Editorial Diógenes, 1978), p. 189; and Liss, *Roots of Revolution*, pp. 10–15.

7. Castro, *Socialismo y comunismo*, p. 190.

8. Fidel Castro, *La primera revolución socialista en América* (Mexico City: Siglo XXI, 1980), p. 21.

9. Liss, *Roots of Revolution*, pp. 70–74.

10. Fidel Castro, *Fidel Castro Denounces Sectarianism* (Havana: Ministry of Foreign Relations, 1962), p. 44. Speech of March 26, 1962.

11. Liss, *Roots of Revolution*, pp. 83–91; and Castro, *Socialismo y comunismo*, p. 190.

12. Liss, *Roots of Revolution*, p. 115.

13. Communist Party of Cuba, *First Congress of the Communist Party of Cuba* (Moscow: Progress Publishers, 1976), p. 30.

14. Liss, *Roots of Revolution*, pp. 113–119.

15. James Nelson Goodsell, ed., *Fidel Castro's Personal Revolution in Cuba 1959–1973* (New York: Knopf, 1975), pp. 10–12.

16. Castro, *Nothing Can Stop*, p. 192.

17. Marta Harnecker, *Fidel Castro's Political Strategy: From Moncada to Victory* (New York: Pathfinder Press, 1987), p. 46.

18. Ibid., p. 8.

19. Fidel Castro, *José Martí: el autor intelectual* (Havana: Editora Política, 1983), p. 181.

20. Fidel Castro, *Fidel in Chile* (New York: International Publishers, 1972), p. 82.

21. Fidel Castro, "Interview with Barbara Walters," *Foreign Policy* 29 (Autumn 1977):30.

22. Fidel Castro, *Discursos,* vol. 1 (Havana: Editorial de Ciencias Sociales, 1975), p. 79.

23. Richard Butler Gray, *José Martí, Cuban Patriot* (Gainesville: University of Florida Press, 1962), pp. 229–236.

24. *Granma Weekly Review,* September 28, 1988, p. 10.

25. Communist Party, *First Congress,* pp. 21–22.

26. Liss, *Roots of Revolution,* pp. 56–57.

27. Ibid., p. 51.

28. Fidel Castro, *Cuba Will Never Adopt Capitalist Methods* (New York: Pathfinder Press, 1988), p. 14. Speech of July 26, 1988.

29. Ibid., p. 15.

30. Liss, *Roots of Revolution,* p. 171; and Martin Kenner and James Petras, eds., *Fidel Castro Speaks* (New York: Grove Press, 1969), p. 113.

31. Fidel Castro and Frei Betto, *Fidel and Religion: Castro Talks on Revolution and Religion with Frei Betto* (New York: Simon and Schuster, 1987), p. 142.

32. Liss, *Roots of Revolution,* p. 54.

33. Ibid., pp. 54–55.

34. Ibid., p. 50.

35. Sheldon B. Liss, *Marxist Thought in Latin America* (Berkeley: University of California Press, 1984), p. 256.

36. C.A.M. Hennessy, "The Roots of Cuban Nationalism," *International Affairs* (London) 39 (3) (July 1963):356.

37. Castro and Betto, *Fidel and Religion,* pp. 282–283.

38. *Granma Weekly Review,* April 22, 1990.

39. Lee Lockwood, *Castro's Cuba, Cuba's Fidel* (New York: Random House, 1969), p. 162.

40. Fidel Castro, *Un encuentro con Fidel: entrevista realizada por Gianni Miná* (Havana: Oficina de Publicaciones de Consejo do Estado, 1987), p. 103.

41. Carlos Tablada, *Che Guevara: Economics and Politics in the Transition to Socialism* (Sydney: Pathfinder/Pacific and Asia, 1989), p. 60.

42. Michael Harrington, *The Twilight of Capitalism* (New York: Simon and Schuster, 1976), p. 179.

43. Herbert L. Matthews, *Revolution in Cuba* (New York: Scribner's, 1975), pp. 255–256.

44. Donald C. Hodges, *The Latin American Revolution: Politics and Strategy from Apro-Marxism to Guevarism* (New York: William Morrow, 1974), p. 147.

45. Hodges, *The Latin American Revolution,* p. 244.

46. Tablada, *Che Guevara,* p. 223.

47. Liss, *Roots of Revolution,* p. 157.

48. Jan Knippers Black et al., *Area Handbook for Cuba* (Washington: Foreign Area Studies of the American University, 1976), p. 140.

49. Jean Stubbs, *Cuba: The Test of Time* (London: Latin American Bureau, 1989), p. 14.

50. Tablada, *Che Guevara,* p. 223.

51. Ibid.

52. *Granma Weekly Review,* April 28, 1989, p. 10.

53. Tablada, *Che Guevara,* p. 222.

54. Liss, *Roots of Revolution,* p. 174.

55. Castro, *Un encuentro,* p. 323.

56. *Militant,* March 9, 1990, p. 13.

57. Mankiewicz and Jones, *With Fidel,* p. 155.

58. Sheldon B. Liss, *Radical Thought in Central America* (Boulder: Westview Press, 1991), p. 4.

59. Fidel Castro, *Fidel Castro habla con Barbara Walters* (Colombia: Carlos Valencia Editores, 1977), p. 45. May 19, 1977.

60. Saul Landau, "Socialist Democracy in Cuba: An Interview with Fidel Castro," *Socialist Revolution* 1 (2) (March-April 1970):135.

61. Fidel Castro, "Important Problems for the Whole of International Revolutionary Thought," *New International* 6 (1987):223.

62. *Militant,* October 13, 1989.

63. Michael Taber, ed., *Fidel Castro Speeches 1984–85: War and Crisis in the Americas* (New York: Pathfinder Press, 1985), p. 125.

64. M. M. Bober, *Karl Marx's Interpretation of History* (New York: Norton, 1965), p. 99.

65. Castro and Betto, *Fidel and Religion,* p. 129.

66. Wayne S. Smith, *The Closest of Enemies: A Personal and Diplomatic Account of U.S.-Cuban Relations Since 1957* (New York: Norton, 1987), p. 262.

67. Lockwood, *Castro's Cuba,* p. 162.

68. Michael Taber, ed., *Fidel Castro Speeches: Cuba's International Foreign Policy 1975–80* (New York: Pathfinder Press, 1981), p. 175.

69. Rolando E. Bonachea and Nelson P. Valdés, eds., *Cuba in Revolution* (Garden City, N.Y.: Anchor Doubleday, 1972), p. 148.

70. Bober, *Karl Marx's,* p. 170.

71. Terence Cannon, *Revolutionary Cuba* (New York: Crowell, 1981), p. 207.

72. Castro, *Socialismo y comunismo,* p. 27.

73. John P. Wallach, "Fidel Castro and the United States Press," in *The Selling of Fidel Castro: The Media and the Cuban Revolution,* ed. William E. Ratliff (New Brunswick: Transaction Books, 1987), pp. 135–136.

74. *Granma Weekly Review,* August 7, 1988, p. 4. Speech of July 26, 1988.

75. Max Azicri, "Twenty-six Years of Cuban Revolutionary Politics: An Appraisal," in *Democracy in Latin America: Visions and Realities,* ed. Susanne Jonas and Nancy Stein (New York: Bergin and Garvey, 1990), p. 156.

76. Declaration of the First National Congress on Education and Culture, Havana, April 1971.

77. Michael Albert and Robin Hahnel, *Socialism Today and Tomorrow* (Boston: South End Press, 1981), p. 236.

78. Tzvi Medin, *Cuba: The Shaping of the Revolutionary Consciousness* (Boulder: Lynne Rienner Publishers, 1990), p. 15.

79. Liss, *Roots of Revolution*, p. 175.

80. Fidel Castro, *Speeches at Three Congresses* (Havana: Editora Política, 1982), p. 111.

81. Kenner and Petras, *Fidel Castro Speaks*, p. xiii.

82. Fidel Castro, *Fidel in Chile* (New York: International Publishers, 1972), pp. 72–73.

83. Caleb Rosado, "Sect and Party: Religion Under Revolution in Cuba," Doctoral Dissertation, Northwestern University, Evanston, Ill., 1985, p. 161.

84. Richard Flacks, *Making History: The Radical Tradition in American Life* (New York: Columbia University Press, 1988), p. 203.

85. Medin, *Cuba: The Shaping*, p. 17; and Fidel Castro, *Second Congress of the Communist Party of Cuba Main Report* (Havana: Political Publishers, 1980), p. 86.

86. Michael Taber, ed., *Fidel Castro Speeches*, vol. 2, *Building Socialism in Cuba* (New York: Pathfinder Press, 1983), p. 314.

87. Communist Party, *First Congress*, p. 247.

88. Bertram Silverman, ed., *Man and Socialism in Cuba* (New York: Atheneum, 1973), p. 377.

89. Tablada, *Che Guevara*, p. 95.

90. Joel C. Edelstein, "The Evolution of Goals and Priorities in the Thought of Fidel Castro Ruz," Doctoral Dissertation, University of California, Riverside, 1975, p. 88.

91. *Militant*, April 25, 1989, p. 10.

92. Lionel Martin, *The Early Fidel: Roots of Castro's Communism* (Secaucus, N.J.: Lyle Stuart, 1978), pp. 38–39.

93. Ibid.

94. Fidel Castro, *We Represent the Immense Majority of History* (New York: Pathfinder Press, 1986), p. 4.

95. Landau, "Socialist Democracy," p. 134.

96. Castro, *Cuba Will Never Adopt*, p. 124. Speech of July 26, 1988.

97. Max Azicri, *Cuba: Politics, Economics and Society* (London: Pinter Publishers, 1988), p. 124.

98. Castro, "Important Problems," p. 22.

99. Fidel Castro, *In Defense of Socialism: Four Speeches on the 30th Anniversary of the Cuban Revolution* (New York: Pathfinder Press, 1989), p. vi.

100. *Granma Weekly Review*, November 12, 1989.

101. Bonachea and Valdés, *Cuba in Revolution*, p. 305.

102. *Granma Weekly Review*, March 24, 1968, pp. 2–8.

103. Mankiewicz and Jones, *With Fidel*, p. 93.

104. Ernesto Cardenal, *In Cuba* (New York: New Directions, 1974), p. 329.

105. Mankiewicz and Jones, *With Fidel*, pp. 105–110.

106. Taber, *Fidel Castro Speeches*, vol. 2, pp. 75–87.

107. Lockwood, *Castro's Cuba*, p. 215.

108. David P. Barkin and Nita R. Manitzas, eds., *Cuba: The Logic of the Revolution* (Andover, Mass.: Warner Modular Publications, 1973), pp. 277–278.

109. Landau, "Socialist Democracy," p. 138.

110. William LeoGrande, "The Theory and Practice of Socialist Democracy in Cuba: Mechanisms of Elite Accountability," *Studies in Comparative Communism* 12 (7) (Spring 1979):41.

111. Landau, "Socialist Democracy," p. 139.

112. Medea Benjamin, Joseph Collins, and Michael Scott, *No Free Lunch: Food and Revolution in Cuba Today* (New York: Grove Press, 1986), pp. 15–16.

113. Taber, *Fidel Castro Speeches 1984–85*, p. xiv.

114. Castro, *Fidel in Chile*, pp. 197–198.

115. Taber, *Fidel Castro Speeches 1984–85*, p. 3.

116. Fidel Castro, *The World Economic and Social Crisis* (Havana: Publishing Office of the Council of State, 1983), p. 168.

117. Taber, *Fidel Castro Speeches 1984–85*, p. 3.

118. *Granma Weekly Review*, December 6, 1987, p. 12.

119. Castro, *Speeches at Three Congresses*, p. 111.

120. *Granma Weekly Review*, February 21, 1988.

121. Mankiewicz and Jones, *With Fidel*, pp. 198–199.

122. Castro, *Speeches at Three Congresses*, pp. 21–22.

123. Castro, *World Economic and Social Crisis*, pp. 19–20.

124. Ibid., pp. 11–16.

125. Castro, *We Represent the Immense*, p. 17.

Chapter 4

1. Fidel Castro, *Lenin's Ideas—Our Lodestar* (Moscow: Novosti Press Agency, 1970), p. 7.

2. Lionel Martin, *The Early Fidel: Roots of Castro's Communism* (Secaucus, N.J.: Lyle Stuart, 1978), p. 39.

3. Sheldon B. Liss, *Roots of Revolution: Radical Thought in Cuba* (Lincoln: University of Nebraska Press, 1987), p. 175.

4. Castro, *Lenin's Ideas*, p. 17.

5. Terence Cannon, *Revolutionary Cuba* (New York: Crowell, 1981), p. 249.

6. Jacques Lévesque, *The USSR and the Cuban Revolution* (New York: Praeger, 1978), p. 31.

7. Tad Szulc, *Fidel: A Critical Portrait* (New York: William Morrow, 1986), p. 569.

8. James O'Connor, *The Origins of Socialism in Cuba* (Ithaca: Cornell University Press, 1970), p. 314.

9. Fidel Castro, *Fidel Castro Speaks on Marxism-Leninism* (New York: Fair Play for Cuba Committee, 1961), p. 54.

10. Ibid., p. 47.

11. Fidel Castro, *Ideología, conciencia y trabajo político: 1959–1986* (Havana: Editora Política, 1987), p. 101.

12. John Kirk, *Between God and the Party: Religion and Politics in Revolutionary Cuba* (Tampa: University of South Florida Press, 1989), p. 123.

13. Fidel Castro, *The Debt Is Not Only Unpayable But Also Uncollectible* (Havana: Editora Política, 1985), p. 237.

14. Mirta Aguirre, Denia García Ronda, and Isabel Monal, "El leninismo en la historia me absolverá," *Casa de Las Americas,* November 16, 1975, p. 82.

15. Carlos Tablada, *Che Guevara: Economics and Politics in the Transition to Socialism* (Sydney: Pathfinder/Pacific and Asia, 1989), p. 94.

16. Fidel Castro, *Discursos,* vol. 2 (Havana: Editorial de Ciencias Sociales, 1975), p. 10.

17. John Lewis, *The Marxism of Marx* (London: Lawrence and Wishart, 1972), p. 75.

18. Michael Taber, ed., *Fidel Castro Speeches: Cuba's Internationalist Foreign Policy 1975–80* (New York: Pathfinder Press, 1981), p. 21.

19. Fidel Castro, *El partido marxista-leninista* (Buenos Aires: Ediciones La Rosa Blindada, 1965), pp. 102–103.

20. Liss, *Roots of Revolution,* p. 194.

21. Ibid., pp. 207–209.

22. Fidel Castro, *Socialismo y comunismo: un proceso único* (Mexico City: Editorial Diógenes, 1978), p. 162.

23. Loree A.R. Wilkerson, *Fidel Castro's Political Programs from Reformism to Marxism-Leninism* (Gainesville: University of Florida Press, 1965), p. 80.

24. Richard R. Fagen, *The Transformation of Political Culture in Cuba* (Stanford University Press, 1969), p. 139.

25. Lee Lockwood, *Castro's Cuba, Cuba's Fidel* (New York: Random House, 1969), p. 188.

26. Castro, *El partido marxista-leninista,* pp. 104–105.

27. Tom Bottomore, *Sociology and Socialism* (New York: St. Martin's Press, 1984), pp. 32–33.

28. Richard Flacks, *Making History: The Radical Tradition in American Life* (New York: Columbia University Press, 1988), p. 13.

29. Bottomore, *Sociology and Socialism,* pp. 33–34.

30. Flacks, *Making History,* p. 15.

31. Robert M. Bernardo, *The Theory of Moral Incentives in Cuba* (University: University of Alabama Press, 1971), p. 56.

32. Taber, *Fidel Castro Speeches: Cuba's Internationalist,* p. 27.

33. Edward Boorstein, *The Economic Transformation of Cuba* (New York: Monthly Review Press, 1968), pp. 253–254.

34. Fidel Castro, "Interview with Charles O. Porter," *Northwest Review* 6 (Autumn 1963):78.

35. Martin, *The Early Fidel,* p. 38.

36. Fidel Castro and Frei Betto, *Fidel and Religion: Castro Talks on Revolution and Religion with Frei Betto* (New York: Simon and Schuster, 1987), pp. 281–282.

37. Fidel Castro, *Un encuentro con Fidel: entrevista realizada por Gianni Miná* (Havana: Oficina de Publicaciones de Consejo de Estado, 1987), p. 154.

38. Lewis, *The Marxism of Marx,* pp. 165–166.

39. Castro, *Lenin's Ideas,* p. 15.

40. Frank Mankiewicz and Kirby Jones, *With Fidel: A Portrait of Castro* (Chicago: Playboy Press, 1975), p. 192.

41. Jorge Edwards, *Persona non grata* (Barcelona: Editorial Seix Barral, 1982), p. 346.

42. Fidel Castro, *Second Congress of the Communist Party of Cuba. Main Report* (Havana: Political Publishers, 1980), p. 57.

43. Szulc, *Fidel*, p. 454.

44. Mankiewicz and Jones, *With Fidel*, p. 151.

45. Sheldon B. Liss, *Marxist Thought in Latin America* (Berkeley: University of California Press, 1984), p. 255.

46. Fidel Castro, *Fidel Castro Speaks on Marxism-Leninism* (New York: Fair Play for Cuba Committee, 1961), p. 43.

47. Castro, *Lenin's Ideas*, p. 8.

48. Hartmut Ramm, *The Marxism of Régis Debray: Between Lenin and Guevara* (Lawrence: Regents Press of Kansas, 1978), p. 89.

49. Fidel Castro, *Speeches at Three Congresses* (Havana: Editora Política, 1982), p. 6.

50. Fidel Castro, *Fidel Castro Denounces Sectarianism* (Havana: Ministry of Foreign Relations, 1962), p. 4. Speech of March 26, 1962.

51. Castro, *El partido marxista-leninista*, pp. 37–38.

52. Tablada, *Che Guevara*, p. 13.

53. Castro, *Second Congress*, p. 77.

54. Fidel Castro, "Important Problems for the Whole of International Revolutionary Thought," *New International* 6 (1987):219.

55. Liss, *Roots of Revolution*, p. 193.

56. Caleb Rosado, "Sect and Party: Religion Under Revolution in Cuba," Doctoral Dissertation, Northwestern University, Evanston, Ill., 1985, p. 159.

57. Taber, *Fidel Castro Speeches: Cuba's Internationalist*, p. 24.

58. Rosado, "Sect and Party," pp. 155–156.

59. Ibid., p. 292.

60. Castro, *El partido marxista-leninista*, pp. 41–42.

61. Ibid., p. 104.

62. Fidel Castro, "Interview on CNN," July 25, 1990.

63. Marta Harnecker, *Fidel Castro's Political Strategy: From Moncada to Victory* (New York: Pathfinder Press, 1987), p. 16.

64. Ronald H. Chilcote and Joel C. Edelstein, eds., *Latin America: The Struggle with Dependency and Beyond* (New York: Schenkman Publishing, 1974), p. 20.

65. Fidel Castro, *La Revolución Cubana* (Mexico City: Ediciones Era, 1979), p. 391.

66. Castro, *Fidel Castro Speaks on Marxism-Leninism*, pp. 11–12.

67. David Wirmark, "Entrevista con el Comandante Fidel Castro, Primer Ministro de Gobierno Revolucionario de Cuba el 5 de abril de 1970," *Estudios y Documentos Suecos Sobre Cuba* (Stockholm: Instituto de Estudios Ibero-Americanos, 1971), p. 32.

68. Castro and Betto, *Fidel and Religion*, p. 151.

69. K. S. Karol, *Guerrillas in Power* (New York: Hill and Wang, 1970), p. 384.

70. Liss, *Roots of Revolution*, p. 194.

71. Castro and Betto, *Fidel and Religion*, p. 237.

72. Joel C. Edelstein, "The Evolution of Goals and Priorities in the Thought of Fidel Castro Ruz," Doctoral Dissertation, University of California, Riverside, 1975, pp. 77–79.

73. Castro, *Lenin's Ideas,* p. 17.

74. Fidel Castro, *Nothing Can Stop the Course of History,* interview by Jeffrey M. Elliot and Mervyn M. Dymally (New York: Pathfinder Press, 1986), p. 236.

75. Martin Kenner and James Petras, eds., *Fidel Castro Speaks* (New York: Grove Press, 1969), p. 146.

76. Ibid., p. 147.

77. Castro and Betto, *Fidel and Religion,* p. 235.

78. Michael Albert and Robin Hahnel, "Cuba Si?" *Z Magazine* 3 (6) (June 1990):34.

79. Lockwood, *Castro's Cuba,* pp. 354–355.

80. For a comprehensive treatment of revolutionary mythology, see C. Fred Judson, *Cuba and the Revolutionary Myth: The Political Education of the Cuban Rebel Army, 1953–1963* (Boulder: Westview Press, 1984).

81. Julio Antonio Mella, *Documentos y artículos* (Havana: Editorial Ciencias Sociales, 1975), p. 35.

82. Harold Eugene Davis, *Revolutionaries, Traditionalists, and Dictators in Latin America* (New York: Cooper Square Publishers, 1973), pp. 191–192.

83. Peter G. Bourne, *Fidel: A Biography of Fidel Castro* (New York: Dodd, Mead, 1986), p. 223.

84. Leslie Dewart, *Christianity and Revolution: The Lesson of Cuba* (New York: Herder and Herder, 1963), p. 85.

85. Herbert L. Matthews, *Revolution in Cuba* (New York: Charles Scribner's, 1975), p. 238.

86. Fidel Castro, *Fidel in Chile* (New York: International Publishers, 1972), p. 65.

87. Liss, *Roots of Revolution,* p. 181.

88. *Militant,* January 5, 1990.

89. Fidel Castro, *The World Economic and Social Crisis* (Havana: Publishing Office of the Council of State, 1983), pp. 17–18.

90. *Granma Weekly Review,* December 18, 1988, p. 2.

91. Castro and Betto, *Fidel and Religion,* p. 197.

92. Fidel Castro, "Speech to the National Assembly," April 4, 1989.

93. Matthews, *Revolution in Cuba,* p. 29.

94. Kenner and Petras, *Fidel Castro Speaks,* pp. 85–90.

95. *Militant,* April 28, 1989, p. 9.

96. Fidel Castro, *The U.S. War Drive and the World Economic Crisis* (New York: Pathfinder Press, 1984), p. 13.

97. Wirmark, "Entrevista con el Comandante," p. 32.

98. Castro, *Un encuentro,* p. 202.

99. Taber, *Fidel Castro Speeches: Cuba's Internationalist,* pp. 30–31.

100. *Militant,* August 10, 1990. Speech of July 26, 1990.

101. O'Connor, *The Origins of Socialism,* p. 6.

102. Castro, "Interview with Charles O. Porter," p. 85.

103. *Granma Weekly Review,* September 25, 1988, p. 12.

104. Castro, *Speeches at Three Congresses,* pp. 97–99.

105. *Granma Weekly Review,* July 17, 1988, p. 5.

106. Donald C. Hodges, ed., *The Legacy of Che Guevara: A Documentary Study* (London: Thames and Hudson, 1977), pp. 49–50.

107. Castro, "Interview with Charles O. Porter," p. 25.

108. Fidel Castro, *Our Struggle Is That of Latin America and the Third World.* Interview with *El Día* (Mexico), June 8, 1985 (Havana: Publishing Office of the Council of State, 1985), p. 13.

109. Kenner and Petras, *Fidel Castro Speaks,* pp. 191–192.

110. Fidel Castro, *In Defense of Socialism: Four Speeches on the 30th Anniversary of the Cuban Revolution* (New York: Pathfinder Press, 1989), p. 121.

111. Castro, "Interview with Charles O. Porter," p. 77; and *Militant,* November 16, 1989.

112. Castro, *In Defense of Socialism,* p. 110.

113. Arthur MacEwan, *Revolution and Economic Development in Cuba* (New York: St. Martin's Press, 1981), p. 208.

114. Ibid., p. 48.

115. Fidel Castro, *Cuba Will Never Adopt Capitalist Methods* (New York: Pathfinder Press, 1988), p. 16. Speech of July 26, 1988.

116. Fidel Castro, Speech of April 4, 1989.

117. *Granma Weekly Review,* September 25, 1989.

118. Castro, *Un encuentro,* pp. 23–24.

119. Castro, *Cuba Will Never Adopt,* p. 16.

120. Castro, *Second Congress,* p. 87.

121. *New York Times,* April 2, 1989.

122. Ernesto Cardenal, *In Cuba* (New York: New Directions, 1974), p. 317.

123. *Granma Weekly Review,* September 25, 1988, p. 9.

124. Edelstein, "The Evolution of Goals," p. 11.

125. Joel C. Edelstein, "Economic Policy and Development Models," in *Cuba: Twenty-five Years of Revolution 1959 to 1984,* ed. Sandor Halebsky and John M. Kirk (New York: Praeger, 1985), p. 183.

126. MacEwan, *Revolution and Economic,* p. 104.

127. Frank T. Fitzgerald, *Managing Socialism: From Old Cadres to New Professionals in Revolutionary Cuba* (New York: Praeger, 1990), pp. 51–52.

128. Peter Shearman, *The Soviet Union and Cuba* (London: Routledge and Kegan Paul, 1987), p. 85.

129. Jaime Suchliki, "The Intellectual Background of the Cuban Revolution," *Annals of the Southeastern Conference on Latin American Studies* 3 (1) (March 1972):106.

130. Gerhard Masur, *Nationalism in Latin America* (New York: Macmillan, 1966), p. 207.

131. Castro, *Fidel in Chile,* p. 220.

132. Michael Taber, ed., *Fidel Castro Speeches 1984–85: War and Crisis in the Americas* (New York: Pathfinder Press, 1985), p. 132.

133. Castro, *Socialismo y comunismo,* p. 23.

134. Castro, *Ideología, conciencia*, p. 52.

135. H. Michael Erisman, *Cuba's International Relations: The Anatomy of a Nationalistic Foreign Policy* (Boulder: Westview Press, 1985), p. 10.

136. Fidel Castro, "Interview with Barbara Walters," *Foreign Policy* 29 (Autumn 1977):47.

137. Fidel Castro, "Waves of the Future," in *Latin American Radicalism: A Documentary Report on Left and Nationalist Movements,* ed. Irving Louis Horowitz, Josué de Castro, and John Gerassi (New York: Random House, 1969), p. 522.

138. *Granma Weekly Review,* September 25, 1988, p. 13.

139. Lockwood, *Castro's Cuba,* p. 47.

140. Castro, *Discursos,* vol. 2, p. 10.

141. Castro, "Interview with Charles O. Porter," p. 107.

142. Ibid., p. 81.

143. Mankiewicz and Jones, *With Fidel,* pp. 87–90.

144. Castro, "Interview with Charles O. Porter," p. 84.

145. Max Azicri, "Twenty-six Years of Cuban Revolutionary Politics: An Appraisal," in *Democracy in Latin America: Visions and Realities,* ed. Susanne Jonas and Nancy Stein (New York: Bergin and Garvey, 1990), p. 175.

146. Fidel Castro, *La primera revolución socialista en América* (Mexico City: Siglo XXI, 1980), pp. 176–177.

147. *Granma Weekly Review,* March 4, 1990, p. 2.

148. Louis A. Pérez, Jr., *Cuba: Between Reform and Revolution* (New York: Oxford University Press, 1988), p. 316.

149. Medea Benjamin, "Soul Searching," *NACLA Report on the Americas* 24 (2) (August 1990):28.

150. Castro and Betto, *Fidel and Religion,* p. 290.

151. Taber, *Fidel Castro Speeches 1984–85,* p. 14.

152. Michael Taber, ed., *Fidel Castro Speeches,* vol. 2, *Building Socialism in Cuba* (New York: Pathfinder Press, 1983), pp. 68–70.

153. Ibid., p. 81.

154. Mankiewicz and Jones, *With Fidel,* pp. 70–72.

155. Ibid., pp. 90–91.

156. See Castro, *Second Congress.*

157. Marta Harnecker, ed., *Cuba: Dictatorship or Democracy?* (Westport, Conn.: Lawrence Hill, 1980), p. xxvii.

158. Max Azicri, *Cuba: Politics, Economics and Society* (London: Pinter Publishers, 1988), pp. 112–113.

159. MacEwan, *Revolution and Economic,* p. 177.

160. Harnecker, *Fidel Castro's,* p. 6.

161. Carlos Moore, *Castro, the Blacks, and Africa* (Los Angeles: Center for Afro-American Studies, University of California, Los Angeles, 1988), p. 13.

162. Tablada, *Che Guevara,* p. 28.

163. Taber, *Fidel Castro Speeches,* vol. 2, p. 51.

164. Pérez, *Cuba: Between Reform,* p. 323.

165. Castro, *Cuba Will Never Adopt,* p. 21.

166. Castro, *Fidel in Chile,* p. 81.

167. Matthews, *Revolution in Cuba*, p. 235.

168. Castro, *Fidel Castro Denounces*, p. 68.

169. James D. Rudolph, *Cuba: A Country Study* (Washington: Foreign Area Studies, American University, 1985), p. 181.

170. Communist Party of Cuba, *First Congress of the Communist Party of Cuba* (Moscow: Progress Publishers, 1976), pp. 231–232.

171. Fitzgerald, *Managing Socialism*, p. 139.

172. Taber, *Fidel Castro Speeches*, vol. 2, p. 61.

173. Castro, *Fidel Castro Denounces*, p. 58.

174. Castro, *El partido marxista-leninista*, p. 141.

175. Harnecker, *Cuba: Dictatorship or Democracy?* p. xxi.

176. Castro, *La primera revolución*, p. 231.

177. Medea Benjamin, "Things Fall Apart," *NACLA Report on the Americas* 24 (2) (August 1990):14.

178. Castro, *El partido marxista-leninista*, pp. 22–23.

179. Fidel Castro, "Renewal or Death," *New International* 6 (1987):250. Speech to Communist Party of Cuba, Third Congress, February 7, 1986.

180. Castro, *Ideología, conciencia*, p. 117.

181. Cannon, *Revolution in Cuba*, p. 255.

182. Harnecker, *Cuba: Dictatorship or Democracy?* p. xxxvii.

183. Ibid., p. xxxviii.

184. Castro, *El partido marxista-leninista*, pp. 18, 20–21.

185. MacEwan, *Revolution and Economic*, p. 178.

186. Liss, *Roots of Revolution*, p. 206.

187. Castro, *Fidel Castro Speaks on Marxism-Leninism*, p. 82.

188. Castro, *Socialismo y comunismo*, p. 17.

189. George Black, "Cuba: The Revolution Toward Victory, Always But When?" *Nation* 247 (11) (October 24, 1988):374.

190. E. Grinevich and B. Gvozdarev, *Washington Versus Havana* (Moscow: Progress Publishers, 1988), p. 29.

191. *Granma Weekly Review*, May 7, 1989, p. 1.

192. Communist Party, *First Congress*, p. 260.

193. Castro, *Socialismo y comunismo*, p. 157.

194. Castro, *El partido marxista-leninista*, p. 48.

195. Ibid., p. 40.

196. Castro, *Un encuentro*, p. 126.

197. Maurice Halperin, *The Taming of Fidel Castro* (Berkeley: University of California Press, 1981), pp. 156–157.

198. Harnecker, *Cuba: Dictatorship or Democracy?* p. 241.

199. *Militant*, March 9, 1990.

200. Castro, *Our Struggle Is That of Latin America*, pp. 23–24.

Chapter 5

1. H. Michael Erisman, *Cuba's International Relations: The Anatomy of a Nationalistic Foreign Policy* (Boulder: Westview Press, 1985), p. 8; and Communist Party of

Cuba, *First Congress of the Communist Party of Cuba* (Moscow: Progress Publishers, 1976), p. 260.

2. Erisman, *Cuba's International Relations,* p. 107.

3. *Militant,* October 13, 1989, p. 11.

4. Erisman, *Cuba's International Relations,* p. 109.

5. *Militant,* April 28, 1989, p. 12.

6. Wayne S. Smith, *The Closest of Enemies: A Personal and Diplomatic Account of U.S.-Cuban Relations Since 1957* (New York: Norton, 1987), pp. 187–189.

7. Fidel Castro, *Fidel Castro habla con Barbara Walters* (Colombia: Carlos Valencia Editores, 1977), p. 66.

8. Michael Taber, ed., *Fidel Castro Speeches 1984–85: War and Crisis in the Americas* (New York: Pathfinder Press, 1985), p. xvi.

9. Regino Díaz, "The Unpayable Debt: An Interview with Fidel Castro," in *Democracy in Latin America: Vision and Realities,* ed. Susanne Jonas and Nancy Stein (New York: Bergin and Garvey, 1990), pp. 132–133.

10. Fidel Castro, *The World Economic and Social Crisis* (Havana: Publishing Office of the Council of State, 1983), p. 159.

11. *Granma Weekly Review,* January 13, 1974.

12. Castro, *The World Economic and Social Crisis,* pp. 22–23, 26.

13. Ibid., p. 27.

14. Nelson P. Valdés, "Revolution and Paradigms: A Critical Assessment of Cuban Studies," in *Cuban Political Economy: Controversies in Cubanology,* ed. Andrew Zimbalist (Boulder: Westview Press, 1988), pp. 189–193.

15. Peter G. Bourne, *Fidel: A Biography of Fidel Castro* (New York: Dodd, Mead, 1986), p. 263.

16. Régis Debray, *Revolution in the Revolution?* (New York: Grove Press, 1967), p. 125.

17. Erisman, *Cuba's International Relations,* p. 173.

18. Damián J. Fernández, *Cuba's Foreign Policy in the Middle East* (Boulder: Westview Press, 1988), p. 27.

19. Sergio Arce, *The Church and Socialism: Reflections from a Cuban Context* (New York: New York Circus Publications, 1985), p. 192.

20. Castro, *The World Economic and Social Crisis,* p. 214.

21. Ibid., p. 213.

22. Ibid., p. 20.

23. Ibid., pp. 117–118.

24. Ibid., pp. 171–173, 175.

25. Martin Kenner and James Petras, eds., *Fidel Castro Speaks* (New York: Grove Press, 1969), p. 74.

26. Erisman, *Cuba's International Relations,* p. 20.

27. Fidel Castro and Frei Betto, *Fidel and Religion: Castro Talks on Revolution and Religion with Frei Betto* (New York: Simon and Schuster, 1987), p. 292.

28. John P. Wallach, "Fidel Castro and the United States Press," in *The Selling of Fidel Castro: The Media and the Cuban Revolution,* ed. William E. Ratliff (New Brunswick: Transaction Books, 1987), p. 145.

29. Taber, *Fidel Castro Speeches 1984–85,* p. 125.

30. Ibid., p. 4.

31. Castro, *The World Economic and Social Crisis*, p. 212.

32. *Guardian* (New York), April 19, 1989, p. 14.

33. Michael Taber, ed., *Fidel Castro Speeches: Cuba's Internationalist Foreign Policy 1975–80* (New York: Pathfinder Press, 1981), p. 156.

34. E. Grinevich and B. Gvozdarev, *Washington Versus Havana* (Moscow: Progress Publishers, 1988), p. 47.

35. Fidel Castro, *Nothing Can Stop the Course of History*, interview by Jeffrey M. Elliot and Mervyn M. Dymally (New York: Pathfinder Press, 1986), p. 184.

36. Fidel Castro, *We Represent the Immense Majority of Humanity* (New York: Pathfinder Press, 1986), p. 35.

37. Ibid., p. 11.

38. Fernández, *Cuba's Foreign Policy*, p. 49.

39. *Militant*, October 19, 1990, p. 5.

40. *Granma Weekly Review*, December 24, 1990.

41. Ibid., March 24, 1991.

42. Ibid., March 3, 1991, p. 12.

43. Castro, *The World Economic and Social Crisis*, p. 210.

44. Erisman, *Cuba's International Relations*, pp. 30–31.

45. Castro, *The World Economic and Social Crisis*, p. 215.

46. Julie M. Feinsilver, "Cuba as a World Medical Power: The Politics of Symbolism," *Latin American Research Review* 24 (2) (1989):22–25.

47. Ibid., pp. 1–2.

48. Gabriel García Márquez, "Plying the Word," *NACLA Report on the Americas* 24 (2) (August 1990):46.

49. Feinsilver, "Cuba as a World," p. 4.

50. *Granma Weekly Review*, September 25, 1988, p. 14.

51. Speech to the National Assembly, April 4, 1989.

52. Fidel Castro, *In Defense of Socialism: Four Speeches on the 30th Anniversary of the Cuban Revolution* (New York: Pathfinder Press, 1989), p. 116.

53. *Granma Weekly Review*, February 11, 1990, p. 3.

54. Ibid.

55. *Granma Weekly Review*, March 25, 1990.

56. Fidel Castro, "Interview with CNN," June 25, 1990.

57. Fidel Castro, Speech given in Havana, December 6, 1989.

58. Ibid.

59. Fidel Castro, *Our Struggle Is That of Latin America and the Third World*. Interview with *El Día* of Mexico, June 8, 1985 (Havana: Publishing Office of the Council of State, 1985), pp. 10–11.

60. Jorge I. Domínguez, *To Make a World Safe for Revolution: Cuba's Foreign Policy* (Cambridge: Harvard University Press, 1989), p. 116.

61. See *Revolución* (Havana), December 2, 1961.

62. Fidel Castro, "Interview with Charles O. Porter," *Northwest Review* 6 (Autumn 1963):81.

63. *New York Times*, July 28, 1989.

64. Fidel Castro, "Important Problems for the Whole of International Revolutionary Thought," *New International* 6 (1987):220.

65. Tom Bottomore, *A Dictionary of Marxist Thought* (Cambridge: Harvard University Press, 1983), p. 224.

66. Caleb Rosado, "Sect and Party: Religion Under Revolution in Cuba," Doctoral Dissertation, Northwestern University, Evanston, Ill., 1985, p. 59.

67. Erisman, *Cuba's International Relations,* pp. 61–66; and James Petras, *Critical Perspectives on Imperialism and Social Class in the Third World* (New York: Monthly Review Press, 1978), pp. 2–3.

68. Sheldon B. Liss, *Roots of Revolution: Radical Thought in Cuba* (Lincoln: University of Nebraska Press, 1987), p. 196.

69. Frank Mankiewicz and Kirby Jones, *With Fidel: A Portrait of Castro* (Chicago: Playboy Press, 1975), pp. 84–85; and Max Azicri, *Cuba: Politics, Economics and Society* (London: Pinter Publishers, 1988), p. 118.

70. *Guardian* (New York), February 5, 1989, p. 11.

71. *Granma Weekly Review,* December 18, 1989, p. 5.

72. *Militant,* August 10, 1990.

73. *Granma Weekly Review,* August 28, 1988, p. 4.

74. I recall these remarks from a conversation with Mr. Bonsal at the American University, Washington, D.C., sometime during the early 1960s.

75. Smith, *The Closest of Enemies,* pp. 51–53.

76. Ibid., p. 45.

77. Taber, *Fidel Castro Speeches 1984–85,* p. 13.

78. Liss, *Roots of Revolution,* p. 197.

79. Mankiewicz and Jones, *With Fidel,* p. 205.

80. Taber, *Fidel Castro Speeches: Cuba's Internationalist,* p. 267.

81. Taber, *Fidel Castro Speeches 1984–85,* p. 149.

82. *Granma Weekly Review,* August 28, 1988, p. 2.

83. Joseph Hansen, *Dynamics of the Cuban Revolution* (New York: Pathfinder Press, 1978), p. 57.

84. Liss, *Roots of Revolution,* p. 183; and *Cuba Update,* February–March 1983, p. 8.

85. Fidel Castro, *Speeches at Three Congresses* (Havana: Editora Política, 1982), p. 14.

86. Fidel Castro, *Lenin's Ideas—Our Lodestar* (Moscow: Novosti Press Agency, 1970), pp. 20–21.

87. Domínguez, *To Make a World Safe,* p. 111.

88. Bourne, *Fidel,* p. 237.

89. Liss, *Roots of Revolution,* p. 198.

90. Ibid.

91. Louis A. Pérez, Jr., *Cuba Between Reform and Revolution* (New York: Oxford University Press, 1988), p. 377.

92. Castro, "Interview with Charles O. Porter," p. 80.

93. Castro, *Fidel Castro habla,* p. 69.

94. Sebastian Balfour, *Castro* (New York and London: Longman, 1990), p. 8, as quoted in *Granma Weekly Review,* April 16, 1989.

95. Herbert L. Matthews, *Revolution in Cuba* (New York: Charles Scribner's, 1975), p. 388.

96. Lee Lockwood, *Castro's Cuba, Cuba's Fidel* (New York: Random House, 1969), p. 357.

97. Castro, *We Represent the Immense,* p. 46.

98. *Guardian* (New York), February 27, 1989, p. 12.

99. *New York Times,* April 1, 1989.

100. George Black, "Cuba: The Revolution Toward Victory, Always But When?" *Nation* 247 (11) (October 24, 1988):374.

101. Tony Platt and Ed McCaughan, "Human Rights in Cuba: Politics and Ideology," in *Transformation and Struggle: Cuba Faces the 1990s,* ed. Sandor Halebsky, Rafael Hernández, and John Kirk (New York: Praeger, 1990), p. 11.

102. *Guardian* (New York), April 19, 1989, p. 14.

103. Fidel Castro, *Cuba Will Never Adopt Capitalist Methods* (New York: Pathfinder Press, 1988), pp. 19–20.

104. Balfour, *Castro,* p. 155.

105. Fidel Castro, Speech to the National Assembly of People's Power, April 4, 1989.

106. *Militant,* December 22, 1989, p. 3.

107. *New York Times,* July 28, 1989.

108. *Militant,* August 25, 1989, p. 10.

109. *Militant,* January 5, 1990, p. 11.

110. Fidel Castro, "Comments at Closing Rally of the First Congress of the Communist Party of Cuba," December 22, 1976, as cited in Jane Franklin, "Cuba-Angola: A Chronology 1961–1988," *Cuba Update* (Fall 1988):16–29.

111. Carlos Moore, *Castro, the Blacks and Africa* (Los Angeles: Center for Afro-American Studies, University of California, Los Angeles, 1988), pp. 323–324.

112. *Granma Weekly Review,* December 18, 1988, p. 2.

113. William LeoGrande, *Cuba's Policy in Africa, 1959–1980* (Berkeley: Institute of International Studies, University of California, Berkeley, 1980), pp. 9–10.

114. Erisman, *Cuba's International Relations,* pp. 31–32.

115. Castro, *We Represent the Immense,* p. 36.

116. Fidel Castro, *Un encuentro con Fidel: entrevista realizada por Gianni Miná* (Havana: Oficina de Publicaciones de Consejo de Estado, 1987), p. 120.

117. Ibid., pp. 118–119.

118. Castro, *Nothing Can Stop,* pp. 171–173.

119. Taber, *Fidel Castro Speeches: Cuba's Internationalist,* pp. 91–94; and Castro, *Fidel Castro habla,* p. 53.

120. Pamela S. Falk, *Cuban Foreign Policy: Caribbean Tempest* (Lexington, Mass.: D. C. Heath, 1986), pp. 83–84, 87.

121. Castro, *In Defense of Socialism,* p. 14.

122. Castro, *Nothing Can Stop,* p. 176.

123. Castro, *Un encuentro,* p. 95.

124. Moore, *Castro, the Blacks,* pp. 330–331.

Chapter 6

1. Instituto de Historia de Movimiento Comunista y de la Revolución Socialista de

Cuba, *La Revolución de Octubre y la Revolución Cubana* (Havana: Editora Política, 1987), p. 33.

2. George Black, "Cuba: The Revolution Toward Victory, Always But When?" *Nation* 247 (11) (October 24, 1988):385.

3. Fidel Castro, *The U.S. War Drive and the World Economic Crisis* (New York: Pathfinder Press, 1984), pp. 8–12.

4. Fidel Castro, *Speeches at Three Congresses* (Havana: Editora Política, 1982), p. 34.

5. *Granma Weekly Review*, September 28, 1988.

6. Michael Taber, ed., *Fidel Castro Speeches 1984–85: War and Crisis in the Americas* (New York: Pathfinder Press, 1985), p. 31.

7. Lee Lockwood, *Castro's Cuba, Cuba's Fidel* (New York: Random House, 1969), p. 218.

8. Saul Landau, "Fidel Will Be Around Awhile," *Nation* 250 (25) (June 25, 1990):885.

9. *Militant*, March 9, 1990, p. 13.

10. Fidel Castro, "Waves of the Future," in *Latin American Radicalism: A Documentary Report on Left and Nationalist Movements*, ed. Irving Louis Horowitz, Josué de Castro, and John Gerassi (New York: Random House, 1969), p. 545. Castro seeks the advice of progressive black U.S. leaders such as Jesse Jackson for insights into how power operates in the United States, a practice that has proven unreliable at times. For example, in 1985, a short time after Jackson visited Cuba, Fidel attended a gathering of Latin American heads of state in Uruguay. The Nicaraguan president, Daniel Ortega, informed Fidel that solidarity movements in the United States were successfully pressuring that nation's Congress to halt aid to the counterrevolutionaries (Contras) seeking to overthrow the Nicaraguan government. Castro told Ortega not to place so much faith in those organizations, that Jesse Jackson had told him that the real force for change in the United States was the (barely conceived and impotent) Rainbow Coalition. Ortega complied with Fidel's suggestion and cut some ties to solidarity groups that had more clout than the Rainbow Coalition. It is frightening to think that heads of state sometimes act on advice based on faith but no evidence.

11. Fidel Castro, "Interview with Charles O. Porter," *Northwest Review* 6 (Autumn 1963):81.

12. Lockwood, *Castro's Cuba*, p. 227.

13. *Granma Weekly Review*, April 27, 1990, p. 3.

14. Fidel Castro, *In Defense of Socialism: Four Speeches on the 30th Anniversary of the Cuban Revolution* (New York: Pathfinder Press, 1989), p. 6.

15. Fidel Castro, *Fidel Castro habla con Barbara Walters* (Colombia: Carlos Valencia Editores, 1977), p. 72.

16. Communist Party of Cuba, *First Congress of the Communist Party of Cuba* (Moscow: Progress Publishers, 1976), p. 33.

17. *Granma Weekly Review*, December 18, 1988, p. 2.

18. Max Azicri, *Cuba: Politics, Economics and Society* (London: Pinter Publishers, 1988), p. 211.

19. *Granma Weekly Review*, April 22, 1990.

20. Castro, *In Defense of Socialism*, pp. 3–6.

21. Lockwood, *Castro's Cuba*, p. 221.

22. Castro, *The U.S. War Drive*, p. 6.

23. Fidel Castro, *On Latin America's Unpayable Debt, Its Unforeseeable Consequences and Other Topics of Political and Historical Interest*. Interview granted to EFE News Agency (Havana: Editora Política, 1985), p. 54.

24. Castro, *In Defense of Socialism*, p. 90.

25. Castro, *On Latin America's Unpayable Debt*, p. 14.

26. Fidel Castro, "Interview with Gianni Miná on Human Rights," *Granma Weekly Review*, March 6, 1988, p. 4.

27. Fidel Castro, *Second Congress of the Communist Party of Cuba. Main Report* (Havana: Political Publishers, 1980), p. 80.

28. Michael Taber, ed., *Fidel Castro Speeches*, vol. 2, *Building Socialism in Cuba* (New York: Pathfinder Press, 1983), p. 308.

29. Martin Weinstein, ed., *Revolutionary Cuba in the World Arena* (Philadelphia: Institute for the Study of Human Issues, 1979), pp. 147–198.

30. Jorge I. Domínguez, *To Make a World Safe for Revolution: Cuba's Foreign Policy* (Cambridge: Harvard University Press, 1989), p. 248.

31. Nelson Valdés, Taperecorded talk on Castro and the Revolution, presented at conference: "Thirty Years of the Cuban Revolution: An Assessment" (Halifax, Canada, November 1–4, 1989), tape no. P. 5.

32. Fidel Castro, "Interview with Barbara Walters," *Foreign Policy* 29 (Autumn 1977):49.

33. Taber, *Fidel Castro Speeches 1984–85*, p. 100.

34. Robert F. Smith, *What Happened in Cuba? A Documentary History* (New York: Twayne Publishers, 1963), p. 294.

35. Tad Szulc, *Fidel: A Critical Portrait* (New York: William Morrow, 1986), p. 51.

36. Fidel Castro, *Un encuentro con Fidel: entrevista realizada por Gianni Miná* (Havana: Oficina de Publicaciones de Consejo de Estado, 1987), p. 79.

37. James Nelson Goodsell, ed., *Fidel Castro's Personal Revolution in Cuba 1959–1973* (New York: Knopf, 1975), p. 20.

38. Castro, "Interview with Barbara Walters," p. 49.

39. Taber, *Fidel Castro Speeches 1984–85*, p. 100.

40. *Granma Weekly Review*, August 7, 1988, p. 4.

41. Fidel Castro, *Discursos*, vol. 1 (Havana: Editorial de Ciencias Sociales, 1975), p. 13.

42. Smith, *What Happened in Cuba?* pp. 326–328.

43. Fidel Castro, *Nothing Can Stop the Course of History*, interview by Jeffrey M. Elliot and Mervyn M. Dymally (New York: Pathfinder Press, 1986), pp. 198–199.

44. Frank Mankiewicz and Kirby Jones, *With Fidel: A Portrait of Castro* (Chicago: Playboy Press, 1975), p. 173.

45. *Granma Weekly Review*, October 14, 1990, p. 2.

46. Marco Vázquez Raña, "Interview with Fidel Castro. Entrevista con Fidel Castro," *El Sol de México*, October 4, 1990.

47. Taber, *Fidel Castro Speeches 1984–85*, p. 52.

48. Castro, "Interview with Gianni Miná," p. 6.

49. Wayne S. Smith, *The Closest of Enemies: A Personal and Diplomatic Account of U.S.-Cuban Relations Since 1957* (New York: Norton, 1987), p. 213.

50. Castro, "Interview with Gianni Miná," p. 6.

51. Castro, *Fidel Castro habla,* p. 5.

52. Smith, *The Closest of Enemies,* pp. 268–270.

53. Fidel Castro, "Interview with Carla Anne Robbins, October 19, 1985," *Business Week,* November 4, 1985, p. 50.

54. Taber, *Fidel Castro Speeches 1984–85,* p. 62.

55. Mankiewicz and Jones, *With Fidel,* p. 132.

56. Castro, *Speeches at Three Congresses,* p. 31.

57. H. Michael Erisman, *Cuba's International Relations: The Anatomy of a Nationalistic Foreign Policy* (Boulder: Westview Press, 1985), pp. 160–162.

58. Castro, *Fidel Castro habla,* p. 35.

59. *New York Times Book Review,* March 3, 1991, p. 21.

60. Morris H. Morley, *Imperial State and Revolution: The United States and Cuba, 1952–1986* (London: Cambridge University Press, 1987), p. 74.

61. John P. Wallach, "Fidel Castro and the United States Press," in *The Selling of Fidel Castro: The Media and the Cuban Revolution,* ed. William E. Ratliff (New Brunswick: Transaction Books, 1987), p. 146.

62. Castro, *Fidel Castro habla,* p. 23.

63. Wallach, "Fidel Castro," p. 148.

64. Castro, *Un encuentro,* p. 53.

65. Azicri, *Cuba: Politics,* p. 212.

66. Castro, *Un encuentro,* p. 85.

67. Azicri, *Cuba: Politics,* p. 212.

68. Castro, *Speeches at Three Congresses,* p. 45.

69. Ibid., pp. 52, 64. I verified this statement in conversations with high-level Cuban sources in Havana in January 1982.

70. Castro, *Nothing Can Stop,* p. 8.

71. Castro, *Speeches at Three Congresses,* p. 35.

72. Ibid., p. 34.

73. Castro, "Interview with Gianni Miná," p. 3.

74. Fidel Castro, "Interview with Maria Shriver, February 24, 1988," *Cuba Update* 9 (1–3) (June 1988):9.

75. Castro, "Interview with Gianni Miná," p. 7.

76. *Granma Weekly Review,* June 4, 1989.

77. Castro, *Nothing Can Stop,* p. 191.

78. *Granma Weekly Review,* April 15, 1990, p. 5.

79. Castro, *Speeches at Three Congresses,* p. 62.

80. Castro, *Nothing Can Stop,* pp. 191–193.

81. Ibid.

82. *Granma Weekly Review,* October 30, 1989.

83. *Militant,* August 11, 1989, p. 22.

84. Ibid., August 1, 1989, p. 3.

85. Taber, *Fidel Castro Speeches 1984–85,* p. 142.

86. *Militant,* September 1, 1989, p. 3.

87. Ibid.

88. *Granma Weekly Review,* August 12, 1990, p. 2.

89. Smith, *The Closest of Enemies,* p. 144.

90. Ibid., p. 279.

91. Castro, *Fidel Castro habla,* p. 20.

92. Michael Taber, ed., *Fidel Castro Speeches: Cuba's Internationalist Foreign Policy 1975–80* (New York: Pathfinder Press, 1981), p. 96; and Castro, *Second Congress,* p. 115.

93. Azicri, *Cuba: Politics,* p. 210.

94. Taber, *Fidel Castro Speeches 1984–85,* p. 149.

95. Castro, *Interview with Barbara Walters,* p. 25.

96. Taber, *Fidel Castro Speeches 1984–85,* p. 4.

97. Lockwood, *Castro's Cuba,* p. 113.

98. Mankiewicz and Jones, *With Fidel,* p. 92.

99. Lockwood, *Castro's Cuba,* pp. 147–148.

100. Fidel Castro, "Interview with CNN," June 25, 1990.

101. Wallach, "Fidel Castro," p. 140.

102. Mankiewicz and Jones, *With Fidel,* p. 156.

103. Castro, "Interview with Barbara Walters," pp. 32–33.

104. Fidel Castro, *Ideología, conciencia y trabajo político: 1959–1986* (Havana: Editora Política, 1987), p. 229.

105. Medea Benjamin, "Things Fall Apart," *NACLA Report on the Americas* 24 (2) (August 1990):12–13.

106. Fidel Castro, *José Martí: el autor intelectual* (Havana: Editora Política, 1983), p. 125.

107. John Griffiths, *Castro* (London: Batsford Academic and Educational, 1981), p. 57.

108. *Granma Weekly Review,* April 8, 1990, pp. 11–12.

109. Castro, *Fidel Castro habla,* p. 64; and Fidel Castro, *We Represent the Immense Majority of Humanity* (New York: Pathfinder Press, 1986), p. 35.

110. Taber, *Fidel Castro Speeches 1984–85,* p. 181.

111. Ibid.

112. Martin Kenner and James Petras, eds., *Fidel Castro Speaks* (New York: Grove Press, 1969), p. 105.

113. Erisman, *Cuba's International Relations,* p. 22.

114. Herbert L. Matthews, *Revolution in Cuba* (New York: Charles Scribner's, 1975), p. 423.

115. Robin Blackburn, ed., *Strategy for Revolution: Essays on Latin America by Régis Debray* (New York: Monthly Review Press, 1969).

116. Fidel Castro, Osvaldo Dorticós, and Raúl Roa, *Así se derrotó al imperialismo,* vol. 1, *Preparando la defensa* (Mexico City: Siglo XXI, 1981), pp. 84–86.

117. Regino Díaz, "The Unpayable Debt: An Interview with Fidel Castro," in *Democracy in Latin America: Visions and Realities,* ed. Susanne Jonas and Nancy Stein (New York: Bergin and Garvey Publishers, 1990), p. 117.

118. Sheldon B. Liss, *Marxist Thought in Latin America* (Berkeley: University of California Press, 1984), p. 278.

119. Ibid., p. 38.

120. Ibid., p. 48.

121. Ibid., p. 93.

122. Ibid., p. 155.

123. Ibid., p. 112.

124. Ibid., p. 197.

125. Mankiewicz and Jones, *With Fidel*, p. 91. For additional material on the phenomenon, see Sheldon B. Liss, *Radical Thought in Central America* (Boulder: Westview Press, 1991), chap. 2, "Guatemala."

126. Taber, *Fidel Castro Speeches 1984–85*, p. 91.

127. Castro, "Interview with Charles O. Porter," p. 105.

128. Mankiewicz and Jones, *With Fidel*, p. 64.

129. *Militant,* March 9, 1990, pp. 14–15.

130. Taber, *Fidel Castro Speeches 1984–85*, p. 3.

131. Erisman, *Cuba's International Relations,* p. 157.

132. Castro, *Un encuentro,* p. 79.

133. Castro, Dorticós, and Roa, *Así se derrotó,* p. 66.

134. Communist Party, *First Congress,* p. 272.

135. *Granma Weekly Review,* November 13, 1988, p. 9.

136. Castro, *Second Congress,* p. 107.

137. The exchange of awards took place in Havana between October 31 and November 2, 1988, during a visit by the Mexican president.

138. *Granma International,* November 3, 1991, p. 8.

139. Ronaldo Munck, *Revolutionary Trends in Latin America* (Montreal: Center for Developing-Area Studies, McGill University Monograph Series No. 17, 1984), p. 129.

140. Fidel Castro, Speech of July 6, 1985, in *This Is the Battle for Latin America's Real Independence* (Havana: Editora Política, 1985).

141. Fidel Castro, *Meeting on the Status of Latin American and Caribbean Women* (Havana: Editora Política, 1985), p. 3.

142. Fidel Castro, *The Debt Is Not Only Unpayable But Also Uncollectible* (Havana: Editora Política, 1985), pp. 25–27.

143. Fidel Castro, *Fidel in Chile* (New York: International Publishers, 1972), pp. 42–46.

144. Taber, *Fidel Castro Speeches 1984–85*, p. xiv.

145. Mankiewicz and Jones, *With Fidel*, p. 97.

146. Sergio Roca, ed., *Socialist Cuba: Past Interpretations and Future Challenges* (Boulder: Westview Press, 1988), p. 14.

147. Díaz, "The Unpayable Debt," p. 124.

148. Taber, *Fidel Castro Speeches 1984–85*, p. 190.

149. Catherine A. Sunshine, *The Caribbean: Survival, Struggle and Sovereignty* (Washington: EPICA, 1988), p. 168.

150. Taber, *Fidel Castro Speeches 1984–85*, p. 126.

151. Ibid., p. 8.

152. Ibid., pp. 6–7.

153. Ibid., pp. 10–11.

154. Ibid., p. 7.

155. Ibid., p. 10.

156. Ibid., pp. 175–178.

157. *Cuba Update,* Winter 1989, p. 21.

158. Castro, "Interview with Carla Anne Robbins," p. 50.

159. Taber, *Fidel Castro Speeches 1984–85,* p. 111.

160. Ibid., p. 100.

161. Ibid., p. 101.

162. Ibid., p. 100.

163. Ibid., p. 16.

164. Ibid., p. 8.

165. Ibid., p. 80.

166. Ibid., p. 120.

167. Taber, *Fidel Castro Speeches: Cuba's Internationalist,* p. 297.

168. Castro, *Un encuentro,* pp. 96–97.

169. Taber, *Fidel Castro Speeches 1984–85,* p. 82.

170. Taber, *Fidel Castro Speeches: Cuba's Internationalist,* p. 320.

171. Ibid., p. 312.

172. Ibid., p. 320; Sergio Arce, *The Church and Socialism: Reflections from a Cuban Context* (New York: New York Circus Publications, 1985), pp. 195–196; and *Granma Weekly Review,* July 25, 1980.

173. Taber, *Fidel Castro Speeches: Cuba's Internationalist,* p. 320.

174. Fidel Castro, *Cuba Will Never Adopt Capitalist Methods* (New York: Pathfinder Press, 1988), p. 13.

175. *Granma Weekly Review,* August 7, 1988, p. 4.

176. Taber, *Fidel Castro Speeches 1984–85,* pp. 75–78.

177. Carla Anne Robbins, *The Cuban Threat* (New York: McGraw-Hill, 1983), p. 264.

178. Smith, *The Closest of Enemies,* p. 181.

179. Taber, *Fidel Castro Speeches 1984–85,* p. 130.

180. Fidel Castro, *Our Struggle Is That of Latin America and the Third World.* Interview with *El Día* (Mexico), June 8, 1985 (Havana: Publishing Office of the Council of State), p. 14.

181. Taber, *Fidel Castro Speeches 1984–85,* p. xviii.

182. Ibid., p. 153.

183. Ibid., p. 92.

184. Ibid., pp. 116–117.

185. Castro, *Nothing Can Stop,* pp. 133–135.

186. *Granma Weekly Review,* April 8, 1990, p. 9.

187. Medea Benjamin, "Soul Searching," *NACLA Report on the Americas* 24 (2) (August 1990):23–24.

188. Carlos Franqui, *Diary of the Cuban Revolution* (New York: Viking Press, 1980), p. 9.

189. Castro, *José Martí,* p. 125.

190. Mankiewicz and Jones, *With Fidel,* p. 196.

191. *Militant,* January 5, 1990, p. 9.

192. Sheldon B. Liss, *The Canal: Aspects of United States–Panamanian Relations* (Notre Dame: University of Notre Dame Press, 1967), pp. 97–98.

193. Fidel Castro, *This Is the Battle for Latin America's Real Independence* (Havana: Editora Política, 1985), p. 11.

194. Castro, *Nothing Can Stop,* p. 16.

195. Taber, *Fidel Castro Speeches 1984–85,* p. 212.

196. Díaz, "The Unpayable Debt," p. 13.

197. Sue Branford and Bernardo Kucinski, *The Debt Squads: The U.S., the Banks, and Latin America* (London: Zed Books, 1988), p. 1.

198. Fidel Castro, *We Represent the Immense Majority of Humanity* (New York: Pathfinder Press, 1986), p. 18.

199. Taber, *Fidel Castro Speeches 1984–85,* p. xvi; *Granma Weekly Review,* April 27, 1990, p. 3; and ibid., March 25, 1990.

200. Castro, *Our Struggle Is That of Latin America,* p. 6.

201. Castro, "Interview with Carla Anne Robbins," p. 50.

202. Fidel Castro, *The World Economic and Social Crisis* (Havana: Publishing Office of the Council of State, 1983), p. 166.

203. Carlos Tablada, *Che Guevara: Economics and Politics in the Transition to Socialism* (Sydney: Pathfinder/Pacific and Asia, 1989), p. 168.

204. Mankiewicz and Jones, *With Fidel,* p. 211.

205. Fidel Castro and Frei Betto, *Fidel and Religion: Castro Talks on Revolution and Religion with Frei Betto* (New York: Simon and Schuster, 1987), p. 297.

206. *Granma Weekly Review,* September 25, 1988, p. 16.

207. Ibid.

208. Castro and Betto, *Fidel and Religion,* p. 297.

209. Ibid., pp. 297–299.

210. Castro, *This Is the Battle,* p. 25.

211. Castro, *Our Struggle Is That of Latin America,* p. 35.

212. *Granma Weekly Review,* October 16, 1988, p. 9.

213. Ibid., September 25, 1988, p. 16.

214. Castro, *The World Economic and Social Crisis,* p. 212.

215. Díaz, "The Unpayable Debt," p. 136.

216. Castro, *Our Struggle Is That of Latin America,* pp. 3–5.

217. *Granma Weekly Review,* April 7, 1985, Special Insert, pp. 2–5.

218. Taber, *Fidel Castro Speeches 1984–85,* p. 235.

219. *Militant,* August 9, 1991, p. 11.

Chapter 7

1. Sheldon B. Liss, *Roots of Revolution: Radical Thought in Cuba* (Lincoln: University of Nebraska Press, 1987), p. 97.

2. Saul Landau, "Socialist Democracy in Cuba: An Interview with Fidel Castro," *Socialist Revolution* 1 (2) (March-April 1970):130–133.

3. Waldo Frank, *Cuba: Prophetic Island* (New York: Marzani and Munsell, 1961), p. 149.

4. Fidel Castro, Osvaldo Dorticós, and Raúl Roa, *Así se derrotó al imperialismo,* vol. 1, *Preparando la defensa* (Mexico City: Siglo XXI, 1981), p. 9.

5. Fidel Castro and Frei Betto, *Fidel and Religion: Castro Talks on Revolution and Religion with Frei Betto* (New York: Simon and Schuster, 1987), p. 280.

6. *Granma Weekly Review,* November 7, 1986, p. 1.

7. Frank Mankiewicz and Kirby Jones, *With Fidel: A Portrait of Castro* (Chicago: Playboy Press, 1975), p. 93.

8. Landau, "Socialist Democracy in Cuba," pp. 129–130.

9. Fidel Castro, *Fidel Castro habla con Barbara Walters* (Colombia: Carlos Valencia Editores, 1977), p. 36.

10. Max Azicri, *Cuba: Politics, Economics and Society* (London: Pinter Publishers, 1988), p. 118.

11. Castro, *Fidel Castro habla,* p. 36.

12. David Deutschmann and Deborah Shnookal, eds., *The Right to Dignity: Fidel Castro and the Nonaligned Movement* (Melbourne: Ocean Press, 1989), p. vii.

13. *Granma Weekly Review,* September 25, 1988.

14. Ibid., March 6, 1988, pp. 2–3.

15. Fidel Castro, *Nothing Can Stop the Course of History,* interview by Jeffrey M. Elliot and Mervyn M. Dymally (New York: Pathfinder Press, 1986), p. 200.

16. Fidel Castro, "Interview with Gianni Miná on Human Rights," *Granma Weekly Review,* March 6, 1988.

17. Ibid.; and Michael Taber, ed., *Fidel Castro Speeches 1984–85: War and Crisis in the Americas* (New York: Pathfinder Press, 1985), p. 154.

18. Castro, "Interview with Gianni Miná," p. 6.

19. Milton Fisk, "Cuban Communists Debate New Tack: Tighten the Lines or Let Them Loose," *Guardian* (New York), June 26, 1991, p. 11.

20. Castro, "Interview with Gianni Miná," p. 5.

21. Ibid., p. 4.

22. Barry Reckord, *Does Fidel Eat More Than Your Father? Conversation in Cuba* (New York: Praeger Publishers, 1971), p. 35.

23. Castro and Betto, *Fidel and Religion,* p. 289.

24. Fidel Castro, *Speeches at Three Congresses* (Havana: Editora Política, 1982), pp. 8–10.

25. Herbert L. Matthews, *Revolution in Cuba* (New York: Charles Scribner's, 1975), p. 147.

26. José Portuondo, "The Cuban Revolution and the Intellectual," *New World Review* 32 (9) (October 1964):42.

27. Fidel Castro, *Un encuentro con Fidel: entrevista realizada por Gianni Miná* (Havana: Oficina de Publicaciones de Consejo de Estado, 1987), p. 117.

28. Lee Lockwood, *Castro's Cuba, Cuba's Fidel* (New York: Random House, 1969), p. 113.

29. Mankiewicz and Jones, *With Fidel,* pp. 94–96.

30. Landau, "Socialist Democracy in Cuba," p. 132.

31. Mankiewicz and Jones, *With Fidel,* p. 236.

32. Fidel Castro, "Important Problems for the Whole of International Revolutionary Thought," *New International* 6 (1987):214–215.

33. Castro and Betto, *Fidel and Religion,* p. 29.

34. Lockwood, *Castro's Cuba,* p. 116.

35. *Granma Weekly Review,* March 25, 1990.

36. Ibid., September 25, 1988, p. 13.

37. See Sheldon B. Liss, *Marxist Thought in Latin America* (Berkeley: University of California Press, 1984), chap. 3.

38. Fidel Castro, *Fidel in Chile* (New York: International Publishers, 1972), p. 85.

39. Fidel Castro, "En la clausura del XI Seminario Nacional de Educación Media," *Cuba Socialista* 7 (2) (March-April 1987):44.

40. Theodore MacDonald, *Making a New People: Education in Revolutionary Cuba* (Vancouver: New Star Books, 1985), p. 18.

41. Caleb Rosado, "Sect and Party: Religion Under Revolution in Cuba," Doctoral Dissertation, Northwestern University, Evanston, Ill., 1985, p. 60.

42. Fidel Castro, Speech to the Seventh National Meeting of the Schools of Revolutionary Instruction, June 27, 1962.

43. Tom Bottomore, *A Dictionary of Marxist Thought* (Cambridge: Harvard University Press, 1983), p. 144.

44. Lionel Martin, *The Early Fidel: Roots of Castro's Communism* (Secaucus, N.J.: Lyle Stuart, 1978), p. 94.

45. Richard R. Fagen, *The Transformation of Political Culture in Cuba* (Stanford: Stanford University Press, 1969), p. 136.

46. John Griffiths, *Castro* (London: Bateford Academic and Educational, 1981), p. 34.

47. *Granma Weekly Review,* February 25, 1990, p. 4.

48. MacDonald, *Making a New People,* pp. 207–208.

49. *Granma Weekly Review,* August 7, 1988, p. 4.

50. Fidel Castro, *Socialismo y comunismo: un proceso único* (Mexico City: Editorial Diógenes, 1978), pp. 76–77.

51. MacDonald, *Making a New People,* p. 194.

52. Carlos Tablada, *Che Guevara: Economics and Politics in the Transition to Socialism* (Sydney: Pathfinder/Pacific and Asia, 1989), p. 71.

53. Fidel Castro, *Fidel Castro Speaks on Marxism-Leninism* (New York: Fair Play for Cuba Committee, 1961), p. 43.

54. *Granma Weekly Review,* February 25, 1990, p. 3.

55. Castro, *Fidel Castro Speaks on Marxism-Leninism,* pp. 26–27.

56. Luis Salas, *Social Control and Deviance in Cuba* (New York: Praeger, 1979), p. 185.

57. Fidel Castro, Speech, *Granma Weekly Review,* February 21, 1988, p. 3.

58. Castro, "En la clausura," p. 64.

59. Fagen, *The Transformation of Political Culture,* p. 107.

60. Ibid., p. 127.

61. Communist Party of Cuba, *First Congress of the Communist Party of Cuba* (Moscow: Progress Publishers, 1976), p. 292.

62. Liss, *Roots of Revolution,* p. 193.

63. *Granma Weekly Review,* January 4, 1976, p. 7.

64. Fidel Castro, "Waves of the Future," in *Latin American Radicalism: A Documentary Report on Left and Nationalist Movements,* ed. Irving Louis Horowitz, Josué de Castro, and John Gerassi (New York: Random House, 1969), p. 548.

65. Carlos Franqui, *Diary of the Cuban Revolution* (New York: Viking Press, 1980), p. 70.

66. Liss, *Roots of Revolution,* p. 178.

67. Ibid.

68. Fidel Castro, Speech, *Granma Weekly Review,* March 27, 1988, p. 6.

69. Ibid.

70. Rosado, "Sect and Party," p. 60.

71. Liss, *Roots of Revolution,* p. 204.

72. Alan Riding, "Revolution and the Intellectual in Latin America," *New York Times Magazine,* March 13, 1983, p. 32.

73. Ramón Bonachea, "Castro and the Intellectuals," *New Politics* 7 (Summer 1970):46–47. Fuentes also communicated his personal feelings to me in a private conversation in Akron, Ohio, in the spring of 1983.

74. *New York Times,* April 2, 1989.

75. Martin Kenner and James Petras, eds., *Fidel Castro Speaks* (New York: Grove Press, 1969), pp. 215–219.

76. Andrew Salkey, ed., *Writing in Cuba Since the Revolution* (London: Bogle-L'Overture Publications, 1977), pp. 150–151.

77. Fidel Castro, *In Defense of Socialism: Four Speeches on the 30th Anniversary of the Cuban Revolution* (New York: Pathfinder Press, 1989), p. 134.

78. Ernesto Cardenal, *In Cuba* (New York: Pathfinder Press, 1989), p. 189.

79. Donald W. Bray and Timothy F. Harding, "Cuba," in *Latin America: The Struggle with Dependency and Beyond,* ed. Ronald H. Chilcote and Joel C. Edelstein (New York: Schenkman Publishing, 1974), pp. 712–713.

80. Azicri, *Cuba, Politics,* p. 182.

81. Jan Knippers Black et al., *Area Handbook for Cuba* (Washington: Foreign Area Studies of the American University, 1976), p. 252.

82. Portuondo, "The Cuban Revolution," p. 41.

83. José Antonio Portuondo, "Literature and Society," in *Latin America in Its Literature,* ed. César Fernández Moreno, Julio Ortego, and Ivan A. Schulman (New York: Holmes and Meier, 1980), pp. 287–288.

84. Portuondo, "The Cuban Revolution," p. 37.

85. George Black, "Cuba: The Revolution Toward Victory, Always But When?" *Nation* 247 (11) (October 24, 1988):382.

86. Castro, *Fidel in Chile,* p. 235.

87. Azicri, *Cuba, Politics,* p. 182.

88. Michael Taber, ed., *Fidel Castro Speeches,* vol. 2, *Building Socialism in Cuba* (New York: Pathfinder Press 1983), pp. 70–71.

89. Cynthia McClintock, *Cuban Revolutionary Ideology and the Cuban Intellectual* (Cambridge: Center for International Studies, MIT, July 1975), pp. 36–37.

90. Abel Prieto, "Interview," *Cuba Update* 9 (1–3) (June 1988):35.

91. Roberto Fernández Retamar, "Caliban," *Casa de Las Américas* (September-October 1971), trans. in *Massachusetts Review* 15 (Winter-Spring 1974):68.

92. Fagen, *The Transformation of Political Culture,* p. 140.

93. Fidel Castro, "Words to the Intellectuals," in *Radical Perspectives in the Arts,* ed. Lee Baxandall (Baltimore: Penguin Books, 1972), p. 268.

94. Joel C. Edelstein, "The Evolution of Goals and Priorities in the Thought of Fidel Castro Ruz," Doctoral Dissertation, University of California, Riverside, 1975, p. 146.

95. Gordon K. Lewis, *Main Currents in Caribbean Thought: The Historical Evolution of Caribbean Society in Its Ideological Aspects, 1492–1900* (Baltimore: Johns Hopkins University Press, 1983), p. 292.

96. Castro, "Words to the Intellectuals," pp. 278–279.

97. Fidel Castro, *Granma Weekly Review,* December 10, 1989.

98. Tad Szulc, *Fidel: A Critical Portrait* (New York: Willliam Morrow, 1986), p. 87.

99. Fidel Castro, *La primera revolución socialista en América* (Mexico City: Siglo XXI, 1980), pp. 158–160.

100. *Granma Weekly Review,* September 24, 1989, p. 5.

101. Fidel Castro, Speech, *Granma Weekly Review,* March 27, 1988, p. 6.

102. Liss, *Marxist Thought in Latin America,* p. 245, and *Roots of Revolution,* p. 87.

103. Castro, *Fidel in Chile,* p. 19.

104. MacDonald, *Making a New People,* p. 144.

105. Fidel Castro, *The International Olympic Movement, the Serious Crisis Which Will Arise Regarding the Seoul Games in 1988 and the Only Possible Solution* (Havana: N.p., 1988), p. 5.

106. Ibid., pp. 5–6.

107. Castro, *Nothing Can Stop,* pp. 236–240.

108. Castro, *The International Olympic Movement,* p. 8.

109. Ibid., p. 3.

110. *Granma Weekly Review,* March 13, 1988.

111. Ibid., April 15, 1990, p. 4.

112. Black, "Cuba: The Revolution Toward Victory," p. 374.

Chapter 8

1. Fidel Castro, *This Is Our Line!* (Havana: Ministry of Foreign Relations, 1964), p. 10.

2. Fidel Castro, *El partido marxista-leninista* (Buenos Aires: Ediciones La Rosa Blindada, 1965), pp. 105–108.

3. Terence Cannon, *Revolutionary Cuba* (New York: Crowell, 1981), p. 64.

4. Fidel Castro, Speech, *Granma Weekly Review,* February 21, 1988, p. 3.

5. Martin Weinstein, ed., *Revolutionary Cuba in the World Arena* (Philadelphia Institute for the Study of Human Issues, 1979), p. 148.

6. Richard R. Fagen, *The Transformation of Political Culture in Cuba* (Stanford: Stanford University Press, 1969), pp. 8–11.

7. Michael Taber, ed., *Fidel Castro Speeches,* vol. 2, *Building Socialism in Cuba* (New York: Pathfinder Press, 1983), p. 84.

8. David P. Barkin and Nita R. Manitzas, eds., *Cuba: The Logic of the Revolution* (Andover, Mass.: Warner Modular Publications, 1973), m. 261–269.

9. Fidel Castro, Speech, *Granma Weekly Review,* March 27, 1988, p. 6.

10. Carlos Franqui, *Family Portrait with Fidel* (New York: Random House, 1984), p. 49.

11. *Granma Weekly Review,* August 5, 1979, p. 3.

12. Louis A. Pérez, Jr., *Cuba: Between Reform and Revolution* (New York: Oxford University Press, 1988), p. 367.

13. James O'Connor, *The Origins of Socialism in Cuba* (Ithaca: Cornell University Press, 1970), p. 133.

14. Fidel Castro and Frei Betto, *Fidel and Religion: Castro Talks on Revolution and Religion with Frei Betto* (New York: Simon and Schuster, 1987), p. 250.

15. Fidel Castro, *José Martí: el autor intelectual* (Havana: Editora Política, 1983), p. 212.

16. Medea Benjamin, Joseph Collins, and Michael Scott, *No Free Lunch: Food and Revolution in Cuba Today* (New York: Grove Press, 1986), pp. 160–161.

17. Ibid., p. 168.

18. Ibid., p. 65.

19. *Granma Weekly Review,* August 7, 1988, p. 4.

20. Fidel Castro, *Our Struggle Is That of Latin America and the Third World.* Interview with *El Día* (Mexico), June 8, 1985 (Havana: Publishing Office of the Council of State, 1985), p. 12.

21. Fidel Castro, *The World Economic and Social Crisis* (Havana: Publishing Office of the Council of State, 1983), pp. 207–211.

22. Ibid., pp. 199–207.

23. Michael Taber, ed., *Fidel Castro Speeches 1984–85: War and Crisis in the Americas* (New York: Pathfinder Press, 1985), p. 25.

24. *Granma Weekly Review,* September 25, 1988, p. 10.

25. Adolfo Gilly, *Inside the Cuban Revolution* (New York: Monthly Review Press, 1964), p. 7.

26. Jean Stubbs, *Cuba: The Test of Time* (London: Latin American Bureau, 1989), p. 15.

27. Max Azicri, *Cuba: Politics, Economics and Society* (London: Pinter Publishers, 1988), p. 160.

28. *In These Times,* May 23, 1988, p. 17.

29. Fidel Castro, *In Defense of Socialism: Four Speeches on the 30th Anniversary of the Cuban Revolution* (New York: Pathfinder Press, 1989), pp. 70–71.

30. Max Azicri, "Proceso de rectificación en Cuba," *Areíto* 7 (5–6) (July 1989):28.

31. George Black, "Cuba: The Revolution Toward Victory, Always But When?" *Nation* 247 (11) (October 24, 1988):374.

32. Carlos Tablada, *Che Guevara: Economics and Politics in the Transition to Socialism* (Sydney: Pathfinder/Pacific and Asia, 1989), p. 21.

33. Stubbs, *Cuba,* p. 52.

34. Tablada, *Che Guevara,* p. 20.

35. Ibid., pp. 22–23.

36. *Granma Weekly Review,* January 11, 1989, p. 5.

37. Ibid., March 27, 1988, p. 6.

38. Ibid., September 18, 1988, p. 3.

218   *Notes*

39. Fidel Castro, Speech, July 26, 1988.

40. *Militant,* October 13, 1989, p. 11.

41. Azicri, *Cuba: Politics,* p. 125.

42. Fidel Castro, Speech of July 26, 1967, in *The Quest for Change in Latin America,* ed. W. Raymond Duncan and James Nelson Goodsell (New York: Oxford University Press, 1970), p. 306.

43. Stubbs, *Cuba,* p. 8.

44. *Militant,* April 28, 1989, pp. 10–11.

45. Tablada, *Che Guevara,* p. 20.

46. *New York Times,* July 28, 1988.

47. *Militant,* April 28, 1989, p. 12.

48. Tablada, *Che Guevara,* p. 27.

49. *Granma Weekly Review,* November 19, 1989, p. 2.

50. Fidel Castro, *Socialismo y comunismo: un proceso único* (Mexico City: Editorial Diógenes, 1978), pp. 168–169.

51. Tom Bottomore, *A Dictionary of Marxist Thought* (Cambridge: Harvard University Press, 1983), p. 57.

52. *Militant,* August 4, 1989, p. 9.

53. Ibid., August 14, 1989, pp. 9, 11.

54. Fidel Castro, *Discursos,* vol. 2 (Havana: Editorial de Ciencias Sociales, 1975), p. 105.

55. Carlos Moore, *Castro, the Blacks, and Africa* (Los Angeles: Center for Afro-American Studies, University of California, Los Angeles, 1988), pp. 26–27.

56. Fidel Castro, *El pensamiento de Fidel Castro: selección temática, enero 1959–abril 1961,* vol. 2 (Havana: Editora Política, 1983), p. 394.

57. Moore, *Castro, the Blacks,* p. 21.

58. Castro, *El pensamiento de Fidel Castro,* vol. 2, pp. 393–395.

59. Fidel Castro, "Renewal or Death," *New International* 6 (1987):245.

60. *Granma Weekly Review,* January 11, 1976, p. 7.

61. Pamela S. Falk, *Cuban Foreign Policy: Caribbean Tempest* (Lexington, Mass.: D. C. Heath, 1986), p. 106.

62. Sergio Roca, ed., *Socialist Cuba: Past Interpretations and Future Challenges* (Boulder: Westview Press, 1988), p. 185.

63. Hugh Thomas, *The Cuban Revolution* (New York: Harper and Row, 1977), p. 655.

64. M. M. Bober, *Karl Marx's Interpretation of History* (New York: Norton, 1965), pp. 69–70.

65. *Militant,* April 25, 1989, p. 13.

66. Moore, *Castro, the Blacks,* p. 44.

67. Ibid., pp. 255–256.

68. Ibid., p. 340.

69. Castro, *El pensamiento de Fidel Castro,* vol. 2, p. 437.

70. Vilma Espín, head of the Federation of Cuban Women (FMC), stated in a public talk that I heard in Havana on June 9, 1992, that Fidel had made this statement to Nicaraguan leader Tomás Borge.

71. Communist Party of Cuba, *First Congress of the Communist Party of Cuba* (Moscow: Progress Publishers, 1976), p. 26.

72. Castro, *Discursos,* vol. 2, p. 242.

73. Sheldon B. Liss, *Roots of Revolution: Radical Thought in Cuba* (Lincoln: University of Nebraska Press, 1987), p. 49.

74. Elizabeth Stone, ed., *Women and the Cuban Revolution* (New York: Pathfinder Press, 1981), pp. 51–53.

75. Azicri, *Cuba: Politics,* p. 82.

76. Castro, "Renewal or Death," p. 242.

77. Fidel Castro, *Un encuentro con Fidel: entrevista realizada por Gianni Miná* (Havana: Oficina de Publicaciones de Consejo de Estado, 1987), p. 202.

78. Stone, *Women and the Cuban Revolution,* p. 23.

79. Ibid., p. 48.

80. Ibid., pp. 8–9.

81. Ibid., p. 48.

82. Castro, *Discursos,* vol. 2, p. 242.

83. Stone, *Women and the Cuban Revolution,* pp. 71–72.

84. Ibid., p. 27.

85. Ibid., pp. 71–72.

86. Ibid., p. 99.

87. Lowry Nelson, *Cuba: The Measure of a Revolution* (Minneapolis: University of Minnesota Press, 1972), pp. 151–152.

88. Fidel Castro, *Second Congress of the Communist Party of Cuba. Main Report* (Havana: Political Publishers, 1980), p. 61.

89. Tablada, *Che Guevara,* p. 29.

90. Castro, *Socialismo y comunismo,* p. 152.

91. Joel C. Edelstein, "The Evolution of Goals and Priorities in the Thought of Fidel Castro Ruz," Doctoral Dissertation, University of California, Riverside, 1975, p. 139.

92. Fidel Castro, Speech to the 5th Congress of the Federation of Cuban Women, March 7, 1990.

93. *Granma Weekly Review,* September 25, 1988, p. 12.

94. Sergio Arce, *The Church and Socialism: Reflections from a Cuban Context* (New York: New York Circus Publications, 1985), p. 183.

95. Thomas, *The Cuban Revolution,* p. 259.

96. Arce, *The Church and Socialism,* p. 188.

97. Ibid., p. xi.

98. Castro and Betto, *Fidel and Religion,* p. 86.

99. Ibid., p. 184.

100. Ibid., p. 244.

101. Ernesto Cardenal, *In Cuba* (New York: New Directions, 1974), p. 326.

102. John M. Kirk, *Between God and the Party: Religion and Politics in Revolutionary Cuba* (Tampa: University of South Florida Press, 1989), p. 132.

103. Sheldon B. Liss, *Marxist Thought in Latin America* (Berkeley: University of California Press, 1984), p. 136.

104. Liss, *Roots of Revolution,* p. 150.

105. Arce, *The Church and Socialism*, p. 189.

106. Castro and Betto, *Fidel and Religion*, pp. 273–274.

107. Raúl Gómez Treto, *The Church and Socialism in Cuba* (Maryknoll, N.Y.: Orbis Books, 1988), p. 139.

108. Castro and Betto, *Fidel and Religion*, p. 19.

109. Kirk, *Between God and the Party*, p. 106.

110. Castro and Betto, *Fidel and Religion*, p. 24.

111. Ibid., p. 74.

112. Ibid., p. 186.

113. Kirk, *Between God and the Party*, p. 135.

114. Castro and Betto, *Fidel and Religion*, p. 35.

115. Ibid., p. 32.

116. Caleb Rosado, "Sect and Party: Religion Under Revolution in Cuba," Doctoral Dissertation, Northwestern University, Evanston, Ill., 1985, p. 185.

117. Castro and Betto, *Fidel and Religion*, p. 268.

118. Gómez Treto, *The Church and Socialism*, p. 79.

119. Castro and Betto, *Fidel and Religion*, p. 43.

120. Ibid., p. 13.

121. Ibid., p. 277.

122. Ibid., p. 32.

123. Ibid.

124. Kirk, *Between God and the Party*, p. 117.

125. Castro and Betto, *Fidel and Religion*, p. 123.

126. Arce, *The Church and Socialism*, p. 186.

127. Kirk, *Between God and the Party*, p. 107.

128. Castro and Betto, *Fidel and Religion*, p. 245.

129. Ibid., p. 36.

130. Arce, *The Church and Socialism*, p. 190.

131. Gómez Treto, *The Church and Socialism*, p. 78.

132. Castro and Betto, *Fidel and Religion*, p. 16.

133. Ibid., p. 265.

134. *Granma Weekly Review*, April 8, 1990, p. 8.

135. Ibid., March 25, 1990, p. 11.

136. Ibid., July 9, 1989, p. 4.

137. Castro and Betto, *Fidel and Religion*, p. 17.

138. Gómez Treto, *The Church and Socialism*, p. ix.

139. Milagros Oliva, "U.S. Cardinal O'Connor Visits Cuba," *Granma Weekly Review*, May 1, 1988, p. 9.

140. James Nelson Goodsell, ed., *Fidel Castro's Personal Revolution in Cuba 1959–1973* (New York: Knopf, 1975), p. 9.

141. Kirk, *Between God and the Party*, p. 130.

142. Liss, *Marxist Thought in Latin America*, pp. 283–285.

143. Castro and Betto, *Fidel and Religion*, pp. 275–276.

144. Ibid., p. 19.

145. Arce, *The Church and Socialism*, p. xxi.

146. Castro and Betto, *Fidel and Religion*, p. 276.
147. Ibid., p. 18.
148. Ibid., p. 224.
149. Ibid., p. 221.
150. Ibid., p. 33.
151. Gómez Treto, *The Church and Socialism*, p. 93.
152. K. S. Karol, *Guerrillas in Power* (New York: Hill and Wang, 1970), p. 185.
153. Rosado, "Sect and Party," p. 280.
154. Castro and Betto, *Fidel and Religion*, p. 245.
155. Liss, *Marxist Thought in Latin America*, p. 283.
156. Alice L. Hageman and Philip E. Wheaton, eds., *Religion in Cuba Today: A New Church in a New Society* (New York: Association Press, 1971), pp. 138–139.
157. Margaret E. Crahan, "Cuba: Religion and Revolutionary Institutionalization," in *Socialist Cuba: Past Interpretations and Future Challenges*, ed. Sergio G. Roca (Boulder: Westview Press, 1988), pp. 223–224.
158. Castro and Betto, *Fidel and Religion*, p. 26.
159. Ibid., p. 34.
160. Ibid., p. 214.
161. Ibid., p. 22.
162. Ibid., p. 119.

Chapter 9

1. Peter G. Bourne, *Fidel: A Biography of Fidel Castro* (New York: Dodd, Mead, 1986), p. 99.
2. Nelson P. Valdés, "Revolution and Paradigms: A Critical Assessment of Cuban Studies," in *Cuban Political Economy: Controversies in Cubanology,* ed. Andrew Zimbalist (Boulder: Westview Press, 1988), p. 202.
3. Herbert L. Matthews, *Revolution in Cuba* (New York: Charles Scribner's, 1975), pp. 12–13.
4. Janette Habel, *Cuba: The Revolution in Peril* (London: Verso, 1991), p. 107.
5. Michael Löwy, *The Marxism of Che Guevara: Philosophy, Economics and Revolutionary Warfare* (New York: Monthly Review Press, 1973), pp. 15–17.
6. *Granma Weekly Review,* October 14, 1990, p. 2.
7. Fidel Castro and Frei Betto, *Fidel and Religion: Castro Talks on Revolution and Religion with Frei Betto* (New York: Simon and Schuster, 1987), p. 289.
8. Max Azicri, "Twenty-six Years of Cuban Revolutionary Politics: An Appraisal," in *Democracy in Latin America: Visions and Realities,* ed. Susanne Jonas and Nancy Stein (New York: Bergin and Garvey, 1990), p. 149.
9. James O'Connor, *The Origins of Socialism in Cuba* (Ithaca: Cornell University Press, 1970), p. 11.
10. *Granma Weekly Review,* September 25, 1988, p. 14.
11. *Militant,* April 28, 1988, p. 10.
12. Sheldon B. Liss, *Marxist Thought in Latin America* (Berkeley: University of California Press, 1984), p. 278.

13. Michael Taber, ed., *Fidel Castro Speeches 1984–85: War and Crisis in the Americas* (New York: Pathfinder Press, 1985), p. 2.

14. Fidel Castro, "Interview with Carla Anne Robbins, October 19, 1985," *Business Week*, November 4, 1985, p. 50.

15. Fidel Castro, "CNN Interview," June 25, 1990.

16. Valdés, "Revolution and Paradigms," p. 207.

17. Michael Albert and Robin Hahnel, "Cuba Si?" *Z Magazine* 3 (6) (June 1990):34–35.

18. Valdés, "Revolution and Paradigms," p. 198.

19. Arthur MacEwan, *Revolution and Economic Development in Cuba* (New York: St. Martin's Press, 1981), p. 160.

20. Michael Taber, ed., *Fidel Castro Speeches,* vol. 2, *Building Socialism in Cuba* (New York: Pathfinder Press, 1983), p. 75.

21. Fidel Castro, *Cuba Will Never Adopt Capitalist Methods* (New York: Pathfinder Press, 1988), p. 17.

22. Habel, *Cuba,* p. 198.

23. Ibid., p. 214.

24. *Militant,* December 22, 1989, p. 3.

25. Candice Hughes, "Cubans Teach That Communism Can Be Fun for Young," *Cleveland Plain Dealer,* March 14, 1991, p. 8F.

26. Ibid.

27. Nelson Valdés, Taperecorded talk on Castro and the Revolution, presented at conference: "Thirty Years of the Cuban Revolution: An Assessment," Halifax, Canada (November 1–4, 1989), Tape no. P. 5.

28. Saul Landau, "Fidel Will Be Around Awhile," *Nation* 250 (25) (June 25, 1990):886.

29. Fidel Castro, *Un encuentro con Fidel: entrevista realizada por Gianni Miná* (Havana: Oficina de Publicaciones de Consejo de Estado, 1987), pp. 164–166.

30. Habel, *Cuba,* p. 112.

31. Ibid., p. 195.

32. *Militant,* April 22, 1991, p. 2.

33. Castro, *Un encuentro,* p. 184.

34. Milton Fisk, "Cuban Communists Debate New Tack: Tighten the Lines or Let Them Loose," *Guardian* (New York), June 26, 1991, p. 10.

35. *Granma International,* November 3, 1991, p. 10.

36. Valdés, Taperecorded talk on Castro.

37. Mirta Aguirre, Denia García Ronda, and Isabel Monal, "El leninismo en la historia me absolverá," *Casa de Las Américas,* November 16, 1975, p. 85.

38. Fidel Castro, *On Latin America's Unpayable Debt, Its Unforeseeable Consequences and Other Topics of Political and Historical Interest.* Interview granted to EFE News Agency (Havana: Editora Política, 1985), p. 67.

39. Fidel Castro, *Fidel in Chile* (New York: International Publishers, 1972), p. 115.

Bibliography

Aguirre, Mirta, Denia García Ronda, and Isabel Monal. "El leninismo en la historia me absolverá." *Casa de Las Américas,* November 16, 1975, pp. 64–85.

Albert, Michael, and Robin Hahnel. "Cuba Si?" *Z Magazine* 3 (6) (June 1990):34–36.

_____. *Socialism Today and Tomorrow.* Boston: South End Press, 1981.

Arce, Sergio. *The Church and Socialism: Reflections from a Cuban Context.* New York: New York Circus Publications, 1985.

Azicri, Max. *Cuba: Politics, Economics and Society.* London: Pinter Publishers, 1988.

_____. "Proceso de rectificación en Cuba." *Areíto* 7 (5–6) (July 1989):28–30.

_____. "Twenty-six Years of Cuban Revolutionary Politics: An Appraisal." In *Democracy in Latin America: Visions and Realities.* Susanne Jonas and Nancy Stein, eds. New York: Bergin and Garvey, 1990.

Balfour, Sebastian. *Castro.* New York: Longman, 1990.

Bambirra, Vania. *La revolución cubana: una reinterpretación.* Mexico City: Editorial Nuestro Tiempo, 1974.

Barkin, David P., and Nita R. Manitzas, eds. *Cuba: The Logic of the Revolution.* Andover, Mass.: Warner Modular Publications, 1973.

Barnes, Jack, and Fidel Castro. *Twenty Years of the Cuban Revolution, and Selected Speeches of Fidel Castro.* New York: National Education Department–Socialist Workers Party, April 1979.

Bender, Lynn Darrell. *The Politics of Hostility: Castro's Revolution and United States Policy.* Hato Rey, Puerto Rico: Inter-American University Press, 1975.

Bengelsdorf, Carolee. "On the Problem of Studying Women in Cuba." In *Cuban Political Economy: Controversies in Cubanology.* Andrew Zimbalist, ed. Boulder: Westview Press, 1988.

Benjamin, Jules R. *The United States and the Origins of the Cuban Revolution: An Empire of Liberty in an Age of National Liberation.* Princeton: Princeton University Press, 1990.

Benjamin, Medea. "Soul Searching." *NACLA Report on the Americas* 24 (2) (August 1990):23–31.

_____. "Things Fall Apart." *NACLA Report on the Americas* 24 (2) (August 1990):12–22.

Benjamin, Medea, Joseph Collins, and Michael Scott. *No Free Lunch: Food and Revolution in Cuba Today.* New York: Grove Press, 1986.

Bernardo, Robert M. *The Theory of Moral Incentives in Cuba.* University: University of Alabama Press, 1971.

Black, George. "Cuba: The Revolution Toward Victory, Always But When?" *Nation* 247 (11) (October 24, 1988):373–386.

Black, Jan Knippers, et al. *Area Handbook for Cuba.* Washington: Foreign Area Studies of the American University, 1976.

Blackburn, Robin, ed. *Strategy for Revolution: Essays on Latin America by Régis Debray.* New York: Monthly Review Press, 1969.

Blanksten, George I. "Fidel Castro and Latin America." In *Latin American Politics.* Robert D. Tomasek, ed. Garden City, N.Y.: Anchor Books, 1966.

Blasier, Cole. *The Giant's Rival: The U.S.S.R. and Latin America.* Pittsburgh: University of Pittsburgh Press, 1983.

Bober, M. M. *Karl Marx's Interpretation of History.* New York: Norton, 1965.

Bonachea, Ramón. "Castro and the Intellectuals." *New Politics* 7 (Summer 1970):45–50.

Bonachea, Ramón, and Marta San Martín. *The Cuban Insurrection 1952–1959.* New Brunswick: Transaction Books, 1974.

Bonachea, Rolando E., and Nelson P. Valdés, eds. *Cuba in Revolution.* Garden City, N.Y.: Anchor Doubleday, 1972.

––––––– . *Revolutionary Struggle 1947–1958: The Selected Works of Fidel Castro.* Cambridge: MIT Press, 1972.

Bonsal, Philip W. *Cuba, Castro and the United States.* Pittsburgh: University of Pittsburgh Press, 1971.

Boorstein, Edward. *The Economic Transformation of Cuba.* New York: Monthly Review Press, 1968.

Borge, Tomás. "An Interview with Fidel Castro." *Guardian* (Manchester, England). May 30, 1992.

Bottomore, Tom. *A Dictionary of Marxist Thought.* Cambridge: Harvard University Press, 1983.

––––––– . *Sociology and Socialism.* New York: St. Martin's Press, 1984.

Bourne, Peter G. *Fidel: A Biography of Fidel Castro.* New York: Dodd, Mead, 1986.

Branford, Sue, and Bernardo Kucinski. *The Debt Squads: The U.S., the Banks, and Latin America.* London: Zed Books, 1988.

Bray, Donald W., and Timothy F. Harding. "Cuba." In *Latin America: The Struggle with Dependency and Beyond.* Ronald H. Chilcote and Joel C. Edelstein, eds. New York: Schenkman Publishing, 1974.

Brenner, Philip, William M. LeoGrande, Donna Rich, and Daniel Siegal. *The Cuba Reader: The Making of a Revolutionary Society.* New York: Grove Press, 1989.

Cannon, Terence. *Revolutionary Cuba.* New York: Crowell, 1981.

Cardenal, Ernesto. *In Cuba.* New York: New Directions, 1974.

Castro, Fidel. *An Interview for NBC.* Havana: Editora Política, 1988.

––––––– . *Can Cuba Survive?* Melbourne: Ocean Press, 1992.

––––––– . *Ciencia, tecnología y sociedad 1959–1989.* Havana: Editora Política, 1990.

––––––– . *Conversaciones con periodistas norteamericanos y franceses.* Havana: Editora Política, 1983.

––––––– . "Convertiremos este revés en victoria." *Perspectiva Mundial* 13 (8) (September 1989):10–32.

––––––– . *Cuba: A Trench of Ideas.* Havana: José Martí Publishing House, 1990.

_____. *Cuba Cannot Export Revolution, Nor Can the United States Prevent It.* Speech, Santiago de Cuba, January 1, 1984. Havana: Editora Política, 1984.

_____. *Cuba Will Never Adopt Capitalist Methods.* Speech of July 26, 1988. New York: Pathfinder Press, 1988.

_____. *De los recuerdos de Fidel Castro, el Bogotazo y Hemingway, entrevistas.* Havana: Editora Política, 1984.

_____. "Discurso de Fidel: XI Seminario Naciónal, de Educación Media." *Educación* 17 (65) (June-July 1987):3–29.

_____. *Discursos.* 2 vols. Havana: Editorial de Ciencias Sociales, 1975.

_____. *El partido marxista-leninista.* Buenos Aires: Ediciones La Rosa Blindada, 1965.

_____. *El pensamiento de Fidel Castro: selección temática, enero 1959–abril 1961.* 2 vols. Havana: Editora Política, 1983.

_____. *El socialismo si puede resolver problemas.* Havana: Editora Política, 1991.

_____. "En la clausura del XI Seminario Nacional de Educación Media." *Cuba Socialista* 7 (2) (March-April 1987):43–65.

_____. "En la reunión informativa del Comité Provincial del partido de Cuidad de La Habana." *Cuba Socialista* 7 (2) (June 1987):1–42.

_____. *En la trinchera de la revolución: selección de discursos.* Havana: Editora Política, 1990.

_____. *Esta es la guerra de David contra Goliat.* Havana: Editora Política, 1990.

_____. *Fidel Castro Denounces Sectarianism.* Speech of March 26, 1962. Havana: Ministry of Foreign Relations, 1962.

_____. *Fidel Castro habla con Barbara Walters.* Colombia: Carlos Valencia Editores, 1977.

_____. *Fidel Castro on Chile.* New York: Pathfinder Press, 1982.

_____. *Fidel Castro Speaks on Marxism-Leninism.* New York: Fair Play for Cuba Committee, 1961.

_____. *Fidel en Brasil: selección de intervenciones.* Havana: Editora Política, 1990.

_____. *Fidel in Chile.* New York: International Publishers, 1972.

_____. *Hacia una gran patria Común.* Havana: Editora Política, 1991.

_____. *Hay solo una opción: ¡La patriá, la Revolución y el socialismo!* Havana: Editora Política, 1991.

_____. "I Am a Marxist-Leninist." In *Models of Political Change in Latin America.* Paul E. Sigmund, ed. New York: Praeger, 1970.

_____. *Ideología, conciencia y trabajo político: 1959–1986.* Havana: Editora Política, 1987.

_____. "Important Problems for the Whole of International Revolutionary Thought." Speech to the Deferred Session of the Third Congress of the Communist Party of Cuba, December 2, 1986. *New International* 6 (1987):209–238.

_____. *In Defense of Socialism: Four Speeches on the 30th Anniversary of the Cuban Revolution.* New York: Pathfinder Press, 1989.

_____. "Interview with ABC Television." *I. F. Stone's Bi-Weekly,* May 27, 1963, pp. 3–6.

_____. "Interview with Barbara Walters." *Foreign Policy* 29 (Autumn 1977):22–51.

————. "Interview with Carla Anne Robbins, October 19, 1985." *Business Week*, November 4, 1985, p. 50.

————. "Interview with Charles O. Porter." *Northwest Review* 6 (Autumn 1963):73–110.

————. "Interview with Gianni Miná on Human Rights." *Granma Weekly Review*, March 6, 1988.

————. "Interview with Maria Shriver." February 24, 1988. As noted in *Cuba Update* 9 (1–3) (June 1988):9.

————. *In the Trench of the Revolution*. Havana: José Martí Publishing House, 1990.

————. *José Martí: el autor intelectual*. Havana: Editora Política, 1983.

————. *La cuestión alimentaria, prioridad uno*. Havana: Editora Política, 1991.

————. *La dueda externa*. Havana: Editora Política, 1989.

————. *La primera revolución socialista en América*. Mexico City: Siglo XXI, 1980.

————. *La Revolución Cubana*. Mexico City: Ediciones Era, 1979.

————. *La Revolución Cubana una proeza extraordinaria*. Havana: Editora Política, 1988.

————. *Lenin's Ideas—Our Lodestar*. Moscow: Novosti Press Agency, 1970.

————. *Los derechos humanos 1959–1980*. Havana: Editora Política, 1989.

————. *Meeting on the Status of Latin American and Caribbean Women*. Speech of June 7, 1985. Havana: Editora Política, 1985.

————. *Nothing Can Stop the Course of History*. Interview by Jeffrey M. Elliot and Mervyn M. Dymally. New York: Pathfinder Press, 1986.

————. *Nuestra causa y nuestra pueblo triunfarán*. Havana: Editora Política, 1991.

————. *On Latin America's Unpayable Debt, Its Unforeseeable Consequences and Other Topics of Political and Historical Interest*. Interview granted to EFE News Agency. Havana: Editora Política, 1985.

————. *Our Struggle Is That of Latin America and the Third World*. Interview with *El Día* (Mexico), June 8, 1985. Havana: Publishing Office of the Council of State, 1985.

————. *Political, Economic, and Social Thought of Fidel Castro*. Havana: Editorial Lex, 1959.

————. *Por el camino correcto*. Havana: Editora Política, 1988.

————. *Presente y futuro de Cuba: entrevista concedida a la revista Siempre!* Havana: Oficina de Pubicaciones del consejo de Estado, 1991.

————. *Rectificación: selección temática sobre el proceso de rectificación en Cuba 1986–1990*. Havana: Editora Política, 1990.

————. "Renewal or Death." Speech to Communist Party of Cuba, Third Congress, February 7, 1986. *New International* 6 (1987):239–253.

————. *Second Congress of the Communist Party of Cuba. Main Report*. Havana: Political Publishers, 1980.

————. *Socialismo y comunismo: un proceso único*. Mexico City: Editorial Diógenes, 1978.

————. Speech. In *Granma Weekly Review*, December 6, 1987, p. 12.

————. Speech. In *Granma Weekly Review*, February 21, 1988.

————. Speech. In *Granma Weekly Review*, March 27, 1988.

————. Speech. In *Granma Weekly Review*, September 13, 1987.

_____ . Speech of August 10, 1967. In *The Quest for Change in Latin America*. W. Raymond Duncan and James Nelson Goodsell, eds. New York: Oxford University Press, 1970.

_____ . Speech of July 26, 1967. In *The Quest for Change in Latin America*. W. Raymond Duncan and James Nelson Goodsell, eds. New York: Oxford University Press, 1970.

_____ . *Speeches at Three Congresses*. Havana: Editora Política, 1982.

_____ . *The Debt Is Not Only Unpayable but Also Uncollectible*. Havana: Editora Política, 1985.

_____ . *The International Olympic Movement, the Serious Crisis Which Will Arise Regarding the Seoul Games in 1988 and the Only Possible Solution*. Havana: N.p., 1985.

_____ . *The Rectification Process Is Not Something New*. Havana: José Martí Publishing House, 1990.

_____ . *The U.S. War Drive and the World Economic Crisis*. New York: Pathfinder Press, 1984.

_____ . *The World Economic and Social Crisis*. Havana: Publishing Office of the Council of State, 1983.

_____ . *This Is Our Line!* Havana: Ministry of Foreign Relations, 1964.

_____ . *This Is the Battle for Latin America's Real Independence*. Havana: Editora Política, 1985.

_____ . *This Must Be an Economic War of All the People*. Havana: Editora Política, 1985.

_____ . *Un encuentro con Fidel: entrevista realizada por Gianni Miná*. Havana: Oficina de Publicaciones de Consejo de Estado, 1987.

_____ . *Una batalla de ideas que se transforman en frutos*. Havana: Editora Política, 1987.

_____ . *Unidos en una sola causa bajo una sola bandera*. Havana: Editora Política, 1991.

_____ . "Venceremos." *Defensa de Cuba*, June 27, 1960, pp. 169–223.

_____ . "Waves of the Future." In *Latin American Radicalism: A Documentary Report on Left and Nationalist Movements*. Irving Louis Horowitz, Josué de Castro, and John Gerassi, eds. New York: Random House, 1969.

_____ . *We Represent the Immense Majority of Humanity*. New York: Pathfinder Press, 1986.

_____ . *We Will Never Kneel*. Havana: José Martí Publishing House, 1990.

_____ . "Words to the Intellectuals." In *Radical Perspectives in the Arts*. Lee Baxandall, ed. Baltimore: Penguin Books, 1972.

Castro, Fidel, and Álvaro Prendes. *Así se derrotó al imperialismo*. Vol. 2, *El combate y la victoria*. Mexico City: Siglo XXI, 1978.

Castro, Fidel, and Che Guevara. *To Speak the Truth: Why Washington's Cold War Against Cuba Doesn't End*. New York: Pathfinder Press, 1992.

Castro, Fidel, and Frei Betto. *Fidel and Religion: Castro Talks on Revolution and Religion with Frei Betto*. New York: Simon and Schuster, 1987.

Castro, Fidel, Osvaldo Dorticós, and Raúl Roa. *Así se derrotó al imperialismo*. Vol. 1, *Preparando la defensa*. Mexico City: Siglo XXI, 1981.

Castro, Fidel, and Ricardo Alarcón. *U.S. Hands Off the Mideast: Cuba Speaks Out at the United Nations*. New York: Pathfinder Press, 1990.

Centro de Estudios Sobre América, ed. *The Cuban Revolution into the 1990s*. Boulder: Westview Press, 1992.

Chilcote, Ronald H., and Joel C. Edelstein, eds. *Latin America: The Struggle with Dependency and Beyond*. New York: Schenkman Publishing, 1974.

Chilcote, Ronald H., and Sheryl Lutjens, eds. *Cuba: 1953–1978: A Bibliographic Guide to the Literature*. 2 vols. White Plains, N.Y.: Kraus International, 1986.

Childs, David. *Marx and the Marxists*. London: Ernest Benn, 1973.

Communist Party of Cuba. *First Congress of the Communist Party of Cuba*. Moscow: Progress Publishers, 1976.

Cort, John C. *Christian Socialism*. Maryknoll, N.Y.: Orbis Books, 1988.

Crahan, Margaret E. "Cuba: Religion and Revolutionary Institutionalization." In *Socialist Cuba: Past Interpretations and Future Challenges*. Sergio G. Roca, ed. Boulder: Westview Press, 1988.

———. "Salvation Through Christ or Marx: Religion in Revolutionary Cuba." In *Churches and Politics in Latin America*. Daniel H. Levene, ed. Beverly Hills: Sage Publications, 1980.

Cuba. Ministerio de Relaciones Exteriores. *The Revolution and Cultural Problems in Cuba*. Havana: Ministry of Foreign Relations, 1962.

D'Angelo, Edward, ed. *Cuban and North American Marxism*. Amsterdam: B. R. Grüner, 1984.

Davis, Harold Eugene. *Latin American Thought: A Historical Introduction*. New York: Free Press, 1974.

———. *Revolutionaries, Traditionalists, and Dictators in Latin America*. New York: Cooper Square Publishers, 1973.

Debray, Régis. *Revolution in the Revolution?* New York: Grove Press, 1967.

Deutschmann, David, ed. *Changing the History of Africa: Angola and Namibia*. Melbourne: Ocean Press, 1989.

———. *Che Guevara: A New Society. Reflections for Today's World*. Melbourne: Ocean Press, 1991.

Deutschmann, David, and Deborah Shnookal, eds. *The Right to Dignity: Fidel Castro and the Nonaligned Movement*. Melbourne: Ocean Press, 1989.

Dewart, Leslie. *Christianity and Revolution: The Lesson of Cuba*. New York: Herder and Herder, 1963.

Díaz, Regino. "The Unpayable Debt: An Interview with Fidel Castro." In *Democracy in Latin America: Visions and Realities*. Susanne Jonas and Nancy Stein, eds. New York: Bergin and Garvey Publishers, 1990.

Dolan, Edward F., Jr., and Margaret M. Seariano. *Cuba and the United States: Troubled Neighbors*. New York: Franklin Watts, 1987.

Dolgoff, Sam. *The Cuban Revolution: A Critical Perspective*. Montreal: Black Rose Books, 1976.

Domínguez, Jorge I. *Cuba: Order and Revolution*. Cambridge: Harvard University Press, 1978.

———. *To Make a World Safe for Revolution: Cuba's Foreign Policy*. Cambridge: Harvard University Press, 1989.

Domínguez, Jorge, and Rafael Hernández, eds. *U.S.-Cuban Relations in the 1990s.* Boulder: Westview Press, 1989.

Draper, Theodore. *Castroism: Theory and Practice.* New York: Praeger, 1965.

Dumont, René. *Cuba: Socialism and Development.* New York: Grove Press, 1970.

Eckstein, Susan. "Capitalist Constraints on Cuban Socialist Development." *Comparative Politics* 12 (3) (April 1980):253–274.

_____. "Structural and Ideological Bases of Cuba's Overseas Programs." *Politics and Society* 11 (1) (1982):95–121.

Edelstein, Joel C. "Economic Policy and Development Models." In *Cuba: Twenty-five Years of Revolution 1959 to 1984.* Sandor Halebsky and John M. Kirk, eds. New York: Praeger, 1985.

_____. "The Evolution of Goals and Priorities in the Thought of Fidel Castro Ruz." Doctoral Dissertation, University of California, Riverside, 1975.

Edwards, Jorge. *Persona non grata.* Barcelona: Editorial Seix Barral, 1982.

Erisman, H. Michael. *Cuba's International Relations: The Anatomy of a Nationalistic Foreign Policy.* Boulder: Westview Press, 1985.

Fagen, Richard R. *The Transformation of Political Culture in Cuba.* Stanford: Stanford University Press, 1969.

Falk, Pamela S. *Cuban Foreign Policy: Caribbean Tempest.* Lexington, Mass.: D. C. Heath, 1986.

Farber, Samuel. *Revolution and Reaction in Cuba, 1933–1960: A Political Sociology from Machado to Castro.* Middletown, Conn.: Wesleyan University Press, 1976.

Feinsilver, Julie M. "Cuba as a World Medical Power: The Politics of Symbolism." *Latin American Research Review* 24 (2) (1989):1–34.

Fernández, Damián J. *Cuba's Foreign Policy in the Middle East.* Boulder: Westview Press, 1988.

Fernández Retamar, Roberto. "Caliban." *Casa de Las Américas* (September-October 1971). Translated in *Massachusetts Review* 15 (Winter-Spring 1974).

Fisk, Milton. "Cuban Communists Debate New Tack: Tighten the Lines or Let Them Loose." *Guardian* (New York), June 26, 1991, pp. 10–11.

Fitzgerald, Frank T. *Managing Socialism: From Old Cadres to New Professionals in Revolutionary Cuba.* New York: Praeger, 1990.

_____. "The Direction of Cuban Socialism: A Critique of the Sovietization Thesis." In *Contemporary Caribbean: A Sociological Reader.* Vol. 2. Susan Craig, ed. Maracus, Trinidad and Tobago: Susan Craig, 1982.

Flacks, Richard. *Making History: The Radical Tradition in American Life.* New York: Columbia University Press, 1988.

Frank, Marc. *Cuba Looks to the Year 2000.* New York: International Publishers, 1993.

Frank, Waldo. *Cuba: Prophetic Island.* New York: Marzani and Munsell, 1961.

Franklin, Jane. "Cuba-Angola: A Chronology 1961–1988." *Cuba Update,* Fall 1988, pp. 16–29.

_____. "New York's Cardinal O'Connor Visits Cuba." *Cuba Update* 9 (1–3) (June 1988).

_____. *The Cuban Revolution and the United States: A Chronological History.* Melbourne: Ocean Press, 1992.

Franqui, Carlos. *Diary of the Cuban Revolution.* New York: Viking Press, 1980.

————. *Family Portrait with Fidel.* New York: Random House, 1984.

Fusco, Coco. "Drawing New Lives." *Nation* 247 (11) (October 24, 1988):397–400.

García Márquez, Gabriel. "Fidel, el oficio de la palabra." *Areíto* 2 (56) (July 1989):14–20.

————. "Plying the Word." *NACLA Report on the Americas* 24 (2) (August 1990):40–46.

Gerassi, John. *Fidel Castro: A Biography.* Garden City, N.Y.: Doubleday, 1973.

Geyer, Georgie Anne. *Guerrilla Prince: The Untold Story of Fidel Castro.* Boston: Little, Brown, 1991.

Gil, Federico G. "Antecedents of the Cuban Revolution." *Centennial Review* 5 (3) (Summer 1962):373–393.

Gilly, Adolfo. *Inside the Cuban Revolution.* New York: Monthly Press Review, 1964.

Goldenberg, Boris. "Radicalization of a Latin American State: The Establishment of Communism in Cuba." In *The Anatomy of Communist Takeovers.* Thomas T. Hammond, ed. New Haven: Yale University Press, 1975.

————. *The Cuban Revolution and Latin America.* New York: Praeger Publishers, 1966.

Gómez Treto, Raúl. *The Church and Socialism in Cuba.* Maryknoll, N.Y.: Orbis Books, 1988.

González, Edward. *Cuba Under Castro: The Limits of Charisma.* Boston: Houghton Mifflin, 1974.

Goodsell, James Nelson, ed. *Fidel Castro's Personal Revolution in Cuba 1959–1973.* New York: Knopf, 1975.

Gray, Richard Butler. *José Martí, Cuban Patriot.* Gainesville: University of Florida Press, 1962.

Green, Gil. *Cuba at 25: The Continuing Revolution.* New York: International Publishers, 1983.

————. *Revolution Cuban Style.* New York: International Publishers, 1970.

Griffiths, John. *Castro.* London: Batsford Academic and Educational, 1981.

Grinevich, E., and B. Gvozdarev. *Washington Versus Havana.* Moscow: Progress Publishers, 1988.

Habel, Janette. *Cuba: The Revolution in Peril.* London: Verso, 1991.

Hageman, Alice L., and Philip E. Wheaton, eds. *Religion in Cuba Today: A New Church in a New Society.* New York: Association Press, 1971.

Halebsky, Sandor, and John M. Kirk, eds. *Cuba in Transition: Crisis and Transformation.* Boulder: Westview Press, 1992.

————. *Cuba: Twenty-five Years of Revolution 1959 to 1984.* New York: Praeger, 1985.

Halebsky, Sandor, John M. Kirk, and Rafael Hernández, eds. *Transformation and Struggle: Cuba Faces the 1990s.* New York: Praeger, 1990.

Halperin, Maurice. *The Rise and Decline of Fidel Castro.* Berkeley: University of California Press, 1974.

————. *The Taming of Fidel Castro.* Berkeley: University of California Press, 1981.

Hansen, Joseph. *Dynamics of the Cuban Revolution.* New York: Pathfinder Press, 1978.

————. "Ideology of the Cuban Revolution." *International Socialist Review,* Summer 1960, pp. 74–78.

_____. *The Leninist Strategy of Party Building: The Debate on Guerrilla Warfare in Latin America.* New York: Pathfinder Press, 1979.

Harnecker, Marta. *Fidel Castro's Political Strategy: From Moncada to Victory.* New York: Pathfinder Press, 1987.

_____, ed. *Cuba: Dictatorship or Democracy?* Westport, Conn.: Lawrence Hill, 1980.

Harrington, Michael. *The Twilight of Capitalism.* New York: Simon and Schuster, 1976.

Harris, Richard L. *Marxism, Socialism, and Democracy in Latin America.* Boulder: Westview Press, 1992.

Hart Dávalos, Armando. *Changing the Rules of the Game.* Havana: Letras Cubanas, 1983.

Heilbroner, Robert L. *Marxism: For and Against.* New York: Norton, 1980.

Hennessy, C.A.M. "The Roots of Cuban Nationalism." *International Affairs* (London) 39 (3) (July 1963).

Hodges, Donald C. *The Latin American Revolution: Politics and Strategy from Apro-Marxism to Guevarism.* New York: William Morrow, 1974.

_____, ed. *The Legacy of Che Guevara: A Documentary Study.* London: Thames and Hudson, 1977.

Holt-Seeland, Inger. *Women of Cuba.* Westport, Conn.: Lawrence Hill, 1981.

Horowitz, Irving Louis, ed. *Cuban Communism.* New Brunswick: Transaction Books, 1977.

Huberman, Leo, and Paul M. Sweezy. *Socialism in Cuba.* New York: Monthly Review Press, 1969.

Hughes, Candice. "Cubans Teach That Communism Can Be Fun for Young." *Cleveland Plain Dealer,* March 14, 1991, p. 8F.

Instituto Cubano del Libro. *Pensamiento revolucionario cubano.* Havana: Editorial Ciencias Sociales, 1971.

Instituto de Historia de Movimiento Comunista y de la Revolución Socialista de Cuba. *La Revolución de Octubre y la Revolución Cubana.* Havana: Editora Política, 1987.

Jacoby, Russell. *The Last Intellectuals: American Culture in the Age of Academe.* New York: Basic Books, 1987.

Jorrín, Miguel, and John D. Martz. *Latin-American Political Thought and Ideology.* Chapel Hill: University of North Carolina Press, 1970.

Judson, C. Fred. *Cuba and the Revolutionary Myth: The Political Education of the Cuban Rebel Army, 1953–1963.* Boulder: Westview Press, 1984.

Karol, K. S. *Guerrillas in Power.* New York: Hill and Wang, 1970.

Kenner, Martin, and James Petras, eds. *Fidel Castro Speaks.* New York: Grove Press, 1969.

Kirk, John M. *Between God and the Party: Religion and Politics in Revolutionary Cuba.* Tampa: University of South Florida Press, 1989.

Knutson, April Ane. *Ideology and Independence in the Americas.* Minneapolis: MEP Publications, 1989.

Krich, John. *A Totally Free Man: An Unauthorized Autobiography of Fidel Castro.* Berkeley: Creative Arts Book Co., 1981.

Landau, Saul. "Fidel Will Be Around Awhile." *Nation* 250 (25) (June 25, 1990):884–886.

_____. "Socialist Democracy in Cuba: An Interview with Fidel Castro." *Socialist Revolution* 1 (2) (March-April 1970):126–143.

LeoGrande, William. *Cuba's Policy in Africa, 1959–1980.* Berkeley: Institute of International Studies, University of California, Berkeley, 1980.

_____. "The Theory and Practice of Socialist Democracy in Cuba: Mechanisms of Elite Accountability." *Studies in Comparative Communism* 12 (7) (Spring 1979).

Lévesque, Jacques. *The USSR and the Cuban Revolution.* New York: Praeger, 1978.

Levine, Barry B., ed. *The New Cuban Presence in the Caribbean.* Boulder: Westview Press, 1983.

Lewis, Gordon K. *Main Currents in Caribbean Thought: The Historical Evolution of Caribbean Society in Its Ideological Aspects, 1492–1900.* Baltimore: Johns Hopkins University Press, 1983.

Lewis, John. *The Marxism of Marx.* London: Lawrence and Wishart, 1972.

Liss, Sheldon B. *Marxist Thought in Latin America.* Berkeley: University of California Press, 1984.

_____. *Radical Thought in Central America.* Boulder: Westview Press, 1991.

_____. *Roots of Revolution: Radical Thought in Cuba.* Lincoln: University of Nebraska Press, 1987.

_____. *The Canal: Aspects of United States–Panamanian Relations.* Notre Dame: University of Notre Dame Press, 1967.

Lister, John. *Cuba: Radical Face of Stalinism.* London: Left View Books, 1985.

Lockwood, Lee. *Castro's Cuba, Cuba's Fidel.* New York: Random House, 1969; Boulder: Westview Press, 1990.

Löwy, Michael, ed. *Marxism in Latin America from 1909 to the Present: An Anthology.* Atlantic Highlands, N.J.: Humanities Press, 1992.

_____. *The Marxism of Che Guevara: Philosophy, Economics, and Revolutionary Warfare.* New York: Monthly Review Press, 1973.

MacDonald, Theodore. *Making a New People: Education in Revolutionary Cuba.* Vancouver: New Star Books, 1985.

MacEwan, Arthur. *Revolution and Economic Development in Cuba.* New York: St. Martin's Press, 1981.

MacGaffey, Wyatt, and Clifford R. Barnett. *Twentieth Century Cuba: The Background of the Castro Revolution.* Garden City, N.Y.: Doubleday, 1965.

Mandela, Nelson, and Fidel Castro. *How Far We Slaves Have Come! South Africa and Cuba in Today's World.* New York: Pathfinder Press, 1991.

Mankiewicz, Frank, and Kirby Jones. *With Fidel: A Portrait of Castro.* Chicago: Playboy Press, 1975.

Martin, Lionel. *The Early Fidel: Roots of Castro's Communism.* Secaucus, N.J.: Lyle Stuart, 1978.

Masur, Gerhard. *Nationalism in Latin America.* New York: Macmillan, 1966.

Matthews, Herbert L. *Fidel Castro.* New York: Simon and Schuster, 1969.

_____. *Revolution in Cuba.* New York: Charles Scribner's, 1975.

McClintock, Cynthia. *Cuban Revolutionary Ideology and the Cuban Intellectual.* Cambridge: Center for International Studies, MIT, July 1975.

Medin, Tzvi. *Cuba: The Shaping of Revolutionary Consciousness.* Boulder: Lynne Rienner Publishers, 1990.

Mella, Julio Antonio. *Documentos y artículos*. Havana: Editorial de Ciencias Sociales, 1975.

Mesa-Lago, Carmelo. *Cuba in the 1970s*. Albuquerque: University of New Mexico Press, 1978.

Miller, Nicola. *Soviet Relations with Latin America 1959–1987*. Cambridge: Cambridge University Press, 1989.

Mills, C. Wright. *Listen Yankee: The Revolution in Cuba*. New York: Ballantine Books, 1960.

Minà, Gianni. *An Encounter with Fidel: An Interview by Gianni Minà*. Melbourne: Ocean Press, 1991.

Montaner, Carlos Alberto. *Fidel Castro and the Cuban Revolution: Age, Position, Character, Destiny, Personality, and Ambition*. New Brunswick: Transaction Books, 1989.

Moore, Carlos. *Castro, the Blacks, and Africa*. Los Angeles: Center for Afro-American Studies, University of California, Los Angeles, 1988.

Morley, Morris H. *Imperial State and Revolution: The United States and Cuba, 1952–1986*. London: Cambridge University Press, 1987.

Morray, J. P. *The Second Revolution in Cuba*. New York: Monthly Review Press, 1962.

Mosak, Esther. "Carlos Aldana: On the Battleground of Ideas." *Cuba Update* 13 (3–4) (August-September 1992):36.

Munck, Ronaldo. *Revolutionary Trends in Latin America*. Montreal: Center for Developing-Area Studies, McGill University Monograph Series No. 17, 1984.

National General Assembly of the People of Cuba. *The Second Declaration of Havana. With the First Declaration of Havana*. New York: Pathfinder Press, 1984.

Nelson, Lowry. *Cuba: The Measure of a Revolution*. Minneapolis: University of Minnesota Press, 1972.

O'Connor, James. *The Origins of Socialism in Cuba*. Ithaca: Cornell University Press, 1970.

Oliva, Milagros. "U.S. Cardinal O'Connor Visits Cuba." *Granma Weekly Review*, May 1, 1988, p. 9.

Pérez, Louis A., Jr. *Cuba and the United States: Ties of Singular Intimacy*. Athens: University of Georgia Press, 1990.

———. *Cuba: Between Reform and Revolution*.New York: Oxford University Press, 1988.

———, ed. *Cuba: An Annotated Bibliography*. Westport, Conn.: Greenwood Press, 1988.

Pérez-Stable, Marifeli. "In Pursuit of Cuba Libre." *NACLA Report on the Americas* 24 (2) (August 1990):32–39.

Petras, James. *Critical Perspectives on Imperialism and Social Class in the Third World*. New York: Monthly Review Press, 1978.

Platt, Tony, and Ed McCaughan. "Human Rights in Cuba: Politics and Ideology." In *Transformation and Struggle: Cuba Faces the 1990s*. Sandor Halebsky, Rafael Hernández, and John Kirk, eds. New York: Praeger, 1990.

Portuondo, José Antonio. "Literature and Society." In *Latin America in Its Literature*. César Fernández Moreno, Julio Ortega, and Ivan Schulman, eds. New York: Holmes and Meier, 1980.

———. "The Cuban Revolution and the Intellectual." *New World Review* 32 (9) (October 1964).

Prieto, Abel. "Interview." *Cuba Update* 9 (1–3) (June 1988):35–37.

Ramm, Hartmut. *The Marxism of Régis Debray: Between Lenin and Guevara.* Lawrence: Regents Press of Kansas, 1978.

Ratliff, William E. *Castroism and Communism in Latin America, 1959–1976: The Varieties of Marxist-Leninist Experience.* Washington: American Enterprise Institute, 1976.

———, ed. *The Selling of Fidel Castro: The Media and the Cuban Revolution.* New Brunswick: Transaction Books, 1987.

Reckord, Barry. *Does Fidel Eat More Than Your Father? Conversations in Cuba.* New York: Praeger Publishers, 1971.

Reed, Gail. *Island in the Storm: The Cuban Communist Party's Fourth Congress.* Melbourne: Ocean Press, 1992.

Ridenour, Ron. *Backfire: The CIA's Biggest Burn.* Havana: José Martí Publishing House, 1991.

Riding, Alan. "Revolution and the Intellectual in Latin America." *New York Times Magazine,* March 13, 1983, pp. 28–40.

Robbins, Carla Anne. *The Cuban Threat.* New York: McGraw-Hill, 1983.

Rosado, Caleb. "Sect and Party: Religion Under Revolution in Cuba." Doctoral Dissertation, Northwestern University, Evanston, Ill., 1985.

Roca, Sergio, ed. *Socialist Cuba: Past Interpretations and Future Challenges.* Boulder: Westview Press, 1988.

Rudolph, James D. *Cuba: A Country Study.* Washington: Foreign Area Studies, American University, 1985.

Ruiz, Ramón Eduardo. *Cuba: The Making of a Revolution.* New York: Norton, 1970.

Salas, Luis. *Social Control and Deviance in Cuba.* New York: Praeger, 1979.

Salkey, Andrew, ed. *Writing in Cuba Since the Revolution.* London: Bogle-L'Overture Publications, 1977.

Saruski, Jaime, and Gerardo Mosquera. *The Cultural Policy of Cuba.* Paris: UNESCO, 1979.

Schlesinger, Arthur, Jr. "Four Days with Fidel: A Havana Diary." *New York Review of Books* 39 (6) (March 26, 1992):22–29.

Shearman, Peter. *The Soviet Union and Cuba.* London: Routledge and Kegan Paul, 1987.

Silverman, Bertram, ed. *Man and Socialism in Cuba.* New York: Atheneum, 1973.

Smith, Robert F., ed. *Background to Revolution: The Development of Modern Cuba.* New York: Robert E. Krieger Publishing Co., 1966, 1979.

———. *What Happened in Cuba? A Documentary History.* New York: Twayne Publishers, 1963.

Smith, Wayne S. *The Closest of Enemies: A Personal and Diplomatic Account of U.S.-Cuban Relations Since 1957.* New York: Norton, 1987.

———, ed. *The Russians Aren't Coming: New Soviet Policy in Latin America.* Boulder: Lynne Rienner Publishers, 1992.

Smith, Wayne S., and Esteban Morales Domínguez. *Subject to Solution: Problems in Cuban-U.S. Relations.* Boulder: Lynne Rienner Publishers, 1988.

Stabb, Martin S. *In Quest of Identity: Patterns in the Spanish American Essay of Ideas, 1890–1960.* Chapel Hill: University of North Carolina Press, 1967.

Stone, Elizabeth, ed. *Woman and the Cuban Revolution.* New York: Pathfinder Press, 1981.

Stubbs, Jean. *Cuba: The Test of Time.* London: Latin American Bureau, 1989.

Suchliki, Jaime. "The Intellectual Background of the Cuban Revolution." *Annals of the Southeastern Conference on Latin American Studies* 3 (1) (March 1972):105–120.

Sunshine, Catherine A. *The Caribbean: Survival, Struggle and Sovereignty.* Washington: EPICA, 1988.

Sweezy, Paul M. "Cuba: A Left U.S. View." *Monthly Review* 42 (4) (September 1990):17–21.

Szulc, Tad. *Fidel: A Critical Portrait.* New York: William Morrow, 1986.

Taber, Michael, ed. *Fidel Castro Speeches.* Vol. 2, *Building Socialism in Cuba.* New York: Pathfinder Press, 1983.

———. *Fidel Castro Speeches: Cuba's Internationalist Foreign Policy 1975–80.* New York: Pathfinder Press, 1981.

———. *Fidel Castro Speeches 1984–85: War and Crisis in the Americas.* New York: Pathfinder Press, 1985.

Tablada, Carlos. *Che Guevara: Economics and Politics in the Transition to Socialism.* Sydney: Pathfinder/Pacific and Asia, 1989.

Targ, Harry R. *Cuba and the USA: A New World Order?* New York: International Publishers, 1992.

Thomas, Hugh. *The Cuban Revolution.* New York: Harper and Row, 1977.

Tulchin, Joseph S., and Rafael Hernández, eds. *Cuba and the United States: Will the Cold War in the Caribbean End?* Boulder: Lynne Rienner Publishers, 1991.

Valdés, Nelson. "Ideological Roots of the Cuban Revolutionary Movement." In *Contemporary Caribbean: A Sociological Reader.* Vol. 2. Susan Craig, ed. Maracas, Trinidad and Tobago: Susan Craig, 1982.

———. "Revolution and Paradigms: A Critical Assessment of Cuban Studies." In *Cuban Political Economy: Controversies in Cubanology.* Andrew Zimbalist, ed. Boulder: Westview Press, 1988.

———. Taperecorded talk on Castro and the Revolution. Presented at conference: "Thirty Years of the Cuban Revolution: An Assessment." Halifax, Canada. November 1–4, 1989. Tape no. P. 5.

Vázquez Raña, Mario. "Interview with Fidel Castro. Entrevista con Fidel Castro." *El Sol de México,* October 4, 1990.

Wallach, John P. "Fidel Castro and the United States Press." In *The Selling of Fidel Castro: The Media and the Cuban Revolution.* William E. Ratliff, ed. New Brunswick: Transaction Books, 1987.

Weeks, John, and Phil Gunson. *Panama: Made in USA.* London: Latin American Bureau, 1991.

Weinstein, Martin, ed. *Revolutionary Cuba in the World Arena.* Philadelphia: Institute for the Study of Human Issues, 1979.

Wilkerson, Loree A.R. *Fidel Castro's Political Programs from Reformism to Marxism-Leninism.* Gainesville: University of Florida Press, 1965.

Winocur, Marcos. *Las clases olvidadas en la revolución cubana*. Barcelona: Editorial Crítica, 1979.

Wirmark, David. "Entrevista con el Comandante Fidel Castro, Primer Ministro del Gobierno Revolucionario de Cuba el 5 de abril de 1970." *Estudios y Documentos Suecos Sobre Cuba*. Stockholm: Instituto de Estudios Ibero-Amreicanos, 1971.

Wright, Thomas C. *Latin America in the Era of the Cuban Revolution*. New York: Praeger, 1991.

Zeitlin, Maurice. *Revolutionary Politics and the Cuban Working Class*. New York: Harper and Row, 1970.

Zeitlin, Maurice, and Robert Scheer. *Cuba: Tragedy in Our Hemisphere*. New York: Grove Press, 1963.

Zimbalist, Andrew, ed. *Cuban Political Economy: Controversies in Cubanology*. Boulder: Westview Press, 1988.

_____ . *Cuba's Socialist Economy: Toward the 1990s*. Boulder: Lynne Rienner Publishers, 1987.

Zimbalist, Andrew, and Claes Brundenius. *The Cuban Economy: Measurement and Analysis of Socialist Performance*. Baltimore: Johns Hopkins University Press, 1989.

Zimmer, Phil. "Can Castro Dodge Democratic Reform?" Interview with Sheldon B. Liss. *Akron: The Magazine of the University of Akron* 4 (3) (Spring 1990):21–23.

About the Book & Author

The author of this book takes a highly original approach to understanding the past three decades of Cuban history—he offers an analysis and interpretation of the prolific writings and speeches of Fidel Castro and of numerous interviews with him. Through Castro's own words, Sheldon Liss examines the evolution of the Cuban leader's political and social ideas and evaluates the strengths and weaknesses of the Revolution.

Liss first illuminates how intellectuals and political activists, including José Martí, Antonio Guiteras, and Ernesto "Che" Guevara, influenced Fidel's ideological development. Next, he examines the Cuban and European origins of Castro's political philosophy, probes his views on the deficiencies inherent in capitalism, and details why he established a vanguard Communist party. Throughout the book, Liss places Fidel's ideas in international perspective, outlining, for example, his views of the Cuban-Soviet relationship, his reasoning behind Cuba's support for revolutionary movements in the Third World, and his thoughts on the role of the United States in exacerbating social ills in Latin America. Finally, Liss investigates Castro's controversial views on democracy, human rights, and freedom of artistic and intellectual expression. The book stands as a fine introduction to Cuba's unique brand of Third World Marxism.

Sheldon B. Liss is Distinguished Professor of History at the University of Akron, where he teaches Latin American history and politics. He is the author of numerous books, including *Radical Thought in Central America* (Westview, 1991).

Index